Published b
Sacred Heart School
17, Mangate St, Swaffham, Norfolk, PE37 7QW
www.sacredheartschool.co.uk
info@sacredheartschool.co.uk
01760 721330 / 724577

Editors
Sr M. Francis Ridler, FDC and Vivienne Phillips

Contributions to Chapters
Individually named
Memories from past and present staff and pupils

Founding Chapter
Research and translation by Sr M Magna Andre, FDC
Written and Composed by David Motton

Cover Design
Diana Lamb

Photographs
School archives
Swaffham Town Museum
Sir Henry Bedingfeld

Published in June 2014
Copyright 2014, Daughters of Divine Charity

Printed by
Berforts Information Press
Stevenage, SG1 2BH

ISBN: 978-0-9929554-4-1

Introduction and Acknowledgements

Reaching a 100 years is a fantastic achievement, like being as old as Methuselah. To celebrate this event it was decided to complete our history up to our centenary year of 2014. The first book entitled Convent of the Sacred Heart, 1914 — 1989 spanned the 75 years from the foundation to a landmark in our history, the opening of the Middle School Building, blessed by Bishop Alan Clark. At the centenary weekend, Bishop Alan Hopes will concelebrate Mass with many priests of the diocese of East Anglia in thanksgiving for 100 years of God's guidance and protection.

The first book was edited by a past pupil, Aideen Wayne in her time of sickness. No one knew how sick until her death shortly after the completion of the book. This edition will be a tribute to her energy and generosity in expanding the in-house draft copy compiled and researched by Margaret Hayes Williams and Sr Francis.

To simplify the task of compiling this book, chapters were identified and members of staff requested to supply an overall picture of their Department over the last 25 years.

Archived resources such as the magazines between 1989 and 2007 and weekly newsletters were given a new lease of life. Hours were spent by past and present staff pouring over our vast library of photographs and locating digital photographs on our system. Grateful thanks are extended to those past pupils and staff who answered our call for memories. The PTA and Governors responded in their usual generous fashion.

What seemed, in theory, to be a simple and easy format has proved to be more challenging. Deadlines expected for December 2013 have been stretched to the last possible moment for printing. Instead of panicking Viv Phillips has been the backbone of stability, taking late arrivals and corrections with a philosophical air that 'we will finish the book'. Little did she know that when she agreed to take on the role of Marketing for a few hours a week that this project would rely on her ICT skills to format the book, proof read, cajole and encourage colleagues and Sr Francis in the marathon task before us.

The book has expanded with the material presented: the goal being a 100 page book, 200 sides, but has reached 256 pages. Why did we think there would not be enough material? There are too many people to thank, but Eric St John Foti needs a mention for sorting out the **ISBN** number, introducing us to his biographer, and being his usual reassuring self. The Sisters at Sacred Heart and the rest of the Province have shown much patience, as three holidays have been consumed by Sr Francis on research, as a stickler for historical accuracy — it had to be correct! Unfortunately there are probably many errors and omissions and the Editors apologise in advance for the inadequacies, but do remember only God is perfect!

May the Sacred Heart of Jesus bless our efforts and everyone associated with this history.

Sr.M Francis Ridler, FDC Headteacher 1979-2006 and 2009– present

CONTENTS

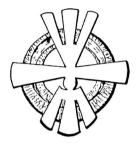

The site for this fine building in the heart of Vienna was given to the Congregation of Divine Charity by Emperor Ferdinand, the predecessor of Franz Joseph, himself a generous benefactor of the Congregation. It was they who prayed at the bier after his assassination, who prepared his body and that of the Empress for the journey to their final resting place.

Chapter 1 MOTHER HOUSE TO MANGATE STREET

by David Motton

IN THE BEGINNING

It was sweet midsummer when three Daughters of Divine Charity set out from their Viennese Mother House on the most fateful journey of their lives.

The fabled Vienna Woods were in full leaf and the Danube, although not a legendary blue, flowed peacefully under the bridges of the beautiful city of Strauss and Mozart, a city of spectacular palaces, symbols of power and wealth of bygone European emperors.

If the Sisters had followed the stately course of the Danube before long they would have entered the dark valleys and roaring white water gorges of the Balkans, troubled lands since ancient times. Even on that summery day, in a cramped student lodging house in Sarajevo a group of future assassins were plotting a murder that would slaughter millions. When the three Sisters boarded a train in Vienna they would have known nothing of this, nor of the horrors that would shortly engulf the whole of Europe, or the awful effect it would have on their pious lives.

The year was 1914.

The Daughters of Divine Charity were not heading to the south and east with the Danube but northwards by rail through Bavaria, Switzerland and France then by steam ferry to England, a land known to them only as a Protestant kingdom where until two generations previously it had been virtually a crime to be a Catholic. However Sister Superior M. Conradine Grassman, Sister M. Donata Reichenwallner and Sister M. Ositha Skrdlant were not travelling entirely unprepared.

*   *   *   *   *

Mother Franzisksa Lechner, who had founded the Congregation of the Daughters of Divine Charity, had dedicated her life to establishing that community which lived by the Rule of Saint Augustine. Its purpose was to furnish working girls of the Industrial Revolution with shelter and care. In time it also engaged in other good works, including the provision of schools.   The

SOROKSÁRI UTCZA ELLER M BUDAPEST

Sister Teresina

She suggested that Swaffham was suitable for a Foundation. In later life she established foundations worldwide, especially in Brazil where her memory is highly regarded.

Congregation itself was founded in Vienna in 1868 but other houses were soon established all over Europe. Sister Donata, for instance, came from the house in Kraków, once the capital of Poland but at that time it had been absorbed into the Austrian Empire. Almost all of these foundations were in great cities, mostly capitals of nations. This was probably because the big cities were where the Industrial Revolution had its most devastating effect on health and morals. It was in the squalid tenements surrounding the factories that young girls were most exposed to physical and moral danger. No longer did they have the family and good neighbourly protection of village life. Mother Franziska had died in 1894. It was in 1913, when Mother M. Ignatia Egger was Superior General of the Congregation, that a combination of circumstances brought about a decision to establish a house for the Sisters of Divine Charity in Swaffham.

For sometime much attention had been focussed on a planned foundation in the United States. It was to collect money raised for this project that Sister Teresina Werner and Sister Lamberta Plundrak had travelled to London in the winter months of 1912. They had stayed with Sister Teresina's sister Augustina, who lived there, and whilst they were there people had suggested that the Daughters of Divine Charity should establish a Congregation in England.

Bishop Amigo had encouraged this idea and had expressed his willingness to have such a congregation in his London Diocese. Letters were exchanged between London and Vienna.

In 1913 Mother M. Ignatia Egger had sent Sister M. Ludiovika Binder, the superior in Kraków and Sister M. Lamberta from Prague to London with the intention of beginning a foundation there. However final decisions were long in the making and communications were painfully slow because the international post of the day was tardy and unreliable. The interested parties had eventually become very weary of the delays.

Meanwhile, one hundred miles to the north of London, in a market town of which the Daughters of Divine Charity had probably never heard, a situation had developed which would affect them all greatly.

After more than three hundred years the Catholic presence had returned to Swaffham.

It had travelled by dusty roads to that town in a motor car, a rare sight in the countryside of early twentieth century England. Missionaries of an organisation called The Motor Mission, an early forerunner of the Catholic Truth Society, had established a church in a building that had once been a theatre, a Salvation Army barracks and most recently used by a Mr Culling as a carpentry store. When the Motor Mission had arrived in Swaffham there were but three Catholics there in a Motor Mission had arrived in Swaffham there were but three Catholics there in a population of two thousand. They were Mr Devaney the Postmaster, his wife and an Irish girl, Kate Dune, who was then working at Messers Bunting.

Mother Most Admirable

The centre piece of the altar in the Chapel of the Mother House in Vienna.

By late in 1913 the Catholic population had grown to eighteen. Father Vendé, a Frenchman, who was then the Mission priest had decided after long and serious consideration to approach several convents in England, France and Ireland to start a foundation in Swaffham in order to support his endeavours and to encourage the small number of Catholics.

He had received nothing but refusals. He had even written to an order in Canada, to no avail.

After so many rejections the good priest was close to despairing that he would ever have a Catholic school in Swaffham, when Hilda Fawkes, his young and very energetic housekeeper and secretary recalled that when her health had failed her a few years previously when she was a novice at a convent in Staffordshire, the Benedictines had sent her to a convent in Austria to recuperate. She told her worried employer that she had noticed that there were some excellent teaching orders in that land.

Father Vendé asked around.

It so happened that a Miss Charlotte Noel of Fincham, an admiral's daughter and a good friend and supporter of the Catholic Church in Swaffham, had known of

Fr Vendé (left) was Mission Priest at Our Lady of Pity from December 1912 until April 1919 when his health began to fail and he spent time as Chaplain at Oxburgh Hall. The Manor House (right) were the premises he first arranged for the Sisters.

Sister Teresina and through Miss Noel's introduction Father Vendé had invited the Daughters of Divine Charity to visit Swaffham.

Then Sister Teresina had travelled to Swaffham, stayed two days and in that time had decided that the market town was a favourable place for a foundation, albeit far different from the Continental conurbations surrounding the Congregation's other houses.

Father Vendé had lost no time in approaching Mr Hammond, the owner of the Manor House in Swaffham, who agreed to let the property to the nuns at £35 per year. He had then consulted his bishop who was delighted with the idea of the foundation, so long as it was self-supporting. Father Vendé could see no problem with this because in his own falsely optimistic words: "Although there was no immediate prospect of having pupils in such a bigoted town, the Foundation was to be encouraged because the nuns were to bring with them pupils from their houses in Austria, Bosnia, Poland and Hungary. " He was also sure that he could encourage pupils to come from his own native France.

Sister Teresina had written immediately to Vienna but Mother Ignatia's reply was too long in coming for Mr Hammond. In November 1913 he had instructed his lawyer to write that a decision had to be made soon.

Mother General Ignatia's eventual reply recalled Sister Teresina to Vienna, saying that the following spring would be better for a foundation to take place. It seemed she feared the winter storms of rural England whilst being oblivious to the terrible storm clouds of war already massing over the whole of Europe.

In December Mr Hammond withdrew his offer of the Manor House.

*   *   *

It was not until after Easter that Mother General Ignatia had written to Father Vendé, advising him that the Sisters would be arriving in June and requesting that he had a house ready for them. It did not give the man much time but he responded with his usual energetic dedication, a characteristic which would eventually take a toll on his health.

He negotiated with Mr Mallon, not an easy man to deal with, for the lease of Ivy House, a small building in very poor condition, for a rent of £35 per year. The lease did however include a large garden and some dilapidated stable buildings to the rear. House and stables were demolished many years ago and the site is now occupied by the front car park and the parish room and presbytery of Our Lady of Pity Catholic Church in Station Street. Mr Mallon offered to sell the whole to the nuns for £800 pounds. Father Vendé did not think it worth more than £500, but as Father Vendé recorded in his diary:

"I rented the house in spite of numerous prejudices and hostile Protestants."

Ivy House did not in any way compare to the fine Manor House that the three Sisters had been offered six months previously.

*   *   *

On Friday the twenty-sixth of June three nuns wearing voluminous capes and habits, and with their faces fringed with elaborately crimped bonnets and wide white collars stepped down from a train in Swaffham Station. Their dress was strange to Swaffham eyes, their German accents were harsh to Swaffham ears.

Father Vendé wrote in his diary:

Swaffham Railway Station

"The whole town was alarmed when the nuns arrived here on June the twenty-fifth (sic) 1914."
Perhaps a Gallic exaggeration but not without some degree of truth in it, although in fact the nuns were met with kindness as they themselves recorded.

For a little group of ladies had gathered on the platform to greet them.

There was Madame Turton, the wife of a retired Indian Army colonel. She offered them the hospitality of her own home until the

Ivy House in Station Street

uninhabitable Ivy House was ready. There was also Miss Winter, the daughter of the Reverend George Winter, a member of a family with a long Anglican clerical tradition. In fact her father had been the vicar of St Peter and St Paul Anglican Parish Church. She lived in Cotmangate, now part of the modern convent, with an older sister and their elderly widowed mother. She was well known in Swaffham as a writer and producer of plays. She had produced her play 'The Pedlar of Swaffham' in the Assembly rooms just two years previously and would write and produce other plays for 'Hospital Week' (the precursor of Carnival Week) in years to come. She was also an accomplished artist.

Also there was Pauline Willis, a lady of some private means. Although she spent much of her time at Kensington Gate, her London address, for she was the Secretary of the Catholic Library and Reading Room in Victoria Street where the Roman Catholic Cathedral now stands, she was a generous benefactor to both the Church and Convent in Swaffham.

Charlotte Noel, whose introduction in the first instance had been instrumental in the nuns coming at all, had travelled from Fincham to greet them. All these ladies were to be good, strong, influential and generous friends for many years to come.

A couple of days later, Lady Sybil Bedingfeld came on a welcoming visit from nearby Oxburgh Hall. The Bedingfeld family had lived in their moated home for several centuries and despite suffering severely for their pains had remained staunch Catholics throughout the penal years of the Reformation until the present day. This would be the first visit of many.

Good friends were needed immediately because for Sister Superior Conradine, Sister Donata and Sister Ositha their troubles had already begun. Ivy House was not an idyllic green clad country home as the name suggested. It was more a crumbling ruin. It needed cleaning, it needed furnishing with the bare essentials of life, it needed to be made ready for the arrival of two more Sisters and seven young boarders who were coming to England to learn the English language. The work was hard, it was unrelenting from morning to night, but fortunately for them the welcoming smiles that had greeted them at the station were soon translated into deeds. Mme Turton, when not being the perfect hostess to the Sisters whom she had invited to eat and sleep in her home, spent every moment of the day cleaning and preparing Ivy House alongside them. Katharine Winter worked with them too, and with Mme Turton would go into town to visit the shops to help the

Sisters buy whatever they needed.

What a difference that must have made. The difference between three strangely dressed foreign ladies whose command of English was then rather poor and their understanding of the distinctive Swaffham version of it even worse, and two upper class ladies with very strong personalities, one the late vicar's daughter and the other the wife of a colonel. The upper class ladies would be greeted with humble smiles by the subservient shop assistants, offered chairs to sit on whilst they made their purchases, and given the personal attention of the proprietor himself. It would have been very unlikely that three foreign Catholic ladies would have received such deference in a such a Protestant English town.

Madame Turton

It took a fortnight, but at last Ivy House was made habitable. One of the rooms in the old stables had been adapted to serve as a chapel, although the Sisters would still have to walk through town to the church in Theatre Street to attend Mass. Their little chapel was no more than a simple table covered with a white cloth on which stood a statue of the Infant of Prague donated by Father Vendé, a small picture of Our Mother Most Admirable and some flowers. But at last, with great relief and thanks to God for His help and blessings, Sister Donata was able to write home to her Motherhouse:

"On Friday 11th July we moved into our little convent for good. We sang Te Deum and were happy to live again in a home of our own."

The Medallion

Both sides of the Medallion worn by the Daughters of Divine Charity in the era of their arrival.

13

The Story of the
Pedlar of Swaffham Market
hath been done into a play by Miss Katharine
Winter and will be presented in the
Assembly Rooms, Swaffham,
on Wednesday, the sixth day of April, at eight
o'the clock, also on the day following, being
Thursday, at the hour of three o'the clock, and
likewise also at eight.

PRICES OF ADMISSION:—
WEDNESDAY EVENING.—Reserved Seats, 2/6; Second Seats, 1/-.
THURSDAY AFTERNOON.—Reserved Seats, 3/-; Second Seats, 2/-; Third
Seats, 1/-.
THURSDAY EVENING.—Reserved Seats, 2/-; Second Seats, 1/-; Third
Seats, 6d.
Plan of the Room may be seen, and Tickets obtained, at Mr. W. J. Coe's, Market
Place, Swaffham.

Scenery especially painted, for the occasion, by
Mr. Bridges, of King's Lynn.

Any profits from the said play will be given to sustain the Fabric of the
Church, which John Chapman helped to re-edify.

Katharine Winter

(Above) 1910 A bill advertising a play
written by Katharine Winter.

(Left) Katharine dressed as Catharine
Chapman, a part in that play which she
performed herself.

The Swaffham Co-operative Society.

The Co-operative general store as it was in 1914. In common with several other general stores in Swaffham in the early twentieth century it sold a wide range of goods, not only all manner of fresh, dry and preserved grocery items as today, but there would be counters for drapery, lingerie, men's wear, boots and shoes.

Now the Foundation was ready to receive the seven boarders and the two Sisters, who were already on their way from Austria.

Before their arrival they had other visitors. Lady Sybil Bedingfeld came by car with Sir Henry, her husband, and her niece. The three of them were shown all over the house and were very interested, so much so that they promised to send their children to the school at the end of summer. The following day, Lady Sybil sent her two children with two governesses to see the premises. The children especially 'the young count' as Sister Donata called him, were both interested in coming to the school with the Sisters.

On Thursday 17th July Sister M. Aloisia and Sister M. Fabiola arrived with seven student boarders. Three of the students came from Kraków and four from Austria.

(Top left) **Peggy and Harry Bedingfeld**

(Top right) **Lady Sybil Bedingfeld**

(Right) **Oxburgh Hall 1914**

Among those students were Teresa Donner, Josephine and Mitzi Pawel. The newcomers were regarded with curiosity by the people of Swaffham. Although some opposition to the coming of Catholics had been voiced by the leaders of other Christian denominations, acceptance seemed to be the rule amongst the ordinary town dwellers

All that was needed now to make the Foundation complete was its consecration one week later by Father Vendé.

Again in Sister Donata's words: *"May our being here achieve the return of souls to the Catholic Church."*

Father Vendé and the seven Austrian boarders.

This picture was taken in the garden of Ivy House during the few days that all the boarders were present in Swaffham in July 1914. Two of the boarders did remain throughout the war and later they joined the Congregation. They were Josephine and Mitzi Pawel, becoming Sister M. Gertrude and Sister M. Teresa respectively.

IN THE SHADOW OF ARMAGEDDON

All was going well. Lady Sybil had invited everyone in the new Sacred Heart Convent to tea at Oxburgh Hall. Sisters and students alike were delighted to be shown around the beautiful old building, with its relics and reminders of its troubled Catholic history.

On Monday the 20th July lessons had begun with the teaching of French and English conversation by Father Vendé and Mme Turton. Some townspeople had expressed a wish for their children to attend the convent school.

Father Vendé received a letter of congratulation from the Bishop of Northampton:

Dear Father Vendé,

Heartiest congratulations on your good news. God grant that the advent of the Sisters may be the consolidation of the work at which you have been labouring so earnestly and under so many difficulties....

Shots rang out in the Balkans. An Austrian Archduke died. Chain lightning flashed around the war clouds over Europe. Austria declared war on Serbia. In support of the Serbs, Russia declared war on Austria, Austria's ally Germany declared war on Russia, France had a treaty with Russia so declared war on Germany which invaded France through Belgium, and in defence of 'brave little Belgium' Britain declared war on the Central Powers of Germany and Austria. These rapid fire declarations happened from first to last within eight days.

In Swaffham the Daughters of Divine Charity had become enemy aliens eight hundred miles from home.

In the market place of Swaffham there was cheering and misguided joy that Britain was at war with the hated Hun.

Inside the Sacred Heart Convent in Station Street Swaffham there was dismay and the offering of fervent prayers.

With so much anti-German feeling in the air, even before Britain actually declared

Soldiers Marching In The Market Place

In 1912 Swaffham had been the centre of a large training exercise in preparation for war. Tents had been pitched in the heart of the town on the aptly named Camping Land.

war, the nuns felt in physical danger. Not only were they concerned for themselves, but they were deeply worried for the Sisters at home. So Sister Donata and Sister Aloisia travelled to London to see the Austrian ambassador and ask for his advice and help. He assured them of his help if it became necessary for them to leave England. He would advise them by telegram when the time came.

However to close down the convent so soon after its establishment which had involved so much hard work, prayer and unstinting help and generosity from friends was not really an option for the Sisters. So a compromise was agreed that Sister Superior Conradine, whose health had begun to fail and who wished to go home, would accompany four of the boarders who could not bear the thought of being totally cut off from their families. On the 4th August Britain declared war and Sister Superior Conradine and four students travelled to London and two days later they joined the Austrian Ambassador and many other Austrians on

The Infant of Prague

This is the actual statue given to the Daughters of Divine Charity by Father Vendé. Although the robes are not original they are very old and are similar in style to those that the Sisters would have made to dress the statue themselves.

their journey home. With diplomatic protection they travelled by ship around the coasts of Spain and Portugal, through the Straits of Gibraltar to Genoa in Italy. After that, all contact with Sister Superior Conradine was lost as was contact with Austria. In fact Sister Conradine died in 1915 soon after her arrival in Austria, in St Andrä, Corinthia.

Four Sisters and three boarders remained in the convent, but they were in dire straits, because no longer could they receive any of the fees that they depended on from the parents of the boarders, nor help from the Mother House itself.

Sister Donata, now acting as Superior, wrote to Bishop Keating explaining the special situation of the Daughters of Divine Charity. He replied "in the kindest manner" that he would come to Swaffham from Northampton and say mass in the convent.

Before the bishop's arrival an unexpected letter arrived from Mother Kostka from the Congregation's house in New York . Sister Superior Conradine had been in touch with Mother Kostka before she left England but there had been no reply until now. With the long letter came twenty pounds, to help the Swaffham Sisters with their needs. Although totally cut off from their Sisters in Europe it was with "the greatest joy" that the nuns in Swaffham could now correspond with Sisters in America.

The bishop announced that he would visit Swaffham on the 23rd September and that he would celebrate Mass in the convent chapel.

The Sisters were delighted at the honour but dismayed at the poverty of their chapel...a table and an Infant of Prague!

"Honour this image and you shall never want."

This prophetic statement associated with the statue of the Infant of Prague appeared to come true. Mme Turton donated a beautiful curtain of dark red velvet, two brass candle sticks and two brass vases and an incense burner and in conjunction with Miss Winter a silver lamp for the eternal light. Miss Noel bought a white altar decorated with gold and a beautiful cross made of brass and some altar linen. She provided fresh flowers. Miss Winter lent the convent a small harmonium and whatever else was missing Father Vendé lent from the church.

The 23rd and 24th September 1914 were joyful and memorable days in the lives of Sister Donata, Sister Ositha, Sister Aloisia and Sister Fabiola and landmark days in the history of the convent.

Bishop Keating arrived in Swaffham shortly after 6pm and made his way straight to the convent. Having greeted the four Sisters one by one he then sat in the parlour and "embarked in a very intimate and fatherly conversation with them all." In this conversation he asked about their situation and showed much concern.

Sister M. Donata Reichenwallner

At 8pm he celebrated Benediction in the church in Theatre Street which was very well filled. Since Swaffham boasted only thirty two Catholics plus eighteen Belgian refugees the number must have been swollen by interested Protestants and it was to them that he addressed the final words of his sermon, which in itself was an explanation of vocations and convents. He was doing his best to quell the hostility that was so blighting the lives of the occupants of Ivy House.

He said: Now you have been blessed for a short time to possess a small convent in Swaffham. Do appreciate this privilege and offer the good Sisters who have come to offer their services, a cordial welcome. Do not listen to words of mistrust and jealousy, which will certainly be heard from some directions, but give the Sisters your full trust. If they do not deserve it, you can always withdraw it from them. But nobody should mistrust them without a reason, because they have come with the most peaceful intention of doing good to you."

At 6am the following morning he went to the convent to say Mass. Before Mass he discussed with the Sisters the possibility of leaving the Blessed Sacrament with them. He knew this would mean a lot to them but he felt that to do so he should first request permission from Rome. But with most of Europe already at war, although Italy was still neutral at this point, no one could know how long this would take.

The Sisters then told him how the Bishop of Kraków had installed the Blessed Sacrament in their house in Wola as soon as he had blessed the house and only afterwards had he applied for permission from Rome.

"Well then," said Bishop Keating, " I shall do as the Austrian bishop did and leave Our Lord here to comfort you. In time of war, I am entitled to do so!"

It is written that tears of joy flew profusely during the Holy Mass of that day. If the truth be known there would hardly have been a dry eye during the breakfast that followed.

Then to make his visit complete, as he was leaving the good bishop told the nuns that he would appoint Father Squirrel, a German speaker and the parish priest at Cromer, as the extraordinary (extraordinarius) confessor for the convent. He would be able to hear their confessions in German. He took this appointment very seriously, to the extent that on one occasion when the Sisters were expecting him there was a rail strike so he cycled from Cromer to Swaffham and back again to hear their confessions. Father Squirrel was many years later, during another war, to serve as the parish priest at Our Lady of Pity, Swaffham (1941-1944) before being called for greater things at St John the Baptist in Norwich.

So ended the most beautiful two days the new Foundation had seen up to then.

Although reassured by Bishop Keating's avowed support the nuns and students found their situation becoming increasingly difficult.

The officially encouraged hatred of Germans and all things German, and in Swaffham this came to mean the German-speaking nuns, went to almost unimaginable lengths. Although there were many good people in Swaffham, as we have seen, there were also, as elsewhere, the zealots and bullies who give patriotism a bad name. The Sisters had to endure threatening and verbal abuse in the streets from the likes of these. Hilda Fawkes, Father Vendé's housekeeper, at times stood face to face with the nuns' tormentors. It was said that she was ready to use her fists to defend them.

In October it was announced that German spies had been discovered lurking in Britain, some disguised as nuns, according to rumour. The patriotically gullible of Swaffham believed that they had a spy in their midst - Sister Ositha, because she was a sturdily built lady of what was then sometimes called 'peasant stock'. This spy hysteria had a more serious effect because a regulation was introduced under which no Germans nor Austrians were allowed to live within fifty miles of the coast. The nuns and their little convent faced expulsion. Unannounced the police arrived with a warrant to search the house. They did so, which must have been a very unpleasant experience for the Sisters to have their few poor possessions picked over and examined. Of course nothing incriminating was found, but the superintendent told them that they were to leave the country and could stay only with special permission. It seemed that the days of the Swaffham convent had come to an end.

So after so much joy came such sorrow. The Sisters applied to the authorities for permission to stay, they offered fervent prayers to Our Lord for His Blessing. A few days later their pleas and prayers were answered. They were allowed to stay.

Whilst Europe continued to blow itself apart with war, and in England German Shepherd dogs were renamed 'Alsatians' and the Royal Family attempted to disown its double German origins from Hanover and Prince Albert's Saxe Coberg Gotha by adopting the truly English name of Windsor, the Daughters of Divine Charity in Swaffham struggled to survive by selling bits of embroidery and by growing vegetables in the garden of Ivy House. They had no local pupils, of course, and the Austrian girls that did linger for a while brought in hardly any income by way of fees because most contact with their homeland was broken.

Lady Bedingfeld heard of their plight and sent five pounds, as did Miss Noel from Fincham. These seem small amounts in today's money but five pounds was the equivalent of six weeks rent. The church collections in 1914 averaged ten shillings (fifty pence) per week. Other gifts are recorded. The Duke of Norfolk donated five pounds and so did Bishop Keating out of his own pocket. The

Benedictine Abbot of Erdington, who knew the Sisters in Prague sent ten pounds. Lady Bedingfeld, Miss Winter, Miss Willis and the Bishop made frequent generous donations which were financial lifelines for the beleaguered Sisters.

Month by month the numbers in the convent declined. Sister Aloisia left England and by a devious route returned to Kraków. In December 1915 Therese Donner returned to Kraków at her parents' request. She had come to Swaffham as a Protestant, but had been baptised as a Catholic and had made her first communion in the convent chapel on the 21st May. A first for the convent and the little chapel!

Two actions of war did little to endear the nuns to the people of Swaffham. The first one was the sinking of the *Lusitania*, a passenger liner on its way to England from America. The torpedoing of this ship with only civilian passengers on board, women and children among them, off the south coast of Ireland caused outrage on both sides of the Atlantic. Some of the passengers were Americans and this atrocity had the effect of drawing the United States into the world war. It was the beginning of 'total war' and the U-boat blockade of Britain. On the mainland the government decided to expel all Germans and Austrians who remained in Britain. Only a few exemptions could be made and then only with the production of exemplary references. The Daughters of Divine Charity were given notice.

Their influential friends in and around Swaffham rallied to their cause as did Superintendent Maries of the local police and Bishop Keating, of course.

The Sisters had to endure a long agonising wait of two months until on the Feast of St Augustine, the patron saint of the Daughters of Divine Charity, notice of permission to stay arrived from the Home Office. To them it was *"...like a seal that our holy patron had set on the foundation. It was new proof that Divine Providence does not deprive us of protection."*

The second 'incident' was when a Zeppelin bombed Swaffham.

In England war had been a distant affair for two hundred years, something that happened abroad in Napoleon's time at Waterloo and a decade or so ago against the Boers of South Africa and the Mahdi and the Fuzzie Wuzzies in the Sudan. A battle had not been fought on English soil since the short lived Monmouth rebellion of 1685. Now war had taken to the air. Civilians were in the front line. Explosives were dropped on to their working class homes. War had come back to England bringing death, damage and widespread fear and anger. As well as bombing London, the Zeppelin airships made frequent attacks on the factories in the Midlands crossing the North Sea and passing over the Norfolk and Lincolnshire coasts on their way. However, one night in January 1916 the captain of one Zeppelin either lost his way and confused Swaffham with Birmingham or decided that he had gone far enough and dropped some bombs on a camp in North Pickenham, a couple more in Swaffham itself, one of which killed a soldier unloading a train in the railway station, before moving on to drop some more

A Zeppelin airship of the type which dropped bombs on Swaffham

bombs on a tented army camp near Oxborough

People vented their fury on the Sisters. The Nonconformist Methodist minister, who had not liked the arrival of Catholics right from the beginning, used this as an opportunity to start up a petition for the removal of the Sisters from Swaffham completely. Undaunted, Sister Donata called upon this man and explained to him that the quiet work that the nuns were doing in their convent was not in anyway a danger to the State. She must have been very persuasive, because nothing more was heard of this petition.

Of course it was not just the Zeppelins, who visited more than once, that brought war to Swaffham. Throughout the land there were countless firesides beside which stood an empty chair from which the man had followed the recruiting serjeant's call to fight for King and Country, leaving his wife to fend for herself and her children. Whether her man would return no one could tell. The cruel truth was that as the months of war crawled by the relentless slaughter of young manhood in the mud of Flanders, the U-boat infested waters of the North Atlantic and elsewhere had left no city, town nor village hamlet in Britain that did not mourn the loss of sons, brothers and husbands. Swaffham was no exception. The war memorial in the market place is testament to that. Not too far from home men of the Sandringham Battalion, recruited from tenants and workers on the Sandringham Estate, had fixed bayonets and marched across a mist streaked battlefield in the Dardenelles. They vanished. Not one of them was seen again. War was no longer an event to be greeted with cheers and jubilation and it was no wonder that anger and blame by association, however unjust, was directed against 'the enemy aliens' living in Station Street.

EXODUS

Another bombshell shattered the peace of the Sisters in the midsummer of 1917. It was three weary war years since they first set foot in Swaffham. They had some cause for joy in this mid-June because Bishop Keating had paid them a brief visit, enjoying lunch with them and a recreation time for the whole community afterwards. He followed this with a service in their little chapel during which he said the litany of St Joseph and a decade of the rosary and gave Benediction. Conscious not only of the Sisters' spiritual needs he also gave Sister Donata ten pounds for the upkeep of the house.

A few days later came the bombshell. Mr Mallon, their landlord, gave them notice to quit. They had until the 20th of September.

Joy dissolved into despair.

The Stables

It was in one of these rooms that the Sisters made their little chapel. The stables were later converted into the priest's quarters and remained in use until the building of the present presbytery.

Where would they find another house in the town where there was so much opposition to them?

Even if they found one, unless there was a suitable room they would have no chapel and would no longer be able to keep the Blessed Sacrament in the house.

How would they finance the cost of removal and refurnishing?

It was no good pleading with Mr Mallon to relent. He was in debt, going bankrupt. He had to sell. He had no option.

In spite of never having met Miss Willis, Father Vendé knew well that she was a good friend of the church and the convent and wrote to her in London, explaining the desperate situation and asking whether she knew of "some charitable soul (meaning her, no doubt) who is likely to help us, to buy or by some means to secure the premises. Buying the house I regret to say would amount to a great deal."

The asking price for Ivy House and the land in Station Street was £750.

Miss Willis replied that she could not possibly pay £750 out of her own income. She added that: *"...she wished she could secure it if you feel it suitable for our needs,"* (which shows how much she identified herself with the mission and the convent) and promised to write to the bishop offering to make a yearly payment towards the purchase. Whether or not her offer was accepted is not clear, but the bishop did manage to arrange a loan from the bank for the full purchase price.

The property was to be sold by auction. Fully aware that there was a very real danger amongst some of the Swaffham citizens to obstruct the nuns in a deliberate conspiracy to bid against them, the bishop countered this by employing Mr Charles Large, a solicitor, to bid for the property in his own name, and then resell it to the bishop afterwards. The eventual price was £670.

The deal was done. The site was bought where now stands the present Church of Our Lady of Pity and the presbytery. The little convent was secure.

And so the Convent of the Sacred Heart survived the final year of war as they had survived the other three - with their good friends standing beside them, with the stern resolve of Sister Superior M. Donata Reichenwallner and with many prayers to their patron St Augustine and also St Joseph for the help and protection of Our Lord.

Such were the wartime struggles and hardships endured by the nuns in Station Street. Great was the suffering from famine and pestilence of those who had remained in Vienna during the war. Their sufferings did not cease with the signing of the Armistice in 1918. Famine and pestilence do not recognise signatures on pieces of paper.

It was not until 1920 that Sister M Ignatia Egger, Mother General, was able to write this poignant letter to the Bishop of Northampton. Quoted here verbatim, her English is strangely stilted in places by the German idiom.

My Lord,

May God bless you for all the numerous favours of your fatherly benevolence and all the help given to our convent (in Swaffham) in the time of need. We shall not omit to beg Our Father in Heaven to keep your Lordship in good health, to take you under His Almighty protection...

She continues:

"The existence and thriving of our convent in England was my great sorrow during the war. But your now impossible to (sic) me to send anyone over to England on account of the expensive voyage and while many of our Sisters fell ill in consequence of the great misery and died. I am sorry to say so - just the most pious and able ones."

In fact, the Sisters in the Mother House had been starving to death.

The Convent of the S. Heart,
Swaffham,
Norfolk.
17.3.1920

My Lord,

May I trouble you about my plans for getting another house soon?
If we want to get on, we must have a bigger house. The one we live in has only 6 rooms, & we want two rooms at least for school purposes. Also I dare not encourage people to send us boarders as we have not sufficient sleeping accomodation, & I had to refuse already several lady-boarders on account of lack of room.
That is why I approached Mr Large, our solicitor in order to make him ask Mr Barnham, the owner of 'Cotman gate' whether & under what conditions he would be willing to sell this property. His answer was that he was not keen on selling it, but would do so if he

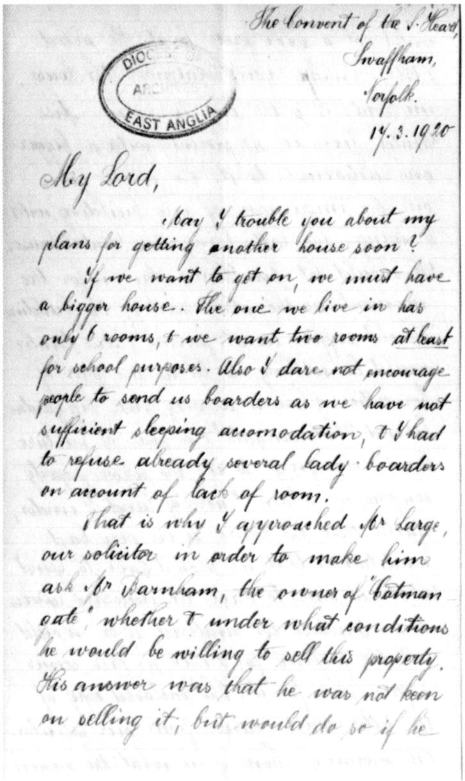

The Letter

The first page of Sr Donata's beautifully hand written letter to Bishop Keating.

* * *

From the end of the war, with hatred and suspicion largely exhausted by the sickening weariness of it all, pupils and boarders had been coming to the convent.

So much so that Ivy House, which only had six rooms, could not accommodate all who wished to come. Sister Superior Donata found that she had to turn some away.

Something had to be done, and Sister Donata was no sluggard in taking action. She sought a larger property and although many doors were closed against her, her attention was first drawn to the Old Grammar School that stood at the southern end of the Camping Land. It had been auctioned but the auction failed. Hoping to secure a bargain Bishop Keating suggested that they make a low offer.

East Cotmangate Street

This is the 'wing' of Cotmangate, the home of Katharine Winter. She lived on in here for a while after the property was bought by the Sisters from the owner, her landlord, Major Barnham of Watton.

Sister Donata did not like the place, and she said so in a long letter to the bishop on 17th March 1920. She detailed a list of defects ranging from the poor state of the building's walls, the smallness of the site should they wish to enlarge in the future to the fact that boys from the nearby Elementary School 'played their wild games in front of the door.' She left no room for doubt as to her opinion of the place. She had in mind a much more suitable, although more expensive, premises.

It was really two properties in one. Cotmangate and Cotmangate West, giving the appearance of one large building with a wing.

Katharine Winter was living in the 'wing', now alone it seemed. She did not own it, she was paying rent, but she thought that the owner, Major Barnham of

Watton, could be persuaded to sell. Sister Donata promptly instructed Mr Large, the solicitor, to approach the owner, and ask under what conditions would he be prepared to sell the property. In her Letter to Bishop Keating Sister Donata extolled all the virtues of Cotmangate and detailed all that she had done so far and enclosed a copy of Mr Barnham's reply suggesting a purchase price of £1800 to Bishop Keating as a fait accomplis!

Cotmangate

A view of the Sacred Heart Convent, as announced by the name plate on the door, soon after its purchase by the Daughters of Divine Charity in 1920

From the bishop's reply it seems that he was rather taken aback by all this, but he agreed, and advised and assisted in many helpful ways. He arranged the finance for the haggled down price of £1300 and again arranged for Mr Large to buy the property in his own name because of possible resistance from the Protestants.

A twist to this business that did not reveal itself until the very last moment was that the tenant of the main building was not a Mr Avann who was living there. He was a subtenant of the actual tenant Reverend Keeling Scott, vicar of St Peter and St Paul!

The Daughters of Divine Charity moved into their new home on 3rd August 1920. This was their Land of Canaan, a land of promise, where amongst its orchard trees, its garden and meadow they would settle and develop their convent over many years to come. Their school would be the *alma mater* of many future citizens of Swaffham.

The Sisters had moved on from being the enemy aliens living in Station Street in a prejudiced and bigoted town to being accepted as an integral part of Swaffham itself. They were on their way to fulfilling Sister Donata's prayer that they would return Catholic souls to Swaffham.

The Garden
This picture, taken in 1929, gives an idea of the extent of the 'meadowland' that lay to the rear of the Cotmangate buildings, although they are already extended to some extent in this view. Classrooms and the gymnasium occupy this space today.

They had achieved this in spite of three major prejudices, for their faith and war paranoia were not the only prejudices which afflicted the three women religious who had remained in Swaffham. There was a great prejudice against women. It was a particular type of prejudice special to that time.

A new breed of women had emerged in the early years of the 20th century. It was a type of young lady who was fearlessly independent in thought and generally self-confident in manner. It was the emergence of a style of womanhood that no longer accepted the role of vapid damsel in the Victorian mode. These young women rejected the claustrophobic comfort of mamma and papa's parlour and the chaperoned walk in the park, the perceived belief that embroidery and reading romantic novels were the limit of feminine mental ability. Women had begun to think for themselves. They took an interest in politics. They became Suffragettes, a feminist protest movement seeking votes for women. They chained themselves to the railings of public buildings, they broke windows, they got themselves arrested. Only twelve months before Sister Donata and the other Sisters had arrived in Swaffham a suffragette had died when she ran as a protest in front of the king's horse in the Derby. The all male Establishment did not like Suffragettes nor any strong minded women like them.

The needs of the Great War, as it had become called, accelerated the process of the widening role of women in all levels of society. When working men marched off to war their womenfolk took over their jobs whether as factory workers, bus conductors, shop assistants, office workers or even as stokers of coke furnaces. Upper class ladies who had previously been chauffeured in limousines along the neatly gravelled roadways of their family estates volunteered to drive clumsy ambulances through the mud and shell holes of war devastated Flanders, quite often under enemy fire. Their protective parents were horrified and fathers would order their daughters home with the firm expectation that they would be obeyed. A few were obeyed, such was the strength of parental authority over unmarried daughters of almost any age.

Katharine Winter, for instance, a vicar's daughter, had Catholic leanings even before the Mission came to Swaffham. She had been expressly forbidden by her staunchly Protestant parent from attending the Catholic Mass. He would have seen it as his duty, being a father from the Victorian era, to protect his daughter from the error of her ways. He would have expected her as a dutiful daughter, although a grown woman, to obey his wishes. Not unsurprisingly to our way of thinking, Katharine disappointed her father in this respect.

The wartime government accepted and even encouraged much of this new concept of women's role in society as a convenient solution to the labour shortage caused by the massive military recruitment programme. But with that temporary proviso they still saw these new, independent women as a threat to the established order, which of course they were. The woman's place was in the home as housewife, mother or dutiful daughter caring for aged parents. The current widespread activities of women outside the home were regarded with great unease.

How the coterie of strong willed, independent ladies supporting the nuns in Swaffham was regarded can be only a matter of conjecture, but the anxiety of the Establishment was made evident from an unlikely source, but it does illustrate how ingrained this prejudice was. Bishop Keating, who was a good friend and a very active supporter of the Foundation, felt the need to express his concern in a private letter that *"Sister Donata is exceeding her authority..."* in her efforts to obtain the premises in Cotmangate Street. In those days it was unusual for a woman to have any authority at all, let alone exceed it!

It was hard for a woman to make progress in that male dominated world, but it was in that climate that Sister Donata did so much to secure the beginnings of the Convent of the Sacred Heart, the Centenary of which is being celebrated this year.

Sacred Heart Convent

Chapter 2 MEMORIES FROM FORMER PUPILS

Childhood Memories of Wartime Swaffham.

I was just 5 years old when war was declared on September 3rd 1939, I started school at the Convent of the Sacred Heart three days later.

The smaller pupils were issued with Mickey Mouse gasmasks and once a week we had to practise putting them on and filing in an orderly manner down to the cellar. Most air raids were at night so we did not often have to do this for real, but if we did lessons would continue in the cellar.

The Head Teacher was Sister Teresa, we did not see her very often but one thing I remember about her was a very pleasant smell like vanilla, probably a toilet water she used. Sister Anthony was my main teacher, every morning directly after prayers she used to make us walk round the class room three times with a book on our heads, we were told this would help us grow up holding our heads high and our backs straight!

All the Sisters wore full length black dresses and hoods with starched white bands round their faces and a bow under the chin, and for work blue aprons. Sister Anthony used to pin up her skirts and play netball with us. I had piano lessons with Sister Winifrede.

All the staff in those days were Nuns even the cooks and gardeners, they worked very hard, all were kind but quite strict. There were more boarders than day girls, most of the pupils just went home for the weekends. There were a few boys but I think only 5 to 7 years old. The total number of pupils was 70.

I have fond memories of Swaffham Convent and I did well there. In 1945 I sat the scholarship for the Grammar School along with 23 other girls and we all passed. I went on to further my education at East Dereham High School.

Many years later when I was Chair of Governors at a primary school I gave my support to encourage children in Key Stage 1 (4-7yrs) I firmly believe the first five years at school are the most important ones in a child's life, they set the pattern for his/her future. I know I was privileged during those years.

I was an only child, we lived in Pedlars Grove, my parents moved there when they married in 1932. My dad was Tom Burton, he had a grocery business, a mobile shop--no supermarkets in those days! He and my Mum used to make up orders in a warehouse and Dad would deliver them in his van, mostly in the Swaffham and Watton area.

Everything had to be weighed then, butter, cheese, lard came in big blocks and sugar in a sack. Dad carried a notebook and when he delivered the groceries to his customer, he would write down next week's order in his book.

Food was rationed and everyone had a ration book. The coupons in these had to be marked, cut out and sent to the Ministry of Food. Later, when I was older, I used to help with this on a Friday night, thus earning my pocket money.

When the war started and petrol was rationed, all the tradesmen in the town organised a pool service. This meant dad would deliver meat and bread with his groceries and the butcher/baker would take our goods to another area. The system worked very well, there was a wonderful spirit with all working together, sadly this usually only happens in times of trouble and stress!

Most families had air raid shelters, either an Anderson, which was a corrugated iron shed buried in the garden, or a Morrison like a heavy iron topped cage in the house. We had quite a big garden which was on two levels, this worked well for an Anderson, it could be put on the rise, covered with earth and plants and from the air it would look like a rockery. It had a small doorway down 4 steps and dad made a narrow bunk from an old car seat. There were two folding chairs a little table, a spirit stove, a small cupboard holding tea, dried milk, sugar, a biscuit tin and on top of the cupboard were cups and saucers. We had electric light, also candles, in case of a power cut.

My father was about 42 when war broke out and considered to be too old for the armed services. He had been a soldier in the Royal Signals towards the end of the 1st World War and to do his bit, he joined the Auxiliary Fire Service.

When the siren sounded warning a raid, dad would grab me out of bed, wrap me in a blanket, always left ready and carry me downstairs. Mum would pick up a small case, which rarely left her side, holding various papers and personal treasures. She would lead the way across the garden to the shelter with a pencil torch, the only light allowed in the blackout. Dad would kiss mum and I goodbye and cycle off to the Fire station, where he would remain until the all clear and sometimes long after. Lots of incendiary bombs were dropped, aiming for the many airfields that surrounded Swaffham. Eventually dad would come home very black and smelling of smoke, the fire service was very different in the 40s and sometimes all they had to fight the fires, was a bucket and stirrup pump. After dad had left, mum would put me to bed in the bunk and read me a story. She always did some knitting and soon the sound of her voice and the click of her knitting needles would send me to sleep. When the raid was over I was given bread and butter, spread with condensed milk, as a special treat before going up to bed. Some raids went on all night and some were soon over, occasionally there would be more than one during the night.

My aunt Winifred Salter, who lived at 25 London Street, was married in 1942 to a sergeant in the Royal Artillery and at first he was stationed in Swaffham. I used to love Sunday mornings, when dad and I went to the market place to watch uncle George drilling the men. He was very loud and stern, not at all like the uncle who played with me at home, I used to try to make him laugh but that never worked when he was on duty. During the war they lived with my gran, they had a Morrison shelter in their front room. On its floor was a large fluffy feather bed, when I was a little girl visiting them I was allowed to play in the Morrison with my dolls.

When the blitz on London started, it was decided that Norfolk was a reasonably safe place to evacuate people who had been bombed out of their homes, or living in danger zones. Dad became Billeting Officer, this meant he was responsible for finding accommodation for these unfortunate people. He still kept the grocery business and mum did more of the work behind the scenes. A telephone was installed at our house, it was fixed to the wall, the earpiece was on a cord to hold at the ear but we had to speak into the part still attached to the wall. A party of evacuees would arrive from London at very short notice and dad had to house them the same day. If this was not possible, they would be bedded down for the night in the Vicarage Room on the Camping Land and the WVS (mum was in this) and Salvation Army would man soup kitchens to feed them. The government provided thick army blankets and camp beds to be used there.

It was a sorry sight, I can remember families who had been bombed out and only had the clothes on their backs, yet still remarkably cheerful just glad to be alive. Usually the parties would consist of 50 to 60 women and children, sometimes a teacher was sent, with perhaps 30 children to look after. All of them were found homes, the townsfolk were wonderful in their response, they always seemed to be homed within 24 hours. Dad requisitioned all empty houses and spare bedrooms. Families were kept together--no easy task! Again the WVS and Salvation Army worked hard to find clothes and equipment for the needy.

Some of the Londoners returned to London very quickly, preferring to risk the bombs, rather than be separated from their friends and loved ones. Most of them stayed and

Convent of the Sacred Heart,

Swaffham,

Norfolk.

THE CONVENT OF THE SACRED HEART keeps a Boarding - and Day School for Girls and Boys (the latter to 9 years of age). The aim of the School is to maintain the atmosphere of a refined and attractive home, to train the boarders for their future life and to afford health and comfort to the students. Pupils can be prepared for the Cambridge School Certificate, Music - and Drawing Examinations.

The Convent is well situated and has good grounds. Sports available, Hockey, Tennis and Basket - Ball.

The Course of Instruction comprises General Subjects:

Religious Knowledge, English, Mathematics, Science, History, Geography, Languages; Plain and Fancy Needlework, Drawing and Painting, Shorthand and Typewriting, Music.

The School Year is divided into the following:

Christmas Term
Easter Term
Midsummer Term

FEES PER TERM

	£ s. d.
Boarders	17 17 0
Weekly Boarders ...	16 16 0
Day Pupils up to 11 years	3 3 0
Day Pupils 11 years and plus	3 15 0

EXTRA FEES

	£ s. d.
Music Lessons	1 10 0
Shorthand	1 10 0
Typewriting	1 1 0
Private Lessons in French, German, Painting	1 10 0
Dancing	1 1 0

All Fees are payable in advance.

Children requiring anything beyond the ordinary school diet are charged accordingly.

Books, Music and Sewing Materials are charged to the pupils.

A prospectus printed in 1946 for The Sacred Heart Convent School
Supplied by Mrs Pauline Coe (former Pupil)

became part of the community, sometimes I meet someone from those days and they tell me what a wonderful job my dad did and how being sent to Swaffham changed their lives.

There were some very sad occasions too:_

My mum was a soft touch, often raiding our own store for the evacuees. Biscuits used to arrive in our warehouse in large square tins to be weighed into bags, there were always broken ones at the bottom and Mum used to save these and many other things for those less fortunate than ourselves. Sometimes she was 'taken for a ride'. There was one lady who arrived from the East End with seven children, we never knew if they were all hers. She was nicknamed throughout the town as Mother Riley, she was given a huge old pram and it usually overflowed with children! She was a merry soul always ready for a laugh and my mother got quite fond of her! When winter came she said I wish I had a warm coat, mum cycled home and returned with a really good coat of hers, with a warm fur collar. A few weeks later mum saw another lady wearing this coat and learned that Mother Riley had sold it for 30 shillings- (£1.50) a lot of money then, (my school fees at the Convent were 50 shillings-a term, plus music lessons and stationery).

Patricia Anne Pearson, (nee Burton), 1939 - 1945

A Pupil From 1968-1978

I started as a day pupil when I was almost 7 years old in 1968 and then started boarding the following September in 1969. I vividly remember walking into the Junior dormitory with my mother on the first night of boarding and seeing rows of beds, knowing that one of these beds would be mine. Being an only child with my own room, I was not keen on this set up but deciding for my mother's sake to keep these thoughts to myself. I remember my mother asking me if I would be OK and as a switched on child, with a mind of my own, answered, "I would cope" and cope I did until 1978 .

In the early days boys also boarded up to the age of 11 years and then left to go on to various secondary schools, be it State or Public schools. I remember there were various Eastern European nuns who seemed to come and go, as well as UK born nuns, some more in touch with life than others .

I settled reasonably well into the routine of boarding school life, rules were in abundance, which as a strong self willed child I enjoyed trying to break where possible. Weekends consisted of long Sunday walks through various Swaffham country footpaths, picking the odd blackberry along the way in summer and stomping in Wellington boots through mud in the winter. As a sporty, lively child I enjoyed these walks, not just because it was exercise but because it was a break from the confines of the school grounds.

I do remember the midnight feasts we had as teenagers, raiding the kitchens and eating with torches.

I made a number of good friends at school and to be honest got on with most people. I

A Garden Fete Display from the 1960's

have kept in touch with some of the girls, going on holidays, attending each other's weddings, meeting up for reunions.

On leaving the Convent I headed back to London, where my family were based and went on to a Public School in the City of London. I later joined the Civil Service, working for various Departments such as ACAS , HSE and OFSTED and for sometime now have been running a business with my husband, running educational music workshops in schools.

I did return to live and work in Norfolk in 1994 for five years. My husband and I have two children, Chantal now 19 years and Marcus 17 years. Our daughter Chantal Robinson-Bailey, attended the Convent in 1998 in the PR class for one year, before we returned to live and work in London. Chantal is currently in her first year at Brunel University studying a physiotherapy degree. Marcus is currently at College studying a BTEC level 3 IT extended course, with the aim of going to University in 2015, to study a Computer Network degree.

My story may be different from others, in the fact that I am of mixed parentage, Caribbean/white and there were virtually no other children of colour during my time at the Convent . However, it saddens me when I hear and read about some black or mixed race people's experiences of school life, in the 1960s and 1970s and the difficulties they experienced . Perhaps I was fortunate, lucky whatever you want to call it, but the Convent for the most part holds memories of a once in a lifetime experience.
Marcella Robinson (now Mrs Marcella Robinson-Bailey) 1968-1978

Three Generations

Early memories of the Convent revolve around Sisters, who although appearing severe to a five year old, were not. I had always known them from time spent every Sunday at Mass with my mother Mrs Winifred Symonds, a staunch Irish Catholic. This was wartime (1943) and though we were an ordinary, hard-working family it seemed normal to be able to go to school there.

Our Reception or Infant class was around the red covered long tables of the dining room, where the boarders and some day pupils had their meals which, by the way always smelt delicious despite rationing.

I lived over the wall in one of the cottages on Mangate Street and as a consequence, always knew you were subject to the rules of the school regarding conduct or manners. Incidentally, my younger brother who also attended the school from 1948, jumped over that wall on his first day there and went home! He was returned very quickly!

This was a time of great hardship for everyone but school seemed fine and I suppose a secure happy place. The Sisters who shared all duties in the daily running of the school, were known to all of the pupils by name and their tasks, and as a consequence when I go to their corner of the Swaffham Cemetery and see their names, I have an instant picture of them and what they did.

The classrooms, the kitchen, the gardens, chickens were all part of our normal day. When the first 'new' building was finished, we were the first class to use it and were in no doubt about the consequences if we didn't look after it! The other long wooden building housed the two senior classes. The history of the school has been well documented and is readily available.

Following in my footsteps, my daughter Sally went to the Convent from the age of six and later served on the PTA for many years. Her daughter then followed. Maybe this is a short ramble but the SHCS will always be something a little bit special to me.
Brian Symonds 1944-1949

I joined the Convent school at the age of six. My parents were working class and scrimped and saved every penny they could to give me a good education. At the time a six year old, or even a sixteen year old, wouldn't appreciate how their parents went without to provide this.

Sr Agnes, was the first Sister to teach me; such a scary sister at the age of six but having continued to visit her until her death, I soon learnt what a loving, caring and dedicated lady she was. It was always a pleasure to visit the town and see her upright walk coming towards you and always having time to share a few moments with you.

Of course I was also taught by Sr Francis, Sr Catherine and also having Sr Margaret as my Sr Superior. I remember pupils leaving classes to have music lessons with Sr Gertrude and the lovely smells coming from the kitchen, as Sr Mary Joseph stood at the kitchen door. Sr Laita was always attending to the gardens but the Sister I am sure most Swaffham residents and pupils will always refer to, is Sr Madeline and her scooter. It didn't seem right seeing the scooter heading towards town being driven by a nun, but she did it and was a memorable character too.

As in all walks of life, I remember happy and sad times spent at the school but the happy times out-weigh the sad. During sad times, I knew school could always help and support. The pastoral care was second to none and I know it still is.

Although looking back, I know I could have done better with results, but I am sure being able to list the Convent of the Sacred Heart as the school I attended on my CV, has always helped me in job interviews. People are always interested in Convent Girls!!!

I was offered every job I applied for, the school always taught good manners, discipline and self confidence and this was continued at home.

Sr Francis always congratulated us all when we entered sports, music or indeed any competitions, she told us we were all winners for entering and taking part. This would always boost your confidence because I remember feeling she was addressing just me when she spoke.

I have happy memories of school trips to France and Germany. Sr Francis and the teaching staff always joined in and gave us many laughs along the way. I remember Sr Francis attempting to drive a bus in Germany (not on the road!!!) and Mrs Gribbon, our HE teacher and Mrs Foxwell our music teacher joining the pupils for a swim.

After leaving the school at the age of 16, I didn't return for some time, but once attitudes change and one grows up, you actually realise how lucky you were. I went back to see the Sisters and to date, they haven't been able to keep me away because once I married and had a daughter of my own, she also attended the school. I became a member of the PTA committee and then went on to become Chairman for several years. The PTA were an active group, always trying to fundraise for various things needed in and around the school. Sr Francis always had a great ability to have the money raised earmarked, but I got a buzz out of that and spent many happy, hardworking years being part of the team. My motto was, that whilst I was helping raise money for the school, my daughter would benefit from whatever was being purchased while she was a pupil there.

Sally Hayes 1970-1981

Were you really a Convent Girl is a question I am often asked.
And yes I was, from the age of six.

I remember going to visit Sr Francis with my mum at a very young age and feeling at home there, and when I was old enough to understand, my parents told me that I would be going to the school when I was six. I remember leaving my 'old school', walking out of the gate and asking if I was starting at the Convent the next day. I was told I had a visit from Father Christmas first, which was very exciting.

After the Christmas holiday, I joined and soon made friends from various places in Norfolk. Most of those friends stayed with me until the day I left, aged 16, and interestingly a few of us have part time jobs together. Employers like the Convent girls because they are organised, well-mannered and disciplined.

I attended the school when Miss Diana Wynter introduced a massive change; boys started in the Senior School. That was sure to put the cat amongst the pigeons but my year soon adapted to our four new boys.

School trips and visits were always on offer and lots of competitions were always suggested for all to take part in. Sport was not my thing but I would always have a go. On the other hand, music was my thing and throughout my time at the school I gained Grade 7 in clarinet, Grade 4 in piano and Grade 6 vocally.

Music played a big part in my time whilst at the SHS. I was a member of the school choir and orchestra and always offered to sing either in a group or as an individual should I be asked. I remember opening the Christmas Carol Concert from the Sports Hall balcony, with the first verse of Once in Royal David's City. It was an honour to be asked to do this but also quite nerve racking. I always volunteered to sing or play at the House Music Festival and was always very proud when Sandringham performed.

Mr Murphy, when he joined the school, brought his love of music too and together we formed the Mangate Street Preachers, a band consisting of musicians from the senior school.

I was an active pupil at the school who was always ready to lend a hand. I helped at all PTA events. My mum was the chairperson for a few years and on the committee for all of my school life, so there was little choice for me, having said that, I loved helping.

I led the Christian Union group for the last two years of my time at Sacred Heart. During my final year I was the House Captain for Sandringham and was also appointed Deputy Head Girl. I gained excellent GCSE results and was the first pupil, aged 13, to gain a GCSE in German (thanks to Sr Emilia)

It isn't until you leave someone or somewhere that you realise what you had and how lucky you were...........will there ever be a 6th Form at the Sacred Heart School?

Charlotte Hayes 2001-2011, Deputy Head Girl 2010-20

Happy Memories

I started at the Convent in 1978 when I joined Sister Agnes' class - Junior 2. I loved the school from my first day and had only been there a matter of weeks when I started talking about boarding!

In Junior 3 I became a boarder, I was in the 'Big Dorm' with 20 other girls, and here are some of the things I remember:

◊   Sister Monica teaching us to crochet
◊   Mrs Beardsley - junior prep
◊   Wednesday night - hair washing night
◊   Piano practice in the basement - scary and haunted!!!
◊   Judo with PC Jackson
◊   Being woken up by Sister Francis and a large noisy bell
◊   Staying in bed until the last possible moment
◊   Getting dressed under the covers in the winter
◊   Top of the Pops on Thursday nights
◊   Getting the toaster for breakfast time
◊   Making up dance rountines to Bucks Fizz - Making Your Mind Up
◊   The fire alarm going off once at about 2am and having to stand outside while the fire brigade checked the boarding house
◊   Learning to Maypole dance for the summer fete
◊   Our production of 'A Christmas Carol'
◊   Swimming on hot summer evenings
◊   Going into town in pairs with a shopping list for the entire boarding house and mostly buying sherbet in different flavours
◊   Senior school and no more summer dresses
◊   Sister Francis roller skating on the infant playground

I was a boarder until my last year in school - 1987, my last dorm was at the top of the house with Dawn, Claire, Katie, Amanda, Rustina and Hannah.
Sister Francis would often sit on Dawn's bed and chat to us, the conversations ere mainly about school, home and our plans for the future but occasionally Sister Francis talked about herself, never giving much away but always supporting us. As I look back now, with two children of my own, I realise what a huge responsiblity Sister Francis had looking after us all, and I am sure we did not make it easy for her.

Thank-you-Sister-Francis.

Joanna Kirkham (nee Black)

Chapter 3 1989-2014 THE HISTORY IN YEARS

✞ 1989 –1990

- **30th September 1989 -** The Middle School, was formally opened by Bishop Alan Clark of East Anglia. This building comprised of:
- ➢ two Science laboratories, ICT suite
- ➢ Home Economics
- ➢ two classrooms for Juniors 3 & 4.,
- ➢ a School Office & Reception area
- ➢ A large statue of the Risen Christ was donated to the school by Fr John Cureton
- ➢ Mother Fidelis Weninger, former General carried a large carved crucifix from Rome
- A History of the School was published, covering the first 75 years of the school 1914-1989.
- The Termly Contribution payment scheme was introduced to pay for school trips.
- Mrs Jane Howarth commenced German Conversation lessons.
- Yvonne, our cook is married to Paul Hooten

Head girl: Hannah Reynolds,
Deputy: Victoria Brett
- **Facilities:** The PTA donated £37,000 towards the costs of the new building. A voluntary levy towards the Building Fund of £15 per term over two years was introduced in May 90.
- **Senior School Activities:**
- ➢ Form 3 to Walsingham - September 89
- ➢ Form 2 Denver Sluice & Mileham
- ➢ Form 4 Castle Acre
- ➢ Forms 1&2 visited Flag Fen
- The annual November '89 trip to London saw visits to:

- ➢ Form 1 St Paul's Cathedral, Form 2 Tower of London, Form 3 Houses of Parliament, Westminster Abbey, & Downing Street, Form 4 National Theatre & Tate Gallery
- ➢ Forms 3 & 4 visit to the Royal Academy and the V&A
- ➢ Form 5 went to Hammersmith to see the TV recording of 'Bread'
- ➢ Form 2 undertook a computer Mathematics project
- ➢ Forms 4 & 5 D of E' Award weekend to Buckenham Mill
- ➢ Form 3 'A Midsummer Night's Dream'- Norwich
- ➢ Forms 1 & 2 'The Merchant of Venice'
- **Competitions**
- Eastern Gas 'Managing your Lifestyle' was won by pupils, Grace Chambers & Johanna Moss.
- We entered the Heinz Baked Bean Competition 'Beany Meany Microwavy' over 1000 schools took part and six entries from Form 2 at our school were selected.
- Anna Marshall became a National Runner up, one of only four finalists representing East Anglia. She won a Sharp's Touch Control Microwave for the school, plus a trophy, book voucher and a recipe book for herself. Lucy Reed was selected as Area runner-up and was presented with £50 for the school and a book voucher for herself.
- Pupils participated in a workshop, led by Northern Ballet, based on the paintings of L.S.Lowry.
- Eleven girls were confirmed by Bishop Peter Smith.

- ♦ **Lower School Activities:**
- ➢ Junior 3 & 4 visited Portsmouth and Isle of Wight, also Windsor Safari Park
- ➢ Junior 4 - London Zoo & Park.
- ➢ A performance of 'Matilda' was attended at the Big Top Theatre
- ➢ Infants visit Snettisham Safari Deer Farm
- ➢ Gepetto's Workshop gave a performance at school for Pre Infants to Form 2
- ➢ Jacko, dressed in old fashioned police uniform rode Constable, a horse injured in the Hyde Park bombings into the school grounds
- ♦ **Boarders** took part in a performance of 'Alice in Wonderland'
- ♦ **Overseas Visits:** In 1990 pupils enjoyed a Ski Trip to Lofer
- ♦ **School Events:**
- ➢ A 'Housecraft Afternoon' took place when pupils made items to go on House stalls at the Christmas Bazaar
- ➢ The Garden Fete raised £1780
- ♦ **Charity:**
- ➢ A Lent Challenge was undertaken, when pupils filled Smartie tubes with 1p pieces, the final total collected was donated to Charity
- ➢ The Annual Sponsored Walk for the whole school raised £3332
- ♦ **Music:**
- ➢ The theme of the Lower School's Christmas Concert was 'Torvic and the Trolls'
- ➢ The Lower School's Summer Performance was 'The Emperor and the Nightingale'
- ➢ The annual House Music Festival was held
- ➢ Pupils entered the Norfolk & Norwich Festival
- ♦ **Ballet, LAMDA and Music** examinations were undertaken with very pleasing results
- ♦ **Sport:**
- ➢ The usual selection of sports - Netball, Hockey, Lacrosse, Rounders, Tennis, Gymnastics, Athletics, Cross Country & Swimming were enjoyed by pupils.
- ➢ Out of school sports offered were a Riding Course at North Runcton & Surfing at Denver.

✞ 1990 – 1991

- ♦ **War ravaged Yugoslavia**.
- ♦ **Staff News:** Sr Angela McMenamin, (Headteacher 1953-1971) died on 19th September. She taught at the Convent from 1929 and entered the Congregation in 1932. Mrs Merrit supplied for Mrs Henden as she was on maternity leave.

Headgirl: Clare Kelly,
Deputy: Hannah Hunt

- ♦ **Facilities:**
- ➢ Seven keyboards & a PA system were given to the school.
- ➢ A new Astroturf Tennis Court was built.
- ♦ **Senior School Activities**: On the annual London trip pupils visited:
- ➢ Form 1 - London Museum & St Paul's
- ➢ Form 2 - Tower of London
- ➢ Form 3 - Planetarium, Madam Tussauds
- ➢ Forms 1 – 4 went to see 'Joseph & His Amazing Technicolor Dreamcoat' in London
- ➢ Forms 3 & 4 -attended the Royal Norfolk Show to carry out a survey
- ➢ Form 1 - The Broads, McDonalds and Flag Fen
- ➢ Form 4 – Hunstanton and Art trip to Fitzwilliam Museum, Cambridge
- ➢ Forms 3 & 4 – English trip to Stratford

- on Avon & Warwick Castle
- D of E Award weekends were held in Derbyshire, Thetford & Ickburgh.
- Confirmation for Catholic members of Form 4 - was held at Walsingham and Form 5 Anglican pupils were confirmed at Hindringham.
- We entered a team in the Crime Prevention Quiz, but lost to Springwood.
- Pupil, Susanne Howard, won the BBC Radio & Hansard Society Competition she also met MP, John Major.

♦ **Lower School Activities:**
- Jodie Wick, Junior 4 won the competition to design the programme for the Swaffham Festival of Youth; the venue for this event was our Gym; our School won the section for the Juniors
- Junior 4- visited Kentwell Hall in costume;
- Infants 1 – 3 visited Cockthorpe Toy Museum; also visited Gressenhall Rural Life Museum.
- Pre Infants saw the 'Firebird' presented by the West Midland Children's Theatre.
- The Lower School saw 'Sleeping Beauty' at the Norwich Puppet Theatre.
- Pupils of the Lower School performed a Christmas Play, 'The Shepherd's Story'.
- The LS performed a Red Indian Musical at the Garden Fete

♦ **Charities:** Overall fund raising throughout the year totalled £4738. Individual charities who benefited included :
- The 'Malcolm Sargeant Concert Fund for Children',
- The Lower School took part in a 'Readathon' and raised £1200 for this charity; they also held a toy sale which raised a further £90
- Non Uniform Day raised £60 for Cancer Research;
- £105 was raised for the Blue Peter Appeal for Romania;
- £382 for poor people in Brazil – non uniform day, unexpected arrival of 8 overgrown schoolgirls and one extremely scruffy, badly behaved boy with a water pistol (Miss Gooderson).
- Forms 1 – 4 raised £305 for Bangladesh by undertaking the assault course at RAF Marham;
- Raffle Tickets were sold for the Theatre Royal Development Fund and raised £30;
- The Sponsored Walk raised a total of £3326, which went towards Computers.
- Harvest Festival raised £133 for CAFOD;
- The Lower School Carol Concert raised £320 for the Blue Peter Romanian Appeal
- The Senior Concert raised a further £320, which was sent to CRISIS at Christmas.
- Pupils also made a collection of letters & comforts to send to troops involved in the 1st Gulf War.

♦ **Music and Dance:**
- Fiona Andrew, sang in the Kings Lynn Amateur Arts Festival & won the competition.
- The Tollhouse Company held a 'Dance Workshop' for the whole school.
- Twenty eight pupils performed in Norfolk and Norwich County Music Festival.
- Our Ballet & LAMDA students achieved excellent results, including 2 Grade 8's & 1 Silver medal.

- **Sport:**
  - ➤ Three girls were selected to play Netball for the County.
  - ➤ Pupils also participated in an after school Riding Course, and Short Tennis Course, took part in Cross Country & Athletics events; & performed in Gymnastics display teams.

✝ 1991-1992

- ◆ The war in Bosnia brought about terrible death and destruction.
- ◆ The Conservative Party, led by John Major, won the 1992 General Election. In our School Election the Tories also won.
- ➤ **Staff News:** Sr Vedrana Ljubic joined us from Yugoslavia as well as student – Zrinka (Ziggy) Beno. Her sister Judita came came for a holiday and was stranded in England due to the war. After their father's death in the war their brother Dormogoj joined them in England and was like Judita given free education by another religious group, the de la Salle brothers in Ipswich.
- ➤ Mrs Marie Mansfield (Maternity leave – had a daughter Katherine),
- ➤ Mr Donald Carter semi-retired, but continued to teach piano to private pupils.
- ➤ Mrs Fryer, cleaner from the Junior School died in February. Pupils sang at her funeral in St Peter & Paul Church.

Headgirl: Grace Chambers,
Deputy: Joanna Moss

- ◆ **Senior School Activities:**
- ➤ On successive London trips pupils went to see 'Joseph & his Amazing Technicolour Dreamcoat' with Jason Donovan
- ➤ Forms 3 & 4 visited the Tate Gallery, Courtauld Institute and Pygmalion at the National Theatre;
- ➤ Form 1 - went to Bridewell Museum
- ➤ Form 2 - went to Tower of London
- ➤ Form 5 ;Gressenhall Rural Life Museum
- ➤ The Tolhurst Company held workshops in school for all year groups.
- ➤ Forms 3 & 4 went on an extended trip to Stratford on Avon, attended a performance of 'Twelfth Night' at the Memorial Theatre and also visited Mary Arden's House and Warwick Castle.
- ➤ Form 2 visited Santon Downham on an Environmental Studies trip. Form 2- visited the Rowntree Factory in Norwich.
- ➤ Form 1 took part in a Puppet Workshop & Show in Norwich.
- ➤ Whilst undertaking the D of E Award Scheme, pupils learned the skills of Photography, Shooting & Pottery and went to Kings Lynn Crown Court as part of the Service Section.
- ➤ A new venture, a Barclays School Bank, was opened by Form 3 under the guiding hand of Mrs Sally Henderson.
- ➤ Form 5- helped to edit the annual School Magazine.
- ➤ Two Pilgrimages were organised in June to Walsingham.
- ➤ Forms 3 & 4 - attended a Science Lecture at the UEA.
- ◆ **Lower School Activities**
- ➤ A visit to the Dinosaur Park at Lenwade and Infants 3 - Junior 4 saw a morning performance of 'Scherhazade'.
- ➤ Junior 1 - visited Caithness Crystal in King's Lynn.
- ➤ Junior 3 & 4 followed the journey of a 'Cucumber Sandwich' at UEA, saw a matinee performance matinee performance of 'Cats' in Norwich,

participated in a re-enactment day at Kentwell Hall & enjoyed a three day visit to Kent including visits to Canterbury Cathedral and tales, Aylesford Priory, the White Cliffs Experience & Windsor Safari Park..

- Junior 4 visited the Egyptian Display at the British Museum.
- **Overseas Visits:** The Ski Trip went to Valloire.
- Forms 2 & 3 visited Rouen,Forges les Eaux, Paris, Bayeux & Arromanches.
- **School Events:-** Lower School pupils took part in the Big Balloon Show. Other events held were a Christmas Play with Karaoke; House Quiz; Computer Club.
- **Charity:** Lenten events included Leap Frog, Sponsored Silence, Shoe Polishing & Car Washing which, all together, raised over £500. On Non-Uniform Day, pupils dressed in clothes of successive decades and Form 1 wore '1920s'. £80 was raised from this event. The Carol Service raised £540 for Yugoslavia
- **Music:** Mr Eddie Seales reformed the Orchestra; starting with 2 saxophones, 5 violins, 2 clarinets, 9 flutes, plus drums, a harp & recorders. Our Orchestra won the first prize at the Swaffham Festival of Youth. Tollhouse Company led another of their Dance Workshops. Christmas Carol Concert included a performance of 'Angels to the Kings'. A Drama Evening was held & included a performance of the 'Easter Cantata'.
- **Ballet / Dance** had many successes, including one by Sarah Skinner, who won a scholarship to the Olga Robinson School of Dancing.
- **Sport:**
- Form 5 took part in Archery lessons.

- The usual sports were played during the year Hockey, Netball. Gymnastics, Tennis, Rounders. Lacrosse, & Swimming.

✝ 1992 – 1993
- Sr Francis had a heart attack in Summer 1992, so Mrs Ann Baker was appointed Acting Headteacher for the year.
- The school adopted the nation's year settings, thus Form 1 became Year 7.
- 1993 edition of the School Magazine changed from A5 to A4 size

Headgirl: Lucy Reed;
Deputy: Debbie Bircham

- **Facilities and Equipment** purchased through the year included Computers, Staging, a Photocopier, Camcorder & a Computerised Weather Station. The Library was computerised.
- **Senior School Activities:** The first Presentation Evening was held.
- D of E group went gliding for the 'skills' element at RAF Marham.
- The tradition of holding First Aid and Self Defence courses began.
- Y10 went on a field trip to the River Nar as part of their Geography GCSE
- Y11's Final Outing was a visit to Norwich;
- Y7 took part in a Science Day at UEA;
- Y5 - 8 went to see the 'Nutcracker' at Norwich;
- Y9-11 to the ballet 'Romeo and Juliet';
- Y7 attended a performance at the Norwich Puppet Theatre.
- The London visit included visits to the Courtauld Institute & Museum of London, Y10 whilst Y9 went to the Houses of Parliament
- **Lower School Activities:** Visits were made to:

- ➤ Y5- 6 Hatfield House
- ➤ Y3 Hunstanton Sea Life World ;
- ➤ Y2 -5 Sandringham Schools Trail Day
- ➤ YPR & R Thrigby Hall
- ◆ **Performances seen included:**
- ➤ 'The Witches' at Norwich Y3 & 4;
- ➤ 'The Merry Pranks of Till' Y2-4;
- ➤ Norwich Puppet Theatre YPR & Y1 and following this visit Gepatto's presented a workshop on puppets at school.
- ➤ The Christmas Concert told the Nativity Story and also included 'Christopher Columbus'.
- ➤ A Staff Pantomime was staged - 'The Village of Three Corners',
- ➤ Pupils performed the Pied Piper at the Garden Fete.
- ➤ Five babies visited Y2.
- ◆ **Overseas**: Y8 went to the French Alps.
- ◆ **School Events:** Christmas Bazaar raised £2,077; The Garden Fete was also held.
- ◆ **Charity:** A vanload of medical supplies was sent to Croatia. Lower School took part in Comic Relief.
- ◆ **Music:** The Orchestra continued to grow. Alexis Jackson, Y6, auditioned for National Childrens' Orchestra. A House Music Festival was held again; and a Music and Drama Evening.
- ◆ **Dance:** Olga Robinson's pupils achieved Examination successes, from Grade 1 to 5 and Medals.
- ◆ **LAMDA** successes were achieved including four Bronze medals.
- ◆ **Sport:** An Equestrian Team went to the Rosebrook Equestrian Centre. They also attended an Equestrian Event held at Stonar School, Wilts.
- ➤ The usual round of sports of Athletics, Netball, Hockey, Gymnastics, Tennis, Rounders were played & the annual Swimming Gala was held.

✝ 1993 – 1994

- ◆ The 80th Anniversary of the school was celebrated.
- ◆ 100th Anniversary of death of Mother Foundress, Francesca Lechner, was commemorated.
- ◆ A visit was made to the School by Mother General, Sister Nicolina Hendges
- ◆ **Staffing News:**
- ➤ Mrs Ann Baker retired after 20 years as Head of Science & Deputy Headteacher; she was Acting Head whilst Sr Francis was ill.
- ➤ Sr Thomas More became Deputy Headteacher

Headgirl: Alex Dalton.

Deputy: Sophie Whigham

- ◆ **Facilities:** Lower School Classrooms repainted.
- ◆ **Senior School Activities:** Visits were made to:
- ➤ Y8 - Nestles Chocolate Factory
- ➤ Y9 - Houses of Parliament & Tate
- ➤ Y9 & 10 -Norwich for a performance of 'She Stoops to Conquer'
- ➤ Y8 - the new Tesco at Dereham.
- ➤ Y8 - attended a presentation of Gamelon Music (Javanese)
- ➤ Y10 Geograpghy River Study, Castle Acre
- ➤ Y11 Historians and Art Group to Gressenhall,
- ➤ Pupils enjoyed performances of 'Dr Faust' at the Puppet Theatre, Norwich;
- ➤ Y10 - 'Cinderella' (Royal Ballet) at Norwich.
- ➤ D of E Bronze Award training at Trimingham, Cromer & learnt pottery as one of their skills.
- ➤ Confirmation groups were held for C of E and Catholic pupils..

- Pupils staged a Passion Play; held a Quiz Evening & took part in a Ballet Workshop by the Northern Ballet Theatre Dancers.
- ◆ **Lower School Activities:**
- YPR, R & 1 went to Banham Zoo;
- Y3 - 7 visited Walsingham;
- Y5 & 6 went on an extended 3 day trip to Yorkshire staying at Hazelwood Castle; visiting Whitby, York Minster and the Jorvik Centre and the Eureka Museum, Halifax.
- Pupils attended a performance of 'Touchwood' in Thetford Forest & presented a performance at the Garden Fete on the theme 'Creation of the World'.
- Y1 – 4 visited Santon Downham,
- YR viewed a private toy collection
- YPR & R enjoyed a show at Norwich Puppet and Mr Pointing Glover brought his collection of owls to show the class
- Y1 &2 went to the theatre to see Button Moon
- Y2 – 4 visited Stranger's Hall and the Theatre Royal to watch BFG
- ◆ **Boarding:**
- There was a Boarding House Inspection;
- A visit was made by a group of French students who stayed in the Boarding House and attended classes
- ◆ **Overseas and Residential:**
- Staff and pupils skied at Folgarida, Italy.
- ◆ **Charity:** Fund raising events included:
- Red Nose Day; Non Uniform Day;
- Sugar Collection for Crisis at Christmas;
- 276 Shoe Boxes to Bosnia plus raising monies for a whole range of other causes and a Pearly King came to thank everyone.

- Some of the Sponsored Walk monies (£500) was sent to the Swaffham Cottage Hospital for a water bed.
- ◆ **Music, Dance & LAMDA Speech:** Another successful year.
- ◆ The House Drama Festival was won by Windsor.
- ◆ Y8's Passion Play for the school
- ◆ **Sport:**
- A Football Competition was held involving some very enthusiastic girls from Y5-11.
- The Equestrian event at Rosebrook Indoor Arena in October 1994 saw two teams entered from the School.

✠ 1994 – 1995

- ◆ Celebrations were held to mark VE / VJ days
- ◆ St Patrick's Day was celebrated with Sr Francis dressed as St Patrick.
- ◆ There was a Crisis in Bosnia affecting several of our convents there.
- ◆ **Staffing News:** Our first Japanese Student Miss Kazuko Sekiguchi joined for a year 'exchange' study.
- Sister Clare O'Carrigan, former teacher celebrated her 100th birthday.
- Year 6 took KS2 SATS for the first time
Headgirl: Helen Childerhouse;
Deputy: Eloise Latham-Smith
- ◆ **Facilities:** The building of a Sports Hall was proposed.
- ◆ **Senior School Activities**: Visits included trips to:
- Museum of Moving Image (MOMI) and the Globe Theatre - Y10;
- National Gallery and Tate - Y7- 9;.
- Local visits made to Norwich Cathedral & the Bridewell Museum Y8.
- Y10 took part in a Science Competition and attended a Science Demonstration

1990 The Eastern Schools Gymnastics Championships Teams

1994 boxes for Bosnia

1989 The Swimming Gala

1989 The 75th Anniversary of the
Daughter's of Divine Charity

1991/92 Sweet making by the boarders

1992/93 An art lesson

1993/94 PR making bread

1994/95 Drama Festival

1995/96 V.E.Day Celebrations

54

Prague

1997/1998 Sponsored Walk

1999 Sr. Emilia & Year 6 Bugs at
Book Fayre in the Sports Hall

1999 Harvest Festival

1999/2000 Music Festival

1998/99 Ballet Class

at the UEA and a Faraday Lecture in Ipswich.

- Environmental Studies for Y 7 & 8 required visits to Gressenhall Workhouse, & River Nar at Castle Acre.; with other visits being made to St Peter & Paul Church in Swaffham; King's Lynn, Thetford Forest, West Stow and Swaffham Museum;
- Y5&6 visited Lowestoft Fish Docks, Somerleyton Hall, Peterborough Cathedral, Fitzwilliam Museum Cambridge and Anglesey Abbey.
- Y10 D of E Award – took Self Defence and First Aid as part of their skills challenge.
- Amy Forbes Robinson, was featured in the EDP, for her study of her great, great grandfather, Sir Johnston Forbes Robertson (Shakespearean actor)
- **Lower School Activities**:
- YR&2 to Dinosaur Park, Lenwade;
- YR -3 &4 to Royal Norfolk Show;
- Y2&3 Great Cressingham Victorian School.
- There was a visit of pet lambs to the School in the spring.
- **Overseas:** May 1995 - A staff, parents and pupils trip to Paris and back was achieved in 48hrs.
- French Trip to Rouen
- **School Events**: New computerized way of producing the magazine was introduced. The School Uniform was changed with several new additions. The School prospectus was updated to a 'coloured' version.
- **Charity:** Concerts, collections, non uniform day and rich / poor lunches raised £1267.35.
- **Music:** Pupils continued to study a wide range of instruments. House Music

Festival
- **Drama:** House Drama Festival, was won by Balmoral
- **Speech:** Mrs Valerie Pickering and Mrs Catherine Hill achieved excellent LAMDA results, including a silver medal.
- **Dance:** A wide range of ballet, tap and modem exams were taken with the usual excellent results.
- **Sport:** Two teams of four entered the Rosebrook Equestrian event
- Many BAGA awards were achieved at Grades 3 - 6.
- The usual sports were played including Netball, Rounders, Tennis, Gymnastics, plus the annual Swimming Gala.

✝ **1995– 1996**
- A School Council was set up in the Senior School. Their first suggestion a 'Paint-a-thon', resulted in a "Rose Window" which is displayed in the gym.
- The Boarders were invited to Eccles Hall School to listen to David Kossof. His unique delivery of Bible Stories was enjoyed by all.
- Students from France, Croatia, Vienna and Brazil were amongst our young visitors during the year
- **Staffing News:**
- Sr Madeline Giquel died in April 1996
- Sr Catherine Maguire Superior since 1979 and Sr Jacinta Cirko (after 4 years here) moved to St Joseph's Convent, Chesterfield.

Headgirl: Sarah Skinner;
Deputy: Jodie Wick
- **Facilities:** Building of the Sports Hall was commenced. Tuck cupboard introduced. Collecting of Tesco Vouchers for computers.

- **Senior School Activities:**
  - Debating Society for Years 7-11 was introduced. The first debate being 'Should men be allowed to wear women's clothes and vice versa?'.
  - The annual London trip
  - St Paul's Y7; Tower of London Y8; Houses of Parliament Y9; The Globe Theatre and the Tate Gallery Y10;
  - West Stow and Castle Acre Y7;
  - Norwich Castle and Fens Y8;
  - Gressenhall Y11.
- **Science Department visits included:**
  - British Telecom, UEA,
  - Natural History Museum
  - Cavendish Laboratories, Cambridge;
  - Sacred Heart Seniors linked up with the Jason Project Florida to see and hear divers over the amazing internet link as they swam with manatee. This was the first link of its kind in the area and schools were invited by RAF Lakenheath.
  - Performances of 'An Inspector Calls' and 'Macbeth' were also attended.
  - First Careers Convention, for Y7-10 organised by Mrs Mansfield.
  - Year 5 & 6 pupils on a three day trip to Kent visited Canterbury Cathedral, Leeds Castle and the Chunnel Exhibition at Dover and stayed at Aylesford Priory.
  - C of E pupils were prepared for Confirmation..
  - D of E Award activities included Pottery with Mrs Heale, Photography, Self Defence, Abseiling and First Aid.
- **Lower School Activities:**
  - Visits were made to West Stow, Snettisham Park Farm, Thrigby Hall, the Dickens Experience at Hermitage Hall and Narborough Trout Farm.
  - A performance of 'Thumbelina' was attended by Year PR
  - School events included an Easter Egg Hunt & an Easter Bonnet Parade.
  - The Tollhouse Company and the Floating Theatre Company visited school
  - Thetford Grammar Y3 & 4 with their teachers spent the day with our pupils.
- **Overseas:**
  - Ski Trip went to Tonabe.
  - Past pupil Rosalin Latham-Smith undertook work experience in Zimbabwe
- **School Events:** 'Take Your Daughters to Work Day' took place for the second year
- **Charities:** £600 was raised for the Holy Childhood Mission and monies sent to a school in Bolivia.
- **Music Drama & Dance :** Pupils participated in the Norfolk County Music Festival. Excellent LAMDA and Dance results achieved once again
- **Sport:** A large squad, under Mrs Margaret Dalton's tuition, entered the East Region Gymnastics Competition. Tennis, Gymnastics, Netball, Hockey, Rounders, Cross Country and Swimming Gala were again undertaken throughout the year.
-

✟ 1996– 1997

- 1997 General Election was won by Labour with Tony Blair as Prime Minister
- This year's Garden Fete, themed 'Olde Time Music Hall', was held at the Swaffham Rugby Club because of construction on the Sports Hall
- To celebrate her Silver Jubilee, Sr Francis went to the USA and visited our 'sister'

school in Staten Island and a school in South Bend where our Sisters teach..

- The School joined, ISA, Independent School Association, which led to an inspection.
- The School gained the Sports Mark Award.
- The Lower School received an excellent Ofsted Report
- The statue of St Joseph in a glass fronted case in the garden was attacked and irreparably damaged by vandals – inside letters and prayers from the 1800's were found.
- **Staff News:**
- ➤ Fr John Cureton retired and Fr Trevor Richardson came as Parish Priest and Chaplain
- ➤ Mrs Jill Williamson retired after 22 years as year R class teacher and returned part time as Curriculum Support Teacher for the Lower School,
- ➤ Mrs Catherine Riedlinger nee Smith and former pupil, joined the Lower School

Headgirl: Franchesca Hunt;
Deputy: Helen Ballantyne

- **Facilities:**
- ➤ Building of the Sports Hall continued through the year with completion in 1997.
- ➤ Norfolk Careers Service continued to work with the school and through matched funding added to our Library.
- ➤ Library set up with six computers.
- ➤ The swimming pool had a new pumping system installed
- **Senior School Activities:**
- ➤ Y10&11 saw the Clothes Show Live '96 in Birmingham;
- ➤ **London Trip**: Y8 The Globe, Y9 Covent Garden Ballet, Y11 London Theatre Museum;

- ➤ GCSE Group went to Norwich to see a performance of 'Blood Brothers'.
- ➤ Y11 visited the Cavendish Laboratory in Cambridge.
- ➤ 'Take Your Daughters to Work Day'
  Lower School Activities:
- ➤ Excellent Nursery Inspection (YPR & R)
- ➤ Visits were made by pupils to West Stow, Walsingham, Narborough Trout Farm, Mr & Mrs Carter's Farm, the Inspire Centre, Gressenhall Museum, Iceni Village and Castle Rising.
- ➤ Pupils also saw a performance at Lydney House by the Norwich Puppet Theatre.
- ➤ Musician, Douglas Combes, entertained the pupils and involved all the staff.
- **School events:**
- ➤ Y5 - 11 received a talk from 'Mr Motivator' who spoke about memory, visions and ways of learning.
- ➤ Y10 held internal elections with imaginary parties as part of their GCSE English
- **Charity:**
- ➤ Concert raised £360 for the Swaffham Cottage Hospital and Fire Service.
- ➤ The school's Blue Peter Leprosy Appeal raised £186; Non Uniform Day was for 'Childline'
- ➤ Bags of sugar for "Crisis" were collected
- **Music & Drama:**
- ➤ The School Choir sang at the 1997 Music Festival at St Andrews Hall.
- ➤ The Orchestra played at the Music and Drama Evening.
- ➤ Y4 - 6 singers performed at the Royal Albert Hall as part of the Junior Proms.
- ➤ A talk was given about string instruments
- ➤ LAMDA Speech -another successful year

- **Sport:**
  - Pupils took part in the Norfolk County Schools Competition for Gymnastics.
  - For the 4th time our Tennis Squad won the County Midland Bank LTA competition and went on to represent Norfolk.

✝ 1997– 1998

- The first Minibus was bought for school
- Executive Committee set up to aid the Trustees
- **Staff News**
  - An 'after-school' Latin Club was set up for pupils, with Mrs Elizabeth Dean leading the group.
  - Mrs Zelos left to have a baby

Headgirl: Kate Scales;

Deputy: Chelsea Mello

- **Facilities:**
  - Re-organisation of the Middle School with specialist teaching introduced from Year 4 upwards.
  - The heating in the Sports Hall was improved
  - Professional Catering Services were employed to run the kitchen
  - The Boarding House was refurbished
  - An outdoor Nursery Play area was established.
- **Senior School Activities**:
  - Ben Osborne, BBC cameraman, came to Swaffham & gave a talk on life in the Antarctic entitled 'Life in the Freezer'.
  - A Careers Convention and Work Experience sessions were introduced;
  - D of E Award expedition took place in Thetford Forest.
  - Y6 - 8 to Gressenhall Rural Life Museum and Ranworth Broad
  - Y9-11 Science Activities at Alton Towers;
  - Y7-9 'As You Like It' at the Globe Theatre;
  - Y10 'An Inspector Calls' at the Garrick Theatre; London.
- **Lower School Activities:**
  - Y5&6 residential trip to Stratford Upon Avon and Warwick Castle, Y6 to Great Cressingham Victorian School;
  - Y1 to the Sealife Centre Hunstanton;
  - Y PR & R to Santon Downham and the Iceni Village at Cockley Cley; ;
  - YR went to the Pensthorpe Waterfowl Trust;
  - Y4 visited Saxon Village at West Stow;
  - Y1&3 went to Thrigby Hall and Castle Rising
  - Y2&4 to Holt and the Norfolk Show;
  - YPR & R to Park Farm, Snettisham;
  - Performances were attended at the Norwich Puppet Theatre;
  - YR - 4 saw a performance of 'Babe the Sheep Pig'; a Nativity Play,
  - Y2-4 attended a Science Lecture at UEA;
- **School events**:-
  - Music Workshop with Douglas Combes;
  - YR - 6 were entertained by Leslie Ashfield (Ventriloquist and Magician);
  - Floating Point Theatre visited;
  - Kevin Crossley-Holland made a literary visit which was enjoyed by Y3 and 4
  - Scholastic Book Fair;
  - Pilgrimage to Walsingham in June;
- **Overseas:** Ski Trip to Montgenevre
- **Past Pupils Re-union** by pupils at the School between 1959 -1967, met up at school on 5th July
- **Charity:**
  - Sponsorship, amounting to £325 was raised, for a past pupil in her Gap Year, to work doing medical work with the Project Trust in South Africa.

Sponsorship, amounting to £436, was also raised for provision of a specialised wheel chair for a local boy.

- ➤ Sugar for 'Crisis at Christmas'; £117 –
- ➤ Jeans for Genes Day;
- ➤ Harvest Supper for Christian Aid.
- ◆ **Music:** another successful year with pupils taking part in Norfolk County Music Festival and attending the 'Last Night of the Proms' at Norwich organized by Paul Donnelly, Assistant Conductor and our school conductor
- ◆ **LAMDA Speech & Drama**
- ➤ Excellent results including four Bronze, two Silver and two Gold medals.

✣ **1998– 1999**
- ◆ Pupils and Staff from our Staten Island School USA, visited.
- ◆ The Nursery received an excellent OFSTED report
- ◆ Book Buddy scheme introduced.

Headgirl: Rebecca Keane;
Deputy: Natasha Jones

- ◆ **Senior School Activities:**
- ➤ On the annual London Trip
- ➤ Y7 visited the Museum of London –
- ➤ Y8 Greenwich Observatory ;
- ➤ Y9 Houses of Parliament ;
- ➤ Y9 & 10 National Gallery & Theatre Museum
- ➤ Y7-9 attended a drama session in Norwich about Edith Cavell.
- ➤ Y8 Environmental Studies to the Norfolk Broads.
- ➤ Y10 & 11 went to the Cavendish Laboratory in Cambridge and made a Geography & Science Field Trip to Kingswood Centre.
- ➤ A 'Careers Convention' was held in school & pupils also took part in 'Take

Your Daughters to Work Day'.
- ➤ A new GCSE examination - 'Travel &Tourism' was introduced.
- ➤ Duke of Edinburgh's Award Scheme pupils' expedition was to Trimingham.
- ◆ **Lower School Activities:**
- ➤ A major change as Y4 joined Y5 and Y6 to form the Middle School.
- ➤ YPR 2 Gressenhall; Y2 Natural Surroundings
- ➤ YR Pensthorpe Wildfowl Trust and Butterfly Park at Ellingham
- ➤ Years R – 4 Harlequin in Trouble at Puppet Theatre, Norwich
- ➤ Y1 & 2 Sea Life Centre, Hunstanton; and were visited by RNLI members
- ➤ Y1 & 2 Greshams for a Music Workshop
- ➤ Y2 & 3 UEA for a Science Workshop;
- ➤ Y3 & 4 Art Sainsbury Centre; Fleggburgh and West Stow Anglo Saxon Village;
- ➤ Y4-6 joined the annual National Pilgrimage to Walsingham
- ➤ Y5 invited by Mr Foti to present flowers and the donated tools for the handicapped collected by the school to Liza Goddard at Hermitage Hall – event on TV;
- ➤ Y5 Kentwell in Tudor costume
- ➤ Y 5/6 to Hammonds High School to take part in a workshop by the Jiving Lindy Hoppers
- ➤ Y6 Great Cressingham Victorian School;
- ➤ Y5 & 6 Kingswood Activity Centre for a multi-activities / ICT weekend;
- ◆ **School events**
- ◆ **A spectacular Book Fayre** with speakers and workshops was held in the Sports Hall with guest speakers: Piers Paul Reed, Georgina Lewis, Paul Jackson, Maurice Lynch, Joe Pearce and James McCallum. The Sports Hall was divided

into creative learning bays.

- YR3 African assembly, story music workshop day for YR – pottery masks made
- Science - the Floating Point Theatre;
- The Matthews Project visited with a play about alcohol and drugs called Fast Eddie – Y7 - 11
- Pupils staged a performance of 'The Day the Animals Sang'
- **Charity:** Pupils fundraising included:
- participation in Non Uniform Day;
- the World's Greatest Coffee Morning for Cancer Relief;
- Sugar Collection for Crisis;
- Sisters Mission in Rushooka, Uganda.
- African Playground £330, Helen Payne a past pupil
- **Music Speech and Drama:**
- Pupils entered for the Norfolk Music Festival.
- Orchestra played at Royal Norfolk Show
- Modern Dance Ballet Performance by Miss Michelle
- LAMDA – all 90 pupils passed
- Hermitage Hall Christmas Performance
- **Sport;**
- Pupils took part & represented the school in Athletics, Cross Country, Rounders, Hockey, Netball, Short Tennis, Gymnastics and Swimming. Volleyball after school
- Years 5, 6, & 7 Rugby Taster Day
- 5 a-side football matches arranged
- Our Ul4 & U16 teams were Western Area Netball champions.
- 3 week Summer School run by Mr Kelly and the parents

✝ 1999-2000

- Millennium Year
- The Sisters gave Y2 – 11 millennium crucifixes, and younger pupils a luminous baby Jesus'.
- Chechnya Nuclear Disaster – Mrs Hill appeals for love to be sent around the world via lighting of candles
- Whole school 'Maths is Fun' Activity Day
- Lunch time Computer Club
- Mother General, Sr Lucyna Mroczek visited the school
- Father Denis Finbow came to school and spoke passionately about Bolivia.
- Reintroduction of beef to the school menu
- YR looking for good homes for explosion of stick insects

Headgirl: Lucinda Halls;
Deputy: Sophie Lewis

- **Senior School Activities:**
- Y4- 9 see Johnny Ball Show – 'Tales of Maths and Legends
- Y5–11 Millennium Dome visit – fantastic
- Y10 Kingswood Centre Field Trip
- Y11 Sizewell Visitors Centre, sites A and B, - Greenwich;
- Y11 EcoTech Wind Turbine,
- Y9 attended a performance of 'The Tempest' at the Globe Theatre, Y10 Tate Gallery.
- **Lower School Activities**: Pupils took part in:
- YR American Indians and their culture day
- YR Great Ellingham Butterfly Farm;
- YPR & R Thrigby Hall Wildlife Park;
- YPR – 1 Santon Downham
- YPR - 1 Gressenhall Rural Life Museum;
- Y1 & 2 Suffolk Wildlife Park;
- Y2 Natural Surroundings at Holt;
- Y3:- Fleggburgh's Bygone Village
- Y3 & 4 Long Sutton Butterfly Park
- Y3 – 6 Diocesan Walsingham pilgrimage
- Y4 West Stow Anglo – Saxon village

- ➢ Y4 – 6 Creative Writing with Fred Sedgwick Castle Acre
- ➢ Y5 Tudor re-enactment at Kentwell Hall
- ➢ Y6 Gt Cressingham – Victorian School
- ➢ 'The Legend of Golden Arrow' at the Garden Fete Performance.
- ◆ **Overseas:** Ski Trip to Prato Nevoso
- ◆ **Charity:**
- ➢ A generous donation was given to the Sisters' Rushooka Mission in Uganda.
- ➢ 105 shoe boxes filled for Romanian children, given via Jennifer and Mrs Ellis
- ➢ Rice for Mozambique Lunch and Lower School Bring and Buy Sale
- ➢ 260 kg of sugar donated for Buckingham Emergency Food Appeal
- ➢ Sponsored Walk for Barn Development and African Mission
- ➢ Y9 snacks for Cancer Research - £107
- ◆ **Music:**
- ➢ Y9 – 11 Instrumental Masterclass at Hammonds School.
- ➢ Whole School millennium Carol Concert
- ➢ Y2 – 8 – Percussion Demonstration - M Bright
- ➢ Hosanna Easter Musical Performance
- ➢ Recorder, Junior Music Group and Choir Clubs
- ➢ Senior choir and instrumentalists took part in Remembrance Service - St Peter Paul Church
- ◆ **Dance:**
- ➢ A Dance Day was held for pupils of all ages.
- ➢ Dance Festival for Y1 – 10 - Miss Michelle
- ◆ **Speech and Drama:**
- ➢ Theatre Studies Makeup Demonstration
- ➢ Y2 – 11 Best of last Millennium Performance
- ➢ Exams were entered by 100 pupils; they also helped to present & perform

productions of 'The Canterbury Tales' and the 'True Story of Good King Wenceslas'
- ◆ **Sport:**
- ➢ Gained Sportsmark Award 2000
- ➢ Lower School Sports Day was rained off;
- ➢ House Swimming Gala
- ➢ Our Cross Country team won at Necton;
- ➢ U14 and UI6 Netball teams did very well in their matches, as did our Hockey Team.
- ➢ Girls had the opportunity to play Tag Rugby representing Breckland;
- ➢ Tennis and Short Tennis were again popular sports undertaken.
- ➢ A visit was made by pupils, to Wimbledon, for the Lawn Tennis Tournament.
- ➢ Badminton Club organized – Friday evenings

✝ 2000– 2001

- ◆ The Year of Science was celebrated.
- ◆ We purchased a life size skeleton, a Betty Bones torso with removable organs and a Computerised Baby Grace who is lent to pupils for the weekend.
- ◆ Pupils achieved excellent GCSE results: 100% A-C rate for the first time.
- ◆ Bishop Peter Smith visited the school
- ◆ The Nursery received another 'Excellent' Ofsted report.
- ◆ Pupils took part in a procession to celebrate the feast of Corpus Christi.

Headgirl: Clare Minto
Deputy: Harriet Holmes
- ◆ **Facilities:**
- ➢ Staines Builders Barn situated at the back of the school, was purchased for £60 000, with plans to convert it to an Arts Centre
- ➢ New Wildlife Pond was constructed

- Conservatory / Walkway adjoining the Sister's Refectory was added
- New Nursery Play Area and Lower School playground re-surfaced
- The PTA assisted with the construction of a Maths Garden and also assisted with the marking out of games on the playground.
- A website was developed for the School.

♦ **Senior School Activities:**
- Collector's World Hermitage Hall - Y9;
- Y10 Biology and Geography Field Trip Holt Hall, Overstrand & West Runcton
- Y7 – 11 London, included the Tate Gallery, Y9 Houses of Parliament, Y8 the National Gallery, Y7 Aquarium & the London Eye;
- Y7 Environmental Studies trip to Hunstanton
- Y9 Ranworth Broads
- Y10/11 lectures at Cavendish Laboratory and Y10 & 11 see Inspector Calls at Theatre Royal
- Y11 Field Trip to River Nar, Castle Acre
- Y11 EcoTech visit, History Group to Gressenhall Museum and Y10 & 11 Art Group to Sainsbury Centre
- Y11 annual Expedition for D of E Award Scheme
- 'The Harry Potter Experience' was a very successful theme for the annual Christmas Bazaar.

♦ **Careers**
- Y10 Pupils went on 2 weeks work experience.
- Y9 &10 Career Activity Day – EcoTech

♦ **Lower School Activities:**
- Y4 West Stow and Y5 Kentwell,
- Y2 Natural Surroundings, Holt,
- Y6 Victorian School
- YPR & R Thetford Forest and Thrigby Hall

- YR had an African Day with Tony Ogogo making masks with Derek Paice and drumming
- YR Great Ellingham Butterfly Park
- Y1 Sea Life Centre, Hunstanton
- Y1 & 2 Green Quay, King's Lynn and Castle Rising
- Y1 – 3 attend a music workshop at Greshams
- Y3 & 4 Sainsbury Centre
- Y4 invited to be present at the opening of the 60's room at Hermitage Hall

♦ **Charity**
- Pencils for Rushooka requested by Sr Caroline Bachman, General Councillor on her visit to us; Sr Nicolina given £375 for Uganda from Lenten money
- Boxes for Romania
- 165 kg of sugar for Crisis at Christmas
- Piano Recital by Don Carter to raise money for Fr Drury's Mission in Equador

♦ **Music:** GCSE Music begins as an after school extra
- YR - 6 participating in a Douglas Coombes Music workshop;
- Y6 to Leys School, to perform in 'Joseph and the Amazing Technicolour Dreamcoat
- Y5 – 9 given the opportunity by Fr Denis Finbow to join in a performance of 'General Mickey', about St John Bosco, at the Corn Exchange, Cambridge for Street Children in Bolivia. A group from Y9 trained as main dancers at Sawston College, Cambridge. A fabulous experience for all who participated in the two perfomances for the public.
- Participation in the County Folk Festival.
- Junior Music Group entertained

parishioners at RC Christmas lunch

- **Speech & Drama:** 66 exams were taken; awards included a Bronze Medal.
- ➢ Christmas Performance Hermitage Hall
- **Dance:** Miss Michelle held jazz dance lessons for pupils working towards their Bronze Jazz Award as well as Ballet lessons
- ➢ **Sport:** pupils participated in -
- ➢ ISA Athletics Tournament at Southend;
- ➢ competed at the Alexander National Stadium at Birmingham;
- ➢ Our U13 Tennis team represented Norfolk.
- ➢ Saturday Football Club with Mr Tony Creed

✢ 2001-2002

- To celebrate the Queen's Jubilee Year, a street party was held at the end of the Jubilee Sponsored Walk.
- Links were renewed with the Staten Island School, USA following the terrorist attacks in New York on 11th September 2001.
- Carol Rap on BBC2 East
- At the School General Election in 2001, the Labour Party & Tony Blair, were re-elected.
- The school took part in The Giant Jump (7th September 2001) in a bid to get into the Guinness Book of Records.
- Sister Lucyna Mroczek Superior General and Sr Nivalda Montenegro, General Councillor of the, Daughters of Divine Charity paid an unofficial visit on their way to Uganda.
- Unofficial 'one way' system established by school travelling up Sporle Road to Station Street.
- **Staff News:**
- ➢ Sister Thomas-More Prentice stepped

down from the post of Deputy Head.
- ➢ Mrs Beth Phimister retired from the Boarding House and was replaced by Miss Joanna Burgiss.
- ➢ Father Trevor Richardson, parish priest of Our Lady of Pity Church, died after a courageous fight against cancer.
- ➢ **Headgirl:** Harriet West
- ➢ **Deputy:** Anne Pickering
- **Facilities:**
- ➢ Mangate Street Station, erected on the Lower School playground, was opened by pupil Daisy Stonach (aged 7) and built by Mick and Jack.
- ➢ The Maths Conservatory Garden completed.
- ➢ Progress was slow on the continuing building works of the Barn Arts Centre
- **Senior School Activities:**
- ➢ Y 3 – 11 tradition begins of 1st day of term to Walsingham for Mass and social occasion
- ➢ Y7 – 9 attended Bloomin Science in Norwich
- ➢ Y7 St Paul's London and Y8 National Gallery
- ➢ Y10 & 11 Science Museum and French Group Cambridge
- ➢ Y10 &11 3-day Biology and Geography Holt Hall
- ➢ Y9 Sainsbury Centre
- ➢ Y8 Kings Lynn Investigation
- ➢ This years D of E Award Expedition group went to Darsham.
- **Lower School Activities:** made visits to:
- ➢ YPR &R High Lodge Thetford Forest;
- ➢ Y1 Denver Windmill
- ➢ YR – 4 Dereham to Wymondham Train
- ➢ Y2 Inspire Science Centre, Norwich
- ➢ True's Yard & Green Quay (Y3 & 5);
- ➢ Y4 Sainsbury Gallery & Norwich Castle
- ➢ Y4 West Stow; Y5 Oxburgh Hall

2004 Book Fair

2001 Garden Fete
The Harry Potter Experience

2004 The Kalai Kaviri Dancers

2002 The Opening of the library by the Mayor of Swaffham Ben Emerson

2004 The Sponsored Walk

2004/05 V.E. week exhibition

2002/03 Swimming Gala

2008 Pirate Day

2000 Tag Rugby Team representing
Breckland

2006

Kingswood

- ➢ Y4-6 Activity Day at Finborough Kids Club
- ➢ Y6 Ecotech
- ◆ **Performances included**:
- ➢ The Tiebreak Theatre -'Storytelling from around the World' (Years 2 – 6) together with attendance at various venues to see 'A Christmas Carol', 'The Borrowers' & 'The Jiving Lindyhoppers'.
- ➢ The Raptor's Trust made a visit to the school with their birds of prey.
- ◆ **Overseas:** Ski Trip by pupils & staff to Le Corbier
- ◆ **Charity:**
- ➢ Frugal lunches were attended at the church during Lent.
- ➢ Money and small items were given to the mission in Rushooka, Uganda.
- ➢ Funds were sent to UNICEF, CAFOD, Macmillan Nurses
- ➢ 69 boxes for Romania
- ➢ Lent offering to Father Joseph's orphanage for abandoned girls in India.
- ➢ Sugar - 281 kg including British Sugar's pledge
- ◆ **Music and Dance:** Pupils participated in the House Music Festival, Dance Display Afternoon
- ◆ **Sport:**
- ➢ Tag Rugby was played and competitors went to the Eton Tennis Tournament.
- ➢ YR–11 Internal Gymnastics Competition
- ➢ County Honours in Tennis were awarded to 4 girls;
- ➢ A group of pupils & staff went to Wimbledon Lawn Tennis Tournament; Annual Swimming Gala was held

✞ **2002– 2003**

- ◆ **The new School Library** was opened by the Mayor of Swaffham, Mr Ben Emmerson, on 27th November . An

appeal was to 'Sponsor a Book' launched and over £900 worth of books was sponsored by parents.
- ◆ **Basic lessons in Japanese** were offered by Miss Yoko Nakaya, to pupils from Y5 upwards.
- ◆ **ISI Inspection** in March when seven inspectors, led by Mr. Tim Holgate, visited for a week!
- ◆ **Three pupils, two members of staff** and two Sisters attended the ordination of Bishop Michael Evans.
- ◆ **Bishop Michael Evans** visited the school on Feast of Corpus Christi to celebrate Mass.
- ◆ **Three pupils attended the Youth 2000 Retreat** at Walsingham .
- ◆ **The Tuck Shop** was withdrawn to encourage healthier eating. During National Vegetarian Week, the food was enjoyed by the staff!
- ◆ **£30,000** awarded by WREN for seating and staging in the Barn
- ◆ **Headgirl:** Donna Palmer
  Deputy: Emily Palmer
- ◆ **Facilities:**
- ➢ Restructuring of the Lower & Middle Schools with Years PR - 6, to be known as Lower School. A School Council was set up for this new group and class Leaders.
- ➢ Miss Sally Gooderson appointed coordinator for the Lower School
- ➢ Fund raising for the Barn Project continued; a grant of £30000 was received from WREN towards retractable seating and staging.
- ➢ The Art and Music Departments moved to the Barn in February 2003.
- ➢ Heightened security at front and back of school CCTV coverage with six cameras

and control from the School Office.

- ♦ **Senior School Activities**:
  - ➢ Kathleen McFarlene Exhibition at Sainsbury Gallery Y10, Cavendish Laboratory Cambridge
  - ➢ Y11 Holkham Hall & Thorpe Park – leavers day
  - ➢ Y11 Travel & Tourism group to Potter Heigham
  - ➢ Y9 & 10 Tower of London and Twelfth Night at the Globe Theatre and 'Inspector Calls' at Theatre Royal Norwich
  - ➢ Y9 True's Yard; Y8 The Broads
  - ➢ West Lexham & Castle Acre (Y7);
  - ➢ Performance attended of 'The Mysteries' at Theatre Royal,' in English, Zulu & Xhosa.
  - ➢ D of E Award Trip to Claxton.
  - ➢ Y7 – 9 Take your Daughters to Work Day and a Careers Convention for the Seniors
  - ➢ The Matthew Project gave a talk to Y7-11 about drugs.
- ♦ **Lower School Activities:**
  - ➢ YPR&R Sea Life, Hunstanton; High Lodge
  - ➢ Y1 Suffolk Wildlife Park; Denver Windmill; Pills and Potions" Exhibition at Swaffham Museum
  - ➢ Y2 Exploring Swaffham, Natural Surroundings
  - ➢ Y2 – 4 saw James and the Giant Peach at Theatre Royal, Norwich
  - ➢ YPR, R & 3 were visited by a Dental nurse
  - ➢ Y3 Fleggborough and Walsingham
  - ➢ Y3 – 8 Corpus Christi Procession at Hermitage Hall
  - ➢ Y4 Castle Museum, West Stow, and Sainsbury Centre
  - ➢ Y4 – 6 Science at Farmland Museum, Wisbech
  - ➢ Y5 Opening by Bishop Michael of Reliquary at Hermitage Hall and Kentwell Hall Tudor re-enactment.
  - ➢ Y6 Gt Cressingham School
  - ➢ Y2-11; Visits & talks given by Astronomer Peter Ingram to pupils and parents
  - ➢ The Rotary Club Handwriting Competition for Years 4 – 6 was won by Sarah Johnson and Russell George.
  - ➢ Y6 Read the Flour Babies and made their own to look after, also decorated a storyteller's coat.
- ♦ **Overseas:**
  - ➢ **Y5 &6 Etaples** with visits to Sea Life Centre, Snail and Bee Farms & Chocolate Factory.
  - ➢ **Y9 Rome Trip** May half term - included seeing Pope John Paul 11 & visits to the Coliseum, St Peter's, the Catacombs, Castel Gandolfo, our Sisters' Generalate in Grottaferata
- ♦ **Charity:** Harvest Festival raised £41, produce donated to the John Chapman Day Centre. Senior School Non-uniform Day £130 for the Breast Cancer Care Appeal; 130 bags of sugar with Silver Spoon matching SS. 60 Shoe boxes filled and sent to Romania. Y2 – 11 were served a Lenten meal of Rice & Dhal Monies raised were sent to the 'Street Children of Columbia' via Fr Michael Johnstone, our parish priest. Smartie tubes were filled with 1p's during Lent and Frugal lunches attended at local churches. Another non-uniform day during March raised money for CAFOD; Y4 Bring & Buy Sale for Blue Peter

Water Appeal; Y9's snacks raised £55 for MacMillan Cancer Research.. The Lower

- ➢ School pupils also collected towels for the sick seals being cared for by RSPCA.
- ♦ **Music:** The Carol Concert at Christmas raised £500 for the Samaritans and the Norwich Homeless
- ➢ Other musical events included:– House Music Festival; Lower School Music afternoon which raised £99 which went towards the purchase of a keyboard with computer link; a Senior School Music Evening. The theme of the Lower School performance at the Garden Fete was "Careers" with Sister Act included.
- ♦ **Speech**: Mrs Pickering's LAMDA pupils staged a Christmas performance at Hermitage Hall
- ♦ **Sport:** Short Tennis / Tennis coaching sessions commenced with Mr John Kirby as an after school activity. Pupils participated in Tennis tournaments at Eton, Windsor and also at Queenswood; also Cross Country, Hockey, Netball, Tennis, Athletics and Rounders events throughout the year. Our U14 Netball team beat eight local schools and went on to represent West Norfolk in a County event. November. Five girls qualified and went on to represent East Anglia in the ISA National Cross Country finals Deryn Ward played for Norfolk County.

✣ 2003– 2004

- ♦ **90th Anniversary of the foundation** of the school: this was celebrated with Mass together with an Exhibition of Art and Pottery in the theatre; Mathematics lessons in imperial measures; drill on the field; German conversation; croquet on the lawn handwriting lessons; and an

introduction to the dunce's hat, cane making and painting pigs

- ♦ **The year had an International flavour** due to the Sisters roots. The Christmas Bazaar was based on Christmas around the world. Y6 held a Chinese Assembly, an Indian priest brought his Kalai Kaviri dancers to perform liturgical and secular dance. We were in awe at their agility and flexibility.
- ➢ YR – 10 visited the Ecotech to take part in an African Dance / Information workshop by the Grassroots from Zimbabwe
- ➢ Pupils from Y7, 8 and 10 offered to host 70 French students at Kingswood Activity Centre when their partner school was unable to attend
- ➢ During the International Week - pupils had the opportunity to learn foreign phrases and sample 'Dishes' from around the World' provided by the Catering staff. This week also incorporated a two day 'Science & Maths Fun Days'.
- ♦ **Five day trip to Prague**, included the sights of the city and a visit to the Nazi transit camp at Terezin,(Theresienstadt).
- ♦ **Ski Trip to Foppolo** had a memorable start as the coach failed to turn up at 2am and the plane took off minus SH. Groups flew from Bristol and Gatwick arriving 24 hours late. After that, it was a wonderful holiday!
- ♦ **The Festival of Reading** held over two days was a wonderful way to celebrate the World of Books. Authors, storytellers, playwrights, illustrators and creative writers filled the Sports Hall, which was transformed into stimulating areas, as a backdrop for our speakers. – Each bay hosted a different

theme, including Dickens, Shakespeare, Jungle, and the Arctic .

- ♦ **National Poetry Day** was celebrated by the whole school. The gym was magnificently displayed with an exhibition of writings by each child in the school.
- ♦ **Wordsworth's Reading Campaign** in aid of Marie Curie Cancer Appeal with as many school children taking part reciting Daffodils on 19th March at 9.15am.
- ♦ Y5 – 9 introduced to the Reading Award Scheme by Mrs Gargett Stringer
- ♦ Sacred Heart Special Train hired for the Boarders from Dereham to Wymondham
- ♦ An off-timetable activity day for those pupils and staff who braved the snow
- ♦ Internet Facility was made available to all, and an 'Agreement' was required for pupils from Y3–11
- ♦ **Staff News:**
- ➢ Mrs Margaret Dalton (PE) was involved in a car accident and was absent for half of the Autumn Term to recover.
- ➢ Lunchtime Latin Club started by Mrs Elizabeth Dean. Years 4 – 6 took up the offer.
- ➢ Individual Portuguese lessons were offered by Sr Emilia Birck in addition to her German lessons

Headgirl: Victoria Lewis

Deputy: Emma Jennings

- ♦ **Facilities:**
- ➢ Lower School and Y7 -8 a Pottery in the Barn Arts Complex.
- ➢ A second Minibus was bought.
- ♦ **Senior School Activities**:
- ➢ Performance of scenes from "Cats", by pupils of all ages with Mr Eddie and Miss Wendy. Pupils presented a Shakespeare Performance of scenes from 'A Midsummer's Night Dream', 'Romeo and Juliet', 'Macbeth' and Twelfth Night' and the Y9 Theatre Studies presented their version of "Charlie and the Chocolate Factory". The Theatre was not quite complete, so held in the gym.
- ➢ The Classical Civilisation Group and the Boarders saw the 'Trojan Women by Euripedes' in Norwich and Antigone at West Acre.
- ➢ London Trip: Y7 – 11 visited the Aquarium, London Eye, National Portrait Gallery, Tate Britain, Tower of London, Houses of Parliament, St Thomas' Old Operating Theatre, the Design Museum and The New London Theatre for the performance of 'Joseph'.
- ➢ Y11 Emotional Intelligence by Elaine Miles
- ➢ Y11 Careers interviews with Eddie Doran
- ➢ Y7-8 Participation, for the first time, in the UK Mathematics Challenge
- ➢ Y10 & 11 Print Workshop with a local artist;
- ➢ Y10.& 11 Visit to the Cavendish Laboratory
- ➢ Y9 took part in a Royal Society Chemistry Competition at Norwich;
- ➢ A group visit the National Stud and Animal Trust
- ➢ An Exhibition in St John's Cathedral, Norwich of pupil's Art Work;
- ➢ D of E Bronze Medal Award exhibition;
- ➢ Participation in the Swaffham Great Pancake Race at the Assembly Rooms;
- ➢ Y11 Leavers Retreat held at Hermitage Hall;
- ➢ Y10 Biology / Geography Field study day at Holt Hall.

- ♦ **Lower School Activities:**
- ➢ Christmas Concert theme of looking at other countries Christmas customs.
- ➢ YPR & R visited Hunstanton Beach and the Sea Life Centre
- ➢ Y2 visited RAF Cottishall;
- ➢ Y4 & 5 Rocket Workshop
- ➢ Y5 &6 Maths / Science Fun Days with invited schools and the inflatable Stardome was available for the whole school;
- ➢ Garden Fete all pupils dressed as toys.;
- ➢ Y6 participation in Evacuees day in King's Lynn
- ♦ **Charities**:
- ➢ Harvest Festival raised £65 for CAFOD;
- ➢ Non-Uniform Day raised £60 for Breast Cancer Awareness;
- ➢ Pupils filled 48 Boxes to send to Romania;
- ➢ Carol Concerts £350 for Sight Savers and Tapping House.
- ➢ A cross of copper coins was made £100;
- ➢ Rich / Poor lunch in the Gym during Lent;
- ➢ School's Sponsored Walk to North Pickenham;
- ➢ Y4 Sponsored Silence raised £230!;
- ♦ **Music:** Pupils took part in performances at Our Lady of Pity's Flower Festival; House Music Festival in October; Royal British Legion Festival of Remembrance in the Parish Church; Harvest Festival; Christmas Concerts; together with a Lower School music afternoon and Senior School music evening.
- ♦ **Speech:** LAMDA successes included several medallions.
- ♦ **Sport:** Our school's team were Tennis finalists in the Nestle League for East of England but beaten by Queenswood;

- ➢ Inter-house and other tournaments took place in Netball, Hockey, Rounders, Tennis, Athletics and Cross Country; pupils went in the new minibus to Wimbledon 2004 and saw, amongst others, Martina Navratilova and Lindsay Davenport.

✠ **2004– 2005**
- ➢ An Appeal was launched for the terrible Tsunami tragedy around the Pacific on Boxing Day. One of our pupils, Rebekah Page, Y7, was in Thailand at the time but was helped to safety, both she and her parents survived this disaster. A past pupils Louise Wilgrass (Cornwell) drowned.
- ♦ The 60th Anniversary of 'Victory in Europe'. A party of Senior pupils went to Arras to see the 1st World War trenches.
- ♦ VE week with Memorabilia in the Barn and gym and talks from Toni Groom and Eddie Doran
- ♦ National Poetry Day in was celebrated on this year's theme of "Food"
- ♦ Fr John Cureton, former parish priest of Our lady of Pity Church, died in July.
- ♦ **Staff News:**
- ➢ Mrs Patricia Woodwards became Boarding Mistress in addition to her LS Teaching Assistant duties.
Headgirl: Gemma Beal;
Deputy: Abigail Daniels-
- ♦ **Facilities:** The Lower School Staffing was reorganised to create a Reception Unit
- ♦ **Senior School Activities:**
- ➢ A Prize Giving / Awards Evening was introduced;
- ➢ Performances were presented by:
- ➢ The Black Cat Theatre Company of

- "Macbeth";
- Performing Arts Group - 'Showstoppers' in the Barn – Annie, Oliver and Bugsy Malone;
- Other events held included a Seder Meal Y8
- Team Building with the Army' Y11
- Y7 - 10 the Imperial War Museum & the Cabinet War Rooms, London;
- Potter Heigham and Cromer Y11 Travel & Tourism group);
- Newmarket Stud;
- Y9 & 10 Career Skills at Excel Centre, London and Swanton Morley Army Camp;
- Ice Skating in Norwich, sponsored by Waitrose; visited an Exhibition of Art at Norwich Castle Y7; also the Cavendish Laboratory.
- Work Experience at a school owned by our Sisters in Prague and organized by Sr Anna, and undertaken by three Y10 pupils.
- Pupils worked with Peruvian artist, Jose Gomez
- Pupils took part in the 'Hardspell' after being finalists in the schools Spelling Bee and Ottakar's Poetry Competition.
- 1st serious drama event in the Barn, Y9 and 10 performed excerpts from Macbeth, Romeo and Juliet and The Taming of the Shrew

♦ **Lower School Activities:**
- Sports Day and Prize Giving.
- Puppet Workshop.
- YPR -6 Imperial War Museum, Duxford;
- Sticky Earth Café & fossil hunting, Hunstanton
- Y6 Great Cressingham; Y5 Kentwell;
- Y4 West Stow; Norwich Castle
- A Chess Club for interested pupils.
- Swaffham Arts provided Circus Skills

- A friendship bench was made for the playground
♦ **Overseas:** Y5& 6 extended trip to Berck sur Mer including visits to the Snail Farm, a Market, the Chocolate Factory, plus pupils joined a class in a French school.
- Y8 and 9 two day trip to the Somme Battlefields, in Northern France
♦ **Charity:**
- Rich / Poor lunch in Lent;
- Sugar Collection for CRISIS at Christmas;
- A Big Hair Day!
- Money was also raised and goods sent to the devastated Indian Ocean region.
- A Coffee Morning was held to promote the views of the 'Fair Trade' group.
♦ **Music & Drama:**
- House Music Festival and usual concerts were held.
- Excellent examination results achieved by Mrs Pickering's pupils
♦ **Sport:**
- Both U14 & U16 teams played hockey in their leagues.
- Netball continued to be popular and our U13's played and won a championship.
- Pupils entered the Norfolk and ISA Cross Country Competition, but for the snow, some of our girls would have travelled to Warwickshire to represent East Anglia in the ISA National Cross Country Competition.
- There were successes in the U14 Athletics Competition, coming first in the 4x100m relay.
- Inter-house Competitions were held and there was the annual school Swimming Gala as well as a Gala event against Hethersett Old Hall, who won.
- A Golf Taster day was held

✠ 2005– 2006

- Mother Foundress' Celebration in Vienna, to mark her being made 'A Servant of God', was attended by Sr Thomas More Prentice.
- The theme of this year's National **Poetry Day** was "The Future"
- There were visits during the year by groups of students from Poland and the Czech Republic
- On 5th July 2006, one of our Year 7 pupils, Daisy Stonach, collapsed with a massive heart attack while in the swimming pool. It was a shocking and frightening event. Daisy was a lively and talented girl with much to give. The whole school community mourned her death with great sorrow and a Mass was held in the Sports Hall with some 350 attendees, including the Headteacher & staff from Hammonds and the first paramedic on the scene of the tragic incident.
- Sr Danuta Wloczka visited from Poland, with a group of her students, for 10 days

Headgirl: Rosie Cross

Deputy: Eleanor Dale

- **Facilities:**
- Sound Systems in the Gym & Sports Hall;
- Swimming pool refurbishment, monies raised from PTA events held.
- **Senior School Activities**: Visits were made to:
- N Norfolk Coast (Y9); Holkham Hall (Y9&10);
- Oxburgh Hall (Y8); Kings Lynn (Y8);
- Westacre – (GCSE Drama Group);
- Astronomy Conference, Cambridge (Y9);
- London Trip- Art Galleries & Museums (Y8 - 10 – Art group);
- Salters Festival of Chemistry at UEA (Y7&8);
- Retreat Hermitage Hall (Y11);
- Narborough Hall (Y10 Art Group);
- Castle Acre (Y7);
- Norfolk Broads (Y8); The Brecks (Y8);
- Wells Lifeboat Station (Y9);
- Holt Hall extended Biology/ Geography (Y10);
- Prize Giving in November;
- Y7– 9Take Your Daughters to Work Day
- An International Week was celebrated with Austria, Egypt, China, USA and India being chosen countries;
- A Shakespeare Evening was held with performances from Y9 &10 "A Midsummer Night's Dream" and "The Tempest";
- Onatti French Theatre presentation;
- Performance by the Black Cat Theatre Company of 'Much Ado about Nothing;
- Staff v pupils Chess Match; staff won
- Emily Wright (Y7) won 1st Prize in the ISA essay competition;
- **Lower School Activities:**
- A Homework Diary was introduced for YR-3;
- At Christmas pupils took part in the play "The Day the Animals Sang";
- Lower School Pottery Exhibition staged in the Barn
- Y5&6 Jiving Lindy Hoppers performance ;
- Y2&3 Christmas Concert performance 'Dances from around the World'
- Y6 Great Cressingham Victorian School;
- Y5 Kentwell Hall;
- Y4 West Stow Anglo Saxon village;
- YR John Innes Institute, Norwich;
- Y2&3 Cromer Lifeboat Museum;
- Y3 How Hill;
- Y1&2 Natural Surroundings;

- ➢ Kingswood Activity Centre. A wonderful time was had by Y6 whilst on a team building weekend but it was very cold!
- ♦ **Overseas Trips** The Ski Trip visited Bormio.
- ➢ A party of 28 pupils from Y8 -10 journeyed to Krakow, Poland and stayed at the Convent with our Sisters. They visited the Nazi camp at Auschwitz and the Salt Mines.
- ♦ **Charity:** Fund raising events this year included:
- ➢ Harvest Festival;
- ➢ Non Uniform Day, on the theme of 'Stars and Celebrities' (£180 to 'Starlight');
- ➢ Romanian Boxes (Samaritan's Purse);
- ➢ Operation Christmas Child;
- ➢ Christmas Sugar Collection (101 bags) for CRISIS; Sponsored Bike Ride £748 EDP Breast Cancer Appeal;
- ➢ Y9 Snack monies £75 East Anglian Air Ambulance
- ➢ Rich/Poor Lunch at the beginning of Lent together with a 'Silver' Collection for charities;
- ✞ Sponsored Walk at High Lodge, Thetford raised £5068
- ✞ A cake sale in aid of St Luke's Hospital, Crawley & Quidenham Children's Hospice Y6

✞ 2006– 2007

- ♦ Annual Walsingham Pilgrimage was made by pupils from Years Y3-11 on first day of new academic year.
- ♦ Confirmations were held for our Catholic pupils, by Bishop Michael Evans, at Our Lady of Pity Church, Swaffham and Church of England pupils at St Edmunds, Downham

Market in September.
- ♦ Separate Poetry Days were held for YPR -6 & Y7-9
- ♦ Boarding House Inspection, October.
- ♦ School registered to accept Busy Bees' Childcare vouchers
- ♦ New House point system introduced;
- ♦ Boaters for required for Lower School pupils only
- ♦ Website was re-vamped by Sr Ana Maria Antunovic
- ♦ A 'Daisy Memorial Day' Thanksgiving service was held on 5th July; the simple service was led by Rev John Smith of St Peter & Paul Church with the whole school, friends and members of Daisy's family.
- ♦ After winning the Blue Peter 'Me & My Movie' Competition, Rosalind Peters, Y9, appeared on national television over 2 to 3 weeks and took part in several creative film challenges; nominated and won a Children's BAFTA
- ♦ **Staff News**
- ➢ **Sr Thomas More** celebrated her Golden Jubilee on 22nd June. A whole School Mass was held, concelebrated by Bishop Michael Evans.
- ➢ **Mrs Jane Howarth** attended a review meeting with Lord Dearing, when the subject of the crisis in languages at KS4 was discussed. She was congratulated on the fact that our KS2 pupils undertake French visits.
- ➢ **Mrs Joanna Gribbon**, former staff member & Deputy Head, died in April 2007
Headgirl: Amy Leeder
Deputy: Freya Barlow
- ♦ **Facilities:**
- ➢ Swimming Pool in desperate need of refurbishment – overall cost of

upgrading estimated to be in region of £65000;

- A bench was donated by staff in Daisy's memory.

♦ **Senior School Activities:**

- UEA for the BA Festival of Science Y10&11 London trip included Tate Modern & a theatre
- National Portrait Gallery & the British LibraryY9
- Theatre Royal, Norwich (GCSE PE);
- Santon Downham (Y8);
- Fuel Cells Lecture by Lecturer from Imperial College, at Hammonds Y11 Science group
- Welney Wildlife Trust Y8
- Norwich Playhouse 'Caucasian Chalk Circle' (Y11 GCSE Drama Group);
- Sainsbury Gallery, (Y10, Y11 GCSE Art);
- Castle Museum & Norwich Cathedral Y7
- French Revision Day, Cambridge Y10&11
- Work Experience Week Y10
- D of E Bronze Award expedition weekend & day trip to Wells Y10
- Institute of Astronomy Y10
- Holt Hall Field trip Y10
- Ranworth Broad; Town House Museum & True's Yard, Kings Lynn; Blakeney & Weybourne Y8
- West Acre Studios Y10 Drama Group;
- Gressenhall Workhouse Y10 History
- Cavendish Laboratories, Cambridge Y10&11

♦ **Other school activities**:

- A workshop by The Black Cat Theatre, 'An Inspector Calls', Y10&11
- Team Building with the ArmyY10&11
- Institute of Astronomy, Cambridge, Bridge Building with the Army;
- Onatti French TheatreY5-11

- Gifted & Talented week; Spanish Week;

♦ **Lower School Activities:**

- Visits were made to: Jiving Lindy Hoppers at Hammonds Y5&6
- Denver Windmill Y2&3
- Theatre for Youth production 'Star Quality' Lower School
- Inspire 'Hands On' Science, Norwich Y1
- Castle Museum & Sainsbury Gallery Y4
- Castle Museum, Norwich YR
- Swaffham Museum workshop Y4 &6
- Kentwell Hall Y5
- West Stow Village Y4
- Sheringham Park Y2&3
- Great Cressingham Victorian School Y6
- Swaffham Museum & St Peter Paul Church Y1;
- 'Inspire Science; Paul Jackson, Storyteller YR-6
- UEA Speedy Study Y5
- Will Wright helped Y1 pupils make an animated version of 'The Pedlar of Swaffham'
- Lower School also held a 'Senses' week

♦ **Overseas:**

- Y5 & 6 pupils to France. They visited Berck World War 11 Museum at Ambleteuse, a snail farm, a sweet shop, supermarket & local market, the Museum at Azincourt, a chocolate factory and a French School;

♦ **Charity:**

- A 'Daisy' Memorial Sponsored Walk was held, monies raised for COSMIC;
- Harvest Festival was celebrated and donations collected for CAFOD;
- 'PINK' non-uniform day for CRY £100, COMIC RELIEF £125; Reindeer Drive;
- Snacks Sale for East Anglian Air Ambulance - £103 Y9; Christmas collections filling Shoe Boxes for Samaritans Purse

- Sugar 109 kilos, for BEFA CRISIS
- A 'Charity Week' in February; RNLI dayY10 £400
- Lenten Activities, with monies to the Mission in Rushooka, included - Rich/Poor meal;
- Whole School Charity Day;
- Sponsored Silence raised a total of £230 split between COSMIC & the Mission in Uganda Y6

- **Music & Drama:**
- Wind Band formed in the Spring Term.
- House Music Festival; Senior Choir sang at the RBL Annual Remembrance Service in the Parish Church;
- Whole School Carol Concert £650 CRY & COSMIC in 'Memory of Daisy');
- Presentation of the 'Bard in the Barn'.

- **Sport:**
- First whole day Senior Sports Day.
- Mr John Clements took a group of pupils to the Burghley Horse Trials;
- Football lessons were reintroduced by Mr John Clements. The boys, played a Five-a-side matches against St Nicholas House School.
- Twenty one pupils (Y6-11) took part in the West Norfolk Cross Country Competition & four pupils qualified to go on to the Norfolk Cross Country event at Earlham Park
- Rachel Mumford won U11 Norfolk Cross Country & went on to become County Champions for the second year, competing in the U13 Anglian event
- ISA Cross Country, 4 pupils were selected to represent East Anglia in the Nationals
- Natasha Grapes, aged 10, was selected to the Norfolk U13 County team as goalkeeper
- Pupils entered the West Norfolk Athletics Competition at UEA;
- Y4 - 6 pupils took part in the ISA Junior Athletics Championships in Chelmsford;
- Miss Clair Foster and Mrs Mazoe Young accompanied eight pupils to see the Wimbledon Tennis Championships in London;
  Evening Judo Club organized.

✝ 2007– 2008
- There was no Walsingham Pilgrimage this year, instead there was a Mass held in school and this was followed by a picnic lunch.
- Charges for 'before and after school care' were introduced.
- National Poetry Day was celebrated in October
- A parent questionnaire was distributed in respect of 'boys into the Senior School' for the response to be considered by the Trustees
- **Staff News:**
- Mr Kevin Riches, after 34 years running the Downham Market minibus service, retired and moved to Australia;
- Mrs Wendy Dunton retired after 30 years' service
- Fire Safety Training by Mr Archer, parent, held for all staff

Headgirl: Edwina Powell Bowns
Deputy: Holly Ann Marler
- **Facilities:**
- Extensive renovation work on the Swimming Pool – agreement of costs reached at £27000
- Redecoration throughout the school continued;
- New data projectors, screens & laptops, funded by the PTA £514, for various ICT locations
- Senior School completely rewired at a

great cost;

- ◆ **Senior School Activities:**
- ➢ Rosalind Peters won 1st prize in ISA Favonius Essay Competition.
- ➢ Cavendish Laboratories, Cambridge Y10&11; Sainsbury Gallery, Norwich (Y10 Art Group);
- ➢ Slavery Workshop at Swaffham Museum Y8; Careers Fair, Kings Lynn Y10&11;
- ➢ Tudor study at Hatfield House Y8;
- ➢ 3 day Holt Hall Geography / Biology field trip Y10;
- ➢ French Revision, Cambridge Y10&11
- ➢ Theatre Royal, Norwich (Y9,10&11);
- ➢ Work experience week (Y10);
- ➢ National Theatre, London (Y11 GCSE Drama)
- ➢ Newton & Castle Acre Church Y7;
- ➢ Gressenhall Y10 GCSE History Group; Holkham Hall Y9;
- ➢ Norfolk Broads Y8
- ➢ PC Sharon Page's talk -'Drugs & Alcohol' Y10; Onatti French Theatre 'Les Garcons' Y5-11;
- ➢ Career Interviews with Connexions Y11;
- ➢ Careers Morning Y9;
- ➢ Science Challenge Roadshow Y9 10&11;
- ➢ Buddhism – talk by Mrs Wong Y6&7;
- ➢ Norwich Castle & the Sainsbury Centre Y3 4 7&10; First Aid training Y9; Dance with Melody Y8-11; Workout with the Army Y9&10
- ➢ Shakespeare Evening Y9&10 Drama Group;
- ◆ **Lower School Activities:**
- ➢ Latin lessons with Mrs Elizabeth Dean re-commenced in September (Y4, 5 & 6);
- ➢ Lower School Challenge Week theme 'Food & Farming';
- ➢ 7 chicks were hatched in the Reception class;

- ➢ Mr & Mrs Hollick talk on 'Keeping Hens';
- ➢ Swaffham Museum Time Trail Y4&5;
- ➢ Denver Windmill Y2&3; Sheringham Park Y2;
- ➢ High Lodge, Santon Downham YR&1;
- ➢ Jiving Lindy Hoppers at Hammonds Y5&6;
- ➢ Cockley Cley Farm Y3-6;
- ➢ Melsop Park Farm YPR R 1 2&3;
- ➢ Ward's Farm (YR&1);
- ➢ West Stow Anglo-Saxon village Y3 & 4;
- ➢ Great Cressingham Victorian School Y5;
- ➢ Kentwell Hall Y5;
- ➢ Walsingham – retreat Y6;
- ➢ Ranworth Broad Y8; Castle Acre Y7;
- ➢ Theatre for Youth YR-6;
- ➢ Dr Carse, Founder & Director of 'Kids4Peace' Y5&6;
- ◆ **Boarders:** staged a performance of 'Grease' monies raised for the Sisters' Mission in Rushooka to purchase a well for an African village £142; Outing to Mrs Smith's house.
- ◆ **Overseas: Ski Trip** to St Gervais, France, for pupils from Y7 – 11
- ◆ **Charity:**
- ➢ Harvest Festival with donated fruit & vegetables given to a the Old Maltings & £131 raised & donated for the Sister's Mission
- ➢ Non-uniform Day – 'Pirates' monies for Gift Aid;
- ➢ Operation Christmas Child – filling of Shoe boxes; Collection of Sugar for BEFA;
- ➢ Non uniform Day in February – themes Seniors 'Mystical Beings' & Lower School 'Spots & Stripes' raised for Gift Aid & the Neurofibromatosis Assn; Lenten fundraising included: LS 5p collection for the Sister's Mission in

Uganda £112;

♦ **Music, Drama & Dance:**

➢ Pupils were invited to join 'Back to Broadway Musical Summer School' and had the opportunity of performing at The Norwich Playhouse as the culmination of their tuition.

➢ Events held included: House Music Festival (Y4-11); Senior Choir sang at the Service of Remembrance in the Parish Church;

➢ School Christmas Concert (YR-11);

➢ **Modern Dance Classes** were offered as an 'after-school' club by Mrs Pearson

➢ **Ballroom & Latin American Dance**:

➢ A new 'after-school' club was set up by Mrs Helen McDermott for all pupils

♦ **LAMDA** Excellent results from the 55 entrants with 6 pupils achieving Distinction;

♦ **Sport:**

➢ An Equestrian team was established by Miss Foster;

➢ Trip to Olympia Horse Show, London

➢ A Judo Club was set up as an 'after school' activity

➢ Rachel Mumford selected for Cross Country training for County. She became ISA's National Champion & 800m Champion as well, but was two years too young to represent Norfolk in the Senior ISA Athletics at Colchester. Three pupils then went on to represent the East of England in the National finals; West Norfolk Athletics at UEA; Junior ISA Athletics at Garon Park, Southend.

➢ Rebecca Chapman (Y10), with her partner, won the Norfolk Badminton Doubles Championships.

➢ Juliet Fenton (Y6) selected to receive coaching by the English Ladies Golf Association.

➢ Natasha Grapes (Y7) continues her Hockey success playing for Norfolk's U14 and East of England U12 teams. Her sister, Francesca is a regular player with Norfolk's U15 team.

➢ Our U13 team were West Norfolk Netball champions;

➢ Visits/ competitions included: Wembley to see England Netball v Malawi (Group of Y9 10&11);

➢ Pupils took part in Hockey & Netball matches & Tournaments, both at home & away. Swimming Gala at Hethersett Old Hall School; Football Taster Day with Norwich City Football Club coach (YR-9); Cross Country at Dereham Neatherd School, Earlham & Eccles Hall School.

✠ **2008– 2009**

♦ Boys were admitted, into the Senior School

♦ Independent Schools Inspection (with Boarding and Early Years) took place in January, when seven Inspectors visited the School.

♦ The Annual Pilgrimage to Walsingham, Y3-11, took place on the first day of the Academic Year.

♦ National Poetry Day was celebrated on the theme of 'Work'

♦ The weekly newsletter was published 'on line' for the first time available through the school website but hardcopies still available.

♦ A Live Animal Workshop held in school (YR- 9)

♦ **Bishop Michael Evans** visited Our Lady of Pity Church to celebrate Mass on the occasion of **Sr Emilia Birck's** Golden Jubilee & to receive First Vows of **Lucia Mickova** (Sr Weronica)

- At Lynford Hall Sophia Walker was a finalist in the Breckland Child of Courage Awards and Sr Emilia Birck was awarded 'Carer of the Year' in recognition of the advice, and practical help that she had given to the local migrant communities.
- ◆ **Staff News:**
- After seven years at the school Miss Diana Wynter retired at the end of the summer term

(**Headgirl**: Emily Wright
Deputies: Rosalind Peter
      Bryony Holland

- ◆ **Facilities:**
- Parents undertook the task to brighten the Lower School playground with painted fence panels depicting a bus, car etc.
- Miss Gooderson was relocated to a new office in the Lower School.
- The swimming pool, which had been renovated last year and funded by the PTA, was enhanced by an enchanting mural painted by Sister Kassia
- ◆ **Senior School Activities:**
- Mrs Jane Howarth started an after school club giving Spanish lessons for pupils Year 9+
- Swaffham Town Mayor, Mrs Shirley Matthews, talked to Y10 &11 about 'Local Government'
- Onatti French Theatre with their production 'Cache-Cache
- Matthew Project talk Y7–11
- Mr Peter Ingram, BBC Astronomer, with his Astroshow talk Y7 - 10
- Sheringham & Blickling Y8
- EcoTech, Swaffham Y7-9
- Norwich Castle Y7
- Science, Engineering & Technology Day at Breckland Park School, Swaffham

- Y8&9;
- Holt Hall residential trip Y10
- Gressenhall (GCSE History);
- Darley Hall Stud, Newmarket;
- Castle Acre & neighbouring churches Y7
- 'War Horse' at the National Theatre, London, Museum of London Y7, The Globe Y8, The National Gallery Y9, The Old Operating Theatre Y10, National Theatre, Back Stage Tour Y11;
- 'An Inspector Calls, Theatre Royal Norwich Y9&10;
- Gideons presented New Testaments to Year 7;
- Year 7 took part in the Swaffham Pancake Race, and won this event!
- First Aid Course introduced for Y9 pupils;
- D of E Bronze Award pupils Y10 undertook a Camp Craft session.
- ◆ **Lower School Activities:**
- Scholastic Book Fair was held in the Gym;
- Pupils participated in: local Time Trail (Y3);
- A workshop by the 'Jiving Lindy Hoppers' at Hammonds School Y5&6;
- YPR&R pupils celebrated the Chinese New Year with bowls of noodles, chicken and vegetables which they ate with chop sticks;
- Electricity Safety Talk Y3 - 6;
- Great Cressingham Victorian School Y6;
- Kentwell Hall Y5 Kings Lynn Corn Exchange Arts Theatre Y3&4;
- Challenge Week with a theme of 'Drama';
- Y2 efforts were recognised and published in a Children's Poetry Anthology;

- ♦ **Challenge Week activities included**
- ➢ the Image Musical Theatre Company, a Puppet Workshop Y6,
- ➢ Visit to Kings Lynn Corn Exchange Y3&4
- ➢ Morris Dancers;
- ➢ Reception Unit established a small garden
- ♦ **Overseas:** Years 5 & 6 pupils visit the 1st World War Battlefields of Northern France, including the Wellington Quarry at Arras and the memorial to the missing at Thiepval.
- ♦ **Charity:**
- ➢ Harvest Festival raised £350 for the King's Lynn Hospital Neo-natal unit;
- ➢ Non Uniform Day with a 'Sunflowers' theme raised £175 for BREAK;
- ➢ Shoe boxes were filled for 'Operation Christmas Child;
- ➢ the Annual Sugar Collection was made for BEFA (CRISIS at Christmas);
- ➢ Christmas collections for the Mercy Ships Charity £450;
- ➢ Lenten activities included: Rich man / Poor man lunch Y8's 'Seder Meal';
- ➢ Pupils dressed as 'Teachers' whilst staff became 'pupils', raised £170 for the 'Make a Wish' Foundation
- ➢ 5p collection for the Mission in Rushooka £187; another Non-uniform Day, theme 'Neon', raised £152 for Teenage Cancer Trust;
- ➢ Miss Clair Foster, Serena Smith and Rachel Mumford, completed a Junior Triathlon in aid of COSMIC (Children of St Mary's Intensive Care) and CRY (Cardiac Risk in the Young)
- ➢ Mrs Scrafield & Y5 pupils produced and sold a Bee Joke Book, which raised enough money to purchase four hives to send to poor countries.

- ➢ Old tea towels, towels, duvets, blankets, bed linen. were collected and sent to East Winch RSPCA Animal Hospital.
- ♦ **.Music Drama &Dance:**
- ➢ The Senior Choir took part in the Royal British Legion's Remembrance service in the church;
- ➢ Junior Choir sang at 'Petals' Christmas lunch;
- ➢ Two Shakespeare evening performances 'Bard in the Barn', were held in the Theatre (Y9&10)
- ➢ **LAMDA:** There was a Christmas presentation by Mrs Pickering's pupils. excellent examination results included: 36 Merits; 18 Distinction; 4 Bronze Medals for Acting
- ➢ (**Latin American / Ballroom Dance** two evening sessions a week held by Mrs Helen McDermott. Of the 22 girls entered 21 achieved Highly Commended and 1 Commended.
- ♦ **Sport:**
- ➢ The Equestrian team, with Miss Clair Foster, met weekly at Forest Edge Arena, The team's first public appearance in September saw six pupils perform a musical ride at the Arena's highly successful opening weekend.
- ➢ A group of pupils went to the International Horse Show, Olympia, London.
- ➢ A Cycling Proficiency course, after school, was offered to pupils.
- ➢ U12 Netball team became West Norfolk Netball Champions beating 4 local schools, this followed the success of the Years 9 & 11 teams;
- ➢ Mr Jeremy Hodges held a 2 day Tennis Camp during the Easter break;
- ➢ Pupils also took part in Swimming Galas at Hethersett & the ISA Gala at

Ipswich;
- ➢ Year 7 took part in the Mid Norfolk Athletics Championship at the UEA

✟ 2009– 2010

- ♦ **The Annual Pilgrimage** to Walsingham, for Y3-11 took place on the first day of the Academic Year led by Mrs Frances Verne & Sister Linda Pergega together with Fr Michael Johnstone.
- ♦ **Our Astronomy Week**, which coincided with International Space Week, was held in October with 'timetable changes to include Apollo 13 en francais, Music and Movement to Holst's Planets, Aliens in Cookery, Starbursts in Pottery, our awesome universe in Humanities and a Sensory Galactic Area in the Lower School as well as the mysterious Stompe Lessons in Science. A magazine was produced to detail this event.
- ♦ **National Poetry Day** theme was 'Heroes & Heroines'
- ♦ **Local Democracy Week** was marked with School Council Elections taking place
- ♦ Fantastic **GCSE results** achieved by Year 11 2009. **A** very special year group with many particularly academically gifted girls who gained outstanding results – 11 A*s, 10 A* and an A.
- ♦ **The relics of St Teresa of the Child Jesus c**ame to Walsingham, as part of the 'Europe' tour. Sr Linda accompanied by Y5 attended Mass and had a special retreat'
- ♦ **Visitors** from Slovakia: Sisters Dagma, Carmela, St Vincent de Paul Sisters together with Miss Hana & 5 students joined us for a week.
- ♦ **Playdayz** Parent, Baby & Toddler 0-4

years Activity Group, started by Mrs Gemma Wright, March 2009 to meet in the Gym, Monday am.
- ♦ A special Mass was celebrated to mark St George's Day on 23rd April.
- ♦ Centenary Mass at St John the Baptist Cathedral, Norwich was attended by Sr Francis & two pupils.
- ♦ Sister Francis and four pupils from Y9 went to Oxburgh Hall for Fr Benedict's First Mass (past pupil Richard Bedingfeld)
- ♦ All year groups attended the Royal Norfolk Show.
- ♦ Harrison Rayner, Y8, won the competition for the design of the 'Swaffham' shopping bag.

Headgirl: Serena Smith
Deputy: Sophie Willis
- ♦ **Facilities:**
- ➢ Miss Diana Wynter donated a pair of benches
- ➢ Old 1998 minibus – 'retired', PTA contributed £5000 towards the cost of a new vehicle
- ➢ An electrically operated 'security gate was installed at the front entrance to the school
- ➢ **The Lower School Playground** was redesigned with designated areas of play; a new quiet corner, a climbing and more active area, a small games area. The PTA financed new playground equipment voted for by the children and installed in July
- ➢ 'Parentmail' was introduced.
- ♦ **Senior School Activities:**
- ➢ Gideons presented Bibles to Y7;
- ➢ Chess Club Tournament, organized by Mr John Clements - pupils v staff, won by the staff 6-2;
- ➢ Gardening Club set up by Mrs Rachel

Scrafield & Mrs Meg Heale for pupils Y5 upwards
- Visits by: Onatti French Theatre "La Chambre de Jean-Paul";
- Dr Birchett talk Y9&10 HE groups
- Fire Service presentation (Y11);
- Vegetarian Society talk; First Aid Course Y9;
- PC Sharon Page talk on "Drugs" Y8;
- Walsingham Historical Society Y10;
- Morston Quay and Sheringham Y8;
- Norwich Castle Art Gallery Y10 & 11 Art Group)
- Retreat Day to Santon Downham Y7; to Micklefield Church Y8; Whitlingham Country Park Y9; to Castleacre Y10; Hunstanton Y11;
- London Science trip Y10 & 11;
- French Day, Cambridge Y10&11 GCSE French
- 3 day Residential Trip to Holt Hall Y10;
- Impsons the Butchers ; EcoTech Centre Y10;
- Snettisham Deer Safari & lunch Y10 HE group;
- Waitrose Y9 HE group;
- D of E Bronze Award expedition Saxmundham

♦ **Lower School Activities:**
- 'Peter Ingram BBC Astronomer Y4 -6;
- PC Hazel visited, talk on 'safety' YR-6;
- Build your own Politician YPR-6;
- Image Musical Theatre Workshop YR- 6;
- Bird boxes with cameras, donated by the Mumford family were installed outside the LS enabling views of the Great Tit's nests;
- Norwich Playhouse to see "We're Going on a Bear Hunt YR&1; High Lodge YR;
- Journey on a X1 bus to Kings Lynn YPR & R;
- Great Cressingham Victorian School Y6

- Warren Farm, Drymere –Sponsored Walk YR & 1; Waitrose YR; Sheringham Park Y1 - 3
- Swaffham Museum; Market Cross Coffee YR;
- Retreat – Walsingham & Hunstanton Y6;
- West Stow Y4;
- Kentwell Y5;
- Diocesan Primary Retreat Y4;
- Retreat – Castle Acre
- Y3; Castle Acre Priory Y6;

♦ **Overseas: Polish trip** to Krakow & Auschwitz Y11 & parents
- **Ski Trip** to Alpe D'Huez for pupils Y6-10

♦ **Charity:**
- Harvest Festival raised £180 for CAFOD & the Sister's Mission in Rushooka;
- BEFA collection of sugar yielded 53 kilos;
- Non-uniform Day 'Space' theme for the charity 'Starlight' £93;
- Breckland Young People's Enterprise Scheme. Y10 and YR took part and raised £250
- The Lower School Nativity in the Barn Theatre raised £103 YPR-3 and the Christmas Performance in the Gym raised £122 Y4 – 6 which was split between Great Ormond Street Hospital and local charity Rebecca's Wishes;
- 'Bees for Development' Sale £110;
- LS Bring & Buy Toy Sale and Sponsored Silence bought two Ten Men Shelter Boxes £900 from the Rotary Club for the Haiti Earthquake Appeal;
- Lenten Activities included Rich Man / Poor Man meal to raise monies for CAFOD £153 and the Sister's Rushooka Mission £75:
- Non-uniform Day – 'Red, White & Blue' theme raised £166 for the Swaffham

Youth Council's work in a Cambodian Orphanage ;

- LEPRA –total raised by pupils overall - £1095 this included Y6 Cake Stall £42
- Sponsored Walk to Castle Acre raised £2447 of which 10% given to Mrs Anna Carter for her 'Moonwalk' for Breast Cancer, the balance going towards the new play equipment.
- Non uniform Day – 'World Cup' raised monies for Nottingham Hospital Renal Unit;

♦ **Music, Drama & Dance:**
- Tiffany Rivett, (Y 11), took part in a masterclass with the violinist Agnes Lauger at Hethersett
- Senior House Music Festival; Senior Christmas Carol Service £2771;
- Y4 choir sang at the Iceni Care Home, Swaffham;
- The Senior choir took part in the Royal British Legion annual Festival of Remembrance;
- **Latin American Dance**; All pupils gained Highly Commended Certificates in their Spring exams; At the Dance Show 41 Highly Commended presented with certificates. £212 was raised at this event to go towards the new playground equipment.
♦ **'Back to Broadway'** ran a summer school for aspiring thespians
♦ **Sport:**
- Natasha Grapes played in goal for the County U15 team;
- Sophie Newby was selected for trial for the East of England U15 Netball team;
- Hockey coaching sessions continued at Dereham Hockey Club.
- Our U13 U14 & U16 Netball teams held onto their titles of West Norfolk Champions for the third year running.

- Cross Country at Gresham's & ISA Cross Country Championships at Eccles Hall School when 6 and 7 pupils qualified for the National event at Princethorpe;
- Athletics at Colchester Garrison Y7 - 9;
- Mid Norfolk Athletics at UEA; ISA Junior Athletics Competition, Garron Park Southend
- Lower School Sports day & Prizegiving;
- Miss Clair Foster and Mrs Mazoe Young accompanied 8 pupils to Wimbledon
- Mr Hodges formed a Multi-Skills Club;
- Mr Moore commenced after school Roller Skating for boys Y5–9; and roller hockey
- Artistic Roller Skating for Years 2 & 3;
- Norwich City Football Club gave Community Coaching sessions Y1- 6;
- **American Football & Baseball** tasters sessions offered by Mr Jones (parent) as an 'after-school' activity.

✠ **2010– 2011**
- Y3-11, accompanied by the Sisters and staff, visited Walsingham for the Annual Pilgrimage
- Registration – morning & afternoon; now conducted electronically. The weekly newsletter sent to parents, staff & governors by email.
♦ **The Holy Father made his first state visit**
♦ 5 pupils & 2 members of staff represented the School on 17th September when he visited St Mary's College, Twickenham. All pupils watched, via the internet, some took part in the Big Assembly Hyde Park Prayer Vigil.
♦ **National Poetry Day** was marked with

pupils work displayed on the theme of 'Home'. This was well supported by parents at the Poetry Recital.

- In celebration of Easter; pupils in Y3–11 were given an egg to decorate during the holidays and these formed a grand 'Eggshibition'
- All Year groups undertook individual form Retreats to various venues throughout the year.
- **Mother General, Sr Lucyna Mroczeck,** accompanied by the General Secretary, Sr Josefa Rapatz visited the School in October and were entertained by a Special Concert in the Barn
- Year R Staff awarded Early Years County Rating of Green for the work they do with our youngest pupils. (Highest grade)
- **Sr Kasjana's Silver Jubilee** was celebrated with a School Mass.
- **Bishop Michael Evans** died 11th July, The prayers offered for a miracle for his complete recovery obviously contributing to his extended service to the Church.
- **Sister Margaret Carolan**, former Provincial Superior and Headteacher died at the beginning of the summer holidays after a long illness.
- **Staff News:**
  - ➢ Sadly Mrs Jenny Davey lost her fight with cancer, she died in early March. Five pupils represented the school at her funeral on 18th March. Staff took part in the Race for Life organized by Miss Wookey, to support Cancer Research - over £2250 was raised.

Headgirl: Anna Stevenson;
Deputy: Emily Simon

- **Facilities:** .The Jungle Climber was completed and ready for use - part

funded from a £5000 Early Years grant & £4000 from EYPS, £2600 from pupils. 'Officially opened' by past pupil & Chair of PTA, Sally Hayes, on 16th November

- **Countdown to '100 years'** –On 28th June the first event was held – a 'Street Party' in the school grounds. A Shakespeare presentation was performed on Tuesday 5th July, at the Buttercross Swaffham together with excerpts from the forthcoming production of CATs' and a demonstration of Latin American dance from Mrs McDermot's pupils. .
- **Senior School Activities:**
- Gifted & Talented Tridium based on Mathematical patterns was held in the Spring Term; Sandringham being the overall winner. A Mathematics magazine was also produced.
- 'The Crucible' – Y11;
- Carries War' – Y7 & 8.
- Sainsbury Centre Y6-8 & 10-&11;
- Morston Quay & Sheringham Y8;
- The Tudor House, Thetford Y8;
- Kings Lynn Arts Centre Y10&11;
- Castle Rising & Castle Acre Y7;
- Science Museum 'Live in King's Lynn Y6-9;
- Victorian School, Gt Cressingham Y6;
- Royal Norfolk Show Y6-10;
- Humanities Week was held for 3 days for Years 7–11 who had not gone on the trip to Poland. Activities enjoyed during this week, included trips to Banham Zoo; Norwich Castle; rehearsal of 'The Time Machine'; Morris Dancing and a Spoon Workshop;
  - ➢ Residential Geography and Science Field trip to Holt Hall in May Y10
  - ➢ Year 11 went to Clare Priory for their Retreat and spent the day in London,

shopping and attending a show.
- A Careers Convention staged for Y7–10
- **Lower School Activities:**
- 'Stick Man' performance YR 1&2;
- Norwich Castle Museum YR;
- Sainsbury Centre Basket Exhibition Y4–7;
- West Stow Y3&4;
- Kentwell Hall Y5;
- Royal Norfolk Show YR-5;
- Happy Prince performance YPR-6;
- High Lodge (Y1&2);
- YR–4 made Tudor scarecrows, for the Scarecrowfest at Oxburgh Hall;
- Year 3 represented the school at the Diocesan Primary School Mass at Walsingham.
- Sports day & Prizegiving took place on 8th July
- Y6 presented with a dictionary by the Rotary Club.
- **Overseas Trips:**
- Somme Battlefield, France Y7-9;
- Ski Trip for pupils from Y6–11;
- Poland, Auschwitz & Krakow Y10&11;
- Berck sur Mer, France Y5 & 6 in June;
- **Charity:**
- Fashion Show held in the Barn Theatre, proceeds to Breast Cancer Care raising over £765;
- Harvest Festival raised £250 to send aid to the Pakistan Flood victims;
- Sugar collection for BEFA resulted in 65 kilos of sugar; with donations of coffee & tea
- Surreal Friends Exhibition hosted by Y6 8 pupils was a resounding success and raised £285 for Swaffham Home Hospice;
- Smartie tubes filled with 'silver' coins in Lent, £233 sent to Loiangalani, Kenya Water project;

- Non-uniform Day for Breast Cancer Research raised £150; a collection at the Senior Music Evening raised a further £150 for this charity;
- **Past Pupils: The 'Class of 1976** held a reunion to celebrate their 'Big 50'at Stow Bardolph
- **Leavers 2009 re-union** was in the Barn
- **Music Speech & Drama::**
- A group of instrumentalists & the Junior Choir entertained at the Swaffham Twinning Party
- The Senior Choir took part in the Royal British Legion's Remembrance in the Parish Church
- The September LAMDA examinations yielded a total of 23 Merit and 34 Distinctions
- Mr Eddie Godden produced a mini-version of 'Cats' with members of the after school Theatre Club.
- **Sport:**
- Other events saw our teams competing at: Swimming Gala Hethersett Y6 - 8; Cross Country, Greshams U9 & U11; Hockey & Netball matches by our usual teams continued throughout the Autumn & Spring terms.
- Rounders, Tennis, Cross Country & Athletics also appeared on the calendar of competition events. Our U14 teams became champions of the West Norfolk Netball league and our U16 squad became West Norfolk champions as well.
- Speed Stacking (YR–11), when great fun was had by all;
- American Football and Baseball sessions, were offered by parent Mr Jones, as an 'after school activity';
- Pupils, especially boys, were invited to attend a Junior Open Golf Day by the

NC Golf Union;

➤ Some of Year 10 attended the Wimbledon Tennis Championships on Wednesday 29th June

✟ 2011– 2012

- The School took part in the Swaffham & Brecks Food Festival. This new venture saw a number of special events held and included our Harvest Festival in the Parish Church, a Saturday Auction & a Sunday Market Stall of local produce, a 'History of Food Exhibition' featuring food & drink in Tudor times; Elizabeth Truss MP, joined the school for a picnic lunch in the front garden, Y10 & 11 participated in a 'Pop-Up' restaurant.
- The Annual Pilgrimage to Walsingham took place on the first day of the new term, when the Sisters & staff members together with pupils from Years 3-11 enjoyed a calm and relaxing day.
- An assembly was held to commemorate the 'Drina Martyrs'. Sr Thomas More Prentice, Sr Linda Pergega, Mrs Marie Mansfield plus 3 pupils attended the memorial celebration in Sarajevo
- Excellent GCSE results recorded once again with two pupils gaining 10xA* grades; 52% of our pupils gained 10 or more A*-C grades; with 90% achieving A*-C.
- ➤ Whole school 'Gifted & Talented PSHEE week
- ➤ Remembrance Day service & silence was observed at the Town War Memorial & a wreath laid by Head girl and Form Captains from Y4 -11
- Australia Day & Chinese New Year were celebrated in style
- School Inspection took place in March 2012;

- Early Learning Years department visited by a team of Advisors for a RAG rating / Inspection; we were awarded overall green (top grade)
- Visit by pupils from a vocational independent school 'Berufskollet Marienschule', Germany, together with their Headteacher, Mr Wooermann and staff member Mrs Redike, Indira and Elena first students
- Twelve students, from our school in Biala Biasko, Poland stayed in the Convent for a week during June, visiting places of interest locally & London
- Art work from Years R-11 were exhibited at Norfolk & Norwich Open Studio Art Festival – one of 18 schools in the County to do this. Monies raised and donated to the Samaritans.
- Pupils, YR-11, attended the Royal Norfolk Show and pupils of Year 7 manned their Brecks Project
- Early Learning Years Department, renamed as Little Pedlars together with redesigned logo, officially opened by , by our local Mayor Terri Jennison unveiling the new sign on 14th June. Pupils peddled their bikes to the new sign and acted as hosts.
- Art picture of Picasso's 'Weeping Woman' Y 5 – 11) and a stained glass window made in squares Y1-4 ;
- **Staff News:**
- ➤ Two past pupils returned as students Claire Morgan (PE and Asthma Awareness) and Georgina Sullivan helped in Senior School.
- ➤ Mrs Vanessa Burton (Science) maternity leave – welcome to Rose Amelia;
- ➤ Congratulations to Mrs Kathy MacLachlan who married during the Easter break & returned to school as

Mrs Laban;

- Mrs Meg Heale (operation) sick leave cover by Mrs Sally Whyte;
- Mr Paul Donley retired Music teacher died February 2012
- Celebration of Queen's Jubilee, with the front of the school decorated with bunting, and afternoon tea taken in this area.

Headgirl: Emily Hill,

Deputy Heads: Charlotte Hayes
      Rachel Mumford

- ♦ **Senior School Activities:**
- Buddhist Centre;
- Turin Shroud (replica) at St John's Cathedral,
- Blakeney / Sheringham Y8;
- Darley Stud Racing Stables, Newmarket Y8;
- Careers Convention, London Y9;
- Ancient House, Thetford Y9;
- 'An Inspector Calls, Y9 10 & 11;
- Workshop on Nazi Germany, Norwich (GCSE History pupils);
- Science Convention, John Innes Centre Y10;
- Holt Hall 3 day Geography Field trip Y10;
- Brecks visit, including Grimes Graves, Santon Downham & High Lodge Thetford, Y7;
- Retreat – Santon Downham, Y7; Mickfield Church, Suffolk, Y8; Hunstanton Y9; Final Retreat – Clare Priory Y11;
- Teams of 4 pupils from Y7 8 9 & 10 attended the Science Olympiad at the UEA;
- Senior School Prizegiving – new trophies donated and nominated by pupils
- Afghanistan talk by W.O. Edwards

Y6-11;
- Onatti French Theatre ' Les Garcons'; Y7-11;
- Felt Making with Inglisse Y4 8 & 9;
- 'The Soldiers', Norwich GCSE Music;
- Activities / Humanities week held in the Spring, West Lexham Education Centre Y7-11; Swaffham Museum Y5&6;
- D of E Bronze Award expeditions to Thetford Forest & Trimingham & weekend at Croxton Village Hall;
- ♦ **Whole school event**
- 'World of Wings' activities YR-11
- Dance workshop through LEPRA YR-11
- Mary Webb Exhibition, Sainsbury Centre, Y 3-9
- ♦ **Lower School Activities:**
- Eggs collected from Mrs Margaret Smith's hens YR; Denver Windmill to buy flour Y2. This was subsequently made into bread, by Y 1 &2, to sell on our Sunday stall; visit to the Duck Pond YR
- Retreats: Castle Acre Priory Y6 Walsingham Y5
- Thetford Y3
- Halloween Walk YR 1&2
- 'Lighting of Lights' carols in Swaffham Y5 & 6
- Theatre, St John's Cathedral & Plantation Garden, Norwich YR-2
- Parish Church Christmas Tree Festival;
- Great Cressingham Victorian School Y5 & 6
- Radio Norfolk interviewed members of Y6 about the 'Holiday Hats' they had made;
- Two pupils Y6 raised £112 for the Mission in Rushooka with their Sponsored silence;

- ➢ Aromatic wreaths made by YR-2;
- ➢ Norwich Puppet Theatre workshop Y5 &
- ➢ Jasper Cooper, author & artist, workshop & talk Y
- ➢ Sainsbury Centre Y3-
- ♦ **Overseas:**
- ➢ Ski Trip to Aosta / Pila –
- ➢ Prague trip by Senior pupils included a visit to Terezin where pupils saw the fortress, walled garrison town & the Jewish cemetery, sites of Prague and experienced a ballet and opera
- ♦ **Charity:**
- ➢ Harvest Festival monies £1000 to St Peter & Paul Church Restoration Appeal & the Sister's Mission in Rushooka;
- ➢ 'Pink Friday' non-uniform for Breast Cancer Care Charity £343
- ➢ Cake Bake Y10 Macmillan Cancer Care £115
- ➢ Operation Christmas Child - 46 Shoe boxes filled sent to Swaziland;
- ➢ BEFA sugar collection – 80kgs collected;
- ➢ School Carol Concert £284 each for BREAK & EACH); Charity Stall for Disabled Bedouin Children £40
- ➢ Non Uniform Day for 'Scotties Little Soldiers ;
- ➢ Lenten activities included – attendance at Frugal Meals in the Town's churches
- ➢ Smarties monies collection for CAFOD £425
- ➢ Bake sale for British Heart Foundation £6
- ➢ LEPRA £721
- ➢ Rich Man / Poor Man lunch £150 raised & sent to the Sister's Mission in Uganda), Smartie tubes were also filled for this mission;
- ➢ Pupils received named Palm Crosses and offered prayers for that person

during Lent;
- ➢ 'St George's' Non-uniform Day £111 for Epilepsy Action;
- ♦ **Music Drama & Dance:**
- ➢ Y1-3 performed & participated in the Town Carol Concert in the Assembly Rooms;
- ➢ Senior Choir attended & sang at the annual RBL Festival of Remembrance in the Parish church; Entertained elderly residents Y5 & 6;
- ➢ Community Carols to the Town's Dementia Club Y8 & 9
- ➢ LAMDA: December examination results included 6 Merits & 43 Distinctions
- ➢ Easter Eggstravaganza
- ➢ Speech & Drama Evening raised £375 for the Theatre.
- ➢ Latin American / Ballroom Dance: presentation took place and raised £201;
- ♦ **Sport:**
- ➢ Senior ISA Swimming – Ipswich;
- ➢ Hockey, Netball & Rounders & Tennis matches played against local schools; Mid Norfolk Area Cross Country;
- ➢ ISA Cross Country, Gosfield;
- ➢ ISA National Cross Country Competition at Princethorpe College, Rugby;
- ➢ Senior ISA Athletics, Cambridge. The girl's team came 1st out of the 13 teams taking part; Mid Norfolk Athletics,
- ➢ UEA Tennis Tournament Regional finals, Lower School Sports Day & Prizegiving;
- ➢ House Sports Day; Swimming Gala;
- ➢ Mr Jeremy Hodges ran 3 day Indoor Tennis Camps during Spring half term & again in the Summer holidays;
- ➢ Lucy Edwards Y8 attended the West Norfolk Sports Award Personality Presentation as a nominee for the Young

Sports Person of the Year. She was the runner up!

✝ 2012– 2013

- Sister Monica Grebener, died on 4th September in Hunstanton.
- All pupils from Years 7 – 11 and staff accompanied Sr Linda Pergega and attended the Albanian Commemorative Mass at Holy Apostles Church, Pimlico. This was conducted by Archbishop Kevin Nichols in memory of Blessed Mother Teresa. Her picture, created in squares by pupils, took centre stage at this event.
- As part of the Brecks Food Festival weekend, our Harvest Festival was celebrated at the parish Church and followed by lunch in the front garden of the school. This was followed by various other events throughout the weekend including processing through the town, Latin American dancing at the Buttercross, waiting-on at the Pop-Up restaurant, Art & T-towel exhibition in the Assembly Rooms, auction of Harvest baskets & Market Stall of Harvest goods.
- Father Michael Johnstone retired as Parish Priest and to mark this event a School Mass was held. His successor being Fr Gordon Williams.
- National Poetry Day was celebrated in October with production of poems on 'Stars'.
- New uniform supplier sourced, John Lewis, who replaced Bird's, the National Schoolwear Centre, from March 2012. Some changes to the uniform also made with kilts replacing the plain skirts and updating of the sports uniform, obtained from Birds of Dereham.
- ISA Art Competition Regional finals –

achieved first place in four categories of this event.
- Snow, in early January, disrupted the regular school timetable for a week.
- The Garden Club pupils, under the guiding hand of Mrs Kathy Laban, continued their endeavors with enthusiasm. Planting various containers and a selection of small trees recently received, Rowan Birch & Cherry. These trees to be planted at various locations around the school grounds when appropriate.
- Meals Questionnaire circulated prior for analysis in order to ascertain lunch preferences.
- The Reverend Alan Hopes, appointed the new Bishop of East Anglia.
- **Visitors:**
- ➢ Two German students, Mieke and Julia, to the Lower School for a fortnight in the Summer term;
- ➢ Spanish teacher, Mrs Cuenco and her three children visited, in the Summer term, for a fortnight and taught Spanish.
- **Staff News:**
- ➢ Mrs Vivienne Phillips, took on the School's 'Marketing' mantle, advised by Mr George Hayes.
- ➢ Mrs Irene Henden took on the role of SENCO as well as Head of RE;

Headgirl: Juliet Fenton,
Deputies: Sasha Fountain, Hannah Hodges
- **Facilities:**
- ➢ School Office & Reception area were refurbished with separate pupil & parent hatches created;
- ➢ Daily minibus service to & from Downham Market introduced in the Spring Term. Driven by parent, Mr Edward Keating
- ➢ Wood craftsman Karl assisted by

various pupils erected a living Willow 'Domed Structure' on the grass playground near the Sports Hall;

- Additions to the Music Room included a baby grand piano to replace the old one and a large, digital Yamaha Keyboard, donated by, Mrs Mary Gargett-Stringer;

♦ **Senior School Activities:**

- Volunteering at the Missionaries of Charity Soup Kitchen, London Y11
- St John's Cathedral, Norwich celebration of the start of the 'Year of Faith' Y8
- Geography Field trip to Sheringham, Blakeney Point & Morston Y8
- History Workshop, Norwich Playhouse, Doctor's Show' and Pathology event at the Forum, Norwich Y10
- London trip included visit to Clink Museum & the Globe Theatre Y7&8
- 'Germany Live' student conference (Y11);
- 3 day Geography trip to Holt Hall Y10
- Royal Norfolk Show Y7-10, Y7 also manned an exhibition of pupils' photographs for both days at this event;
- Very long day visit to Battlefields of Belgium;
- Enrichment Days, for those not on the Belgium trip, included visits to the Secret Bunker, Kelvedon Hatch, Essex
- 'In-school' taster sessions of Judo, run by coach Mr Neil Turner,
- 'Listening' run by Mr and Mrs King and Mrs McCarthy, Samaritan volunteers for Y9&10;
- Retreat - Buddhist Centre plus Stations of the Cross at St John's Cathedral Y7;
- Retreat – Julian of Norwich Centre Y9
- Weekend Retreat – Chesterfield Y10
- Fr Lush, a Vicar General from Albania gave a talk on 'Mother Teresa' to the whole school;

- Senior School Prizegiving;
- Onatti Theatre presented 'Les Filles'(Y7-11);
- Talks given to Y7-11 by Fr Richard Finn with Dominican brothers Sam & Toby, on 'Christians & War'; & Sir Richard Parsons, former British Ambassador, on the unseen role of a diplomat
- 'Life of Mother Teresa' production by a London based Albanian theatre group Y1-11
- 'The Tempest' workshop Y8 –10
- 'Bard in the Barn',performed by (Y9&10);
- 'Mosaic Memory' Workshop -Carolyn Ash (Y7);
- D of E Bronze Award Group expedition to Trimingham for their final assessment;

♦ **Lower School Activities:**

- Retreat – Thetford RC Church, surrounding area and secret garden (Y3); Castle Acre Priory (Y4&5); Holkham Beach, Walsingham and Wells for fish and chips (Y6);
- The Tiger who came to Tea, at Norwich Playhouse, lunch - St John's Cathedral; later made artistic creations for Exhibition at Norwich Playhouse (YR-2);
- Schools Pilgrimage to Walsingham (Y3);
- Kentwell Hall dressed as Tudors (Y5&6);
- Royal Norfolk Show(Little Pedlars - Y6);
- Holt Hall – Environmental studies (Y6);
- Bewilderwood (YR-6);
- Independent Schools Drama Shakespeare Day with St Nicholas School, Notre Dame and local Greenhoe Middle School for Y5 and 6 pupils
- Simon Rowe from KLFM made recordings for daily schools' educational joke broadcast with each pupil from Y1-

6 taking part;

- Little Pedlars class saw the hatching of six chicks in their classroom and watched their progress
- Sports Day & Prizegiving;

♦ **Overseas:**

- The Battlefields at Ypres, Belgium, led by staff member Mrs Natalie Wilson (some pupils from Y7-11)
- Work experience at Sr Anna Benesova's school in Prague, was undertaken by pupils Elise Sorrell, Joanna Simon & Mollie Ogden Y10 in February half term;

♦ **Charity:**

- Brecks weekend Harvest Basket sales £660) divided between Swaffham & Litcham Home Hospice & the St Peter & Paul Restoration Appeal;
- Macmillan Cancer Care Cake sale;
- BEFA Sugar collection; Operation Christmas Child Shoe Box collection;
- Angels Non uniform Day, plus part of the Carol Concert monies, to CAFOD's World Gifts £379
- Male staff & pupils took part in 'Movember' sponsored event (£200);
- St Peter & Paul Church Christmas Tree Festival raised £80, donated in equal parts to the Church's Restoration Fund & the Mission in Rushooka;
- Pupils knitted blanket squares to raise funds for the Alzheimer's Society, some learnt to knit; including Mr Murphy
- Lenten Activities included Rich Man / Poor Man lunch, attendance at local Frugal Meals;
- Collection of copper coins, silver 'Smartie-tube fill', All monies raised was sent to CAFOD;
- Year 4 House Points for 5p raised £25 for Rushooka
- Non-uniform Day, 'Red' theme for Big

'C' Charity.

- Two Jewellery Sales, organized by Mrs Pat de Swart, raised £706 for local disabled children;
- Music, Speech & Drama evenings raised £686, of which £140 was given to the Mission in Rushooka;
- Charity Bake Sale £50 to Swaffham & Litcham Home Hopice

♦ **Music Drama & Dance:**

- Hannah Hodges was offered a place at the Trinity College Saturday School in London, her primary study being Recorder with Piano as her second instrument.
- Pupils achieved good results in their ABRSM Music examinations. All nine entrants passed; with good results once again;
- Senior Choir Y5-11 attended & sang at the annual RBL Festival of Remembrance in the Parish church;
- Pupils also attended the service at the War memorial & laid a wreath; Timothy Pennington sounded the 'Last Post' and school members of the local cadet forces marched to this event in cadet uniforms;
- Pupils, invited by former pupil, Jenna Fountain, sang at St Peter Mancroft. The Co-op donated £100 for this service which was given to the Mission in Uganda;
- Lower School Christmas & Senior School Concerts (added to non-uniform day figure for CAFOD's World Gifts & £200 to local Barnardos Appeal;
- Pupils attended & performed at the Town Carol Concert Y1-3; Some pupils sang at the Town Lights Switch – on; pupils also sang carols at various venues & care homes around the town;
- Senior Music Evening; Lower School

Music Afternoon, which raised £90 towards the new piano fund plus £30 for the Mission in Uganda;

- ➤ LAMDA: November examination results: exceptionally good once again with 6 Passes, 20 Merits & 11 Distinctions. Eliza Nodes passed her Gold Medal with Distinction;
- ➤ Speech & Drama Evening;
- ➤ Drama Club run by past pupil Miss Laura Hayes for a term. The Junior School Theatre Studies group presented 'Top of the Mops'.
- ➤ Dance: Latin American & Ballroom Performance raised monies for local Home Hospice;
- ♦ **Sport:**
- ➤ Lucy Edwards won a gold medal as part of the U15 Team Norfolk at the UK Sportshall Championships. She ranked first for her age group in the East of England and 9th in the UK.
- ➤ Kick Boxing Championships – Richard Keating Y10 & Thomas McDermott Y4 came first in their individual events, both winning trophies;
- ➤ U16's Netball Team got through to the County Finals (National Schools Competition) at UEA; U11 Boys Football team competed for the first time; Senior ISA Swimming Gala, Ipswich Crown Pools; ISA Cross Country at Gosfield;
- ➤ Wimbledon tickets, one pair for Centre Court and five pairs for Court One, were obtained for Years 10 & 11.

✞ 2013– 2014

- ♦ The new Academic year commenced, with the School Pilgrimage (Y3-11) to Walsingham.
- ♦ Outstanding GCSE results achieved in the Summer 2013 examinations: 90% A*-

C; 75% of which included English & Mathematics. One pupil, Hannah Hodge, gained 11 A* grades.

- ♦ Y6-9 pupils attended a special School's Mass at St John's Cathedral, which was held to mark the end of 'Faith Year'. Some pupils joined the torchlight Eucharistic procession that evening from Norwich Castle, through the town to the Cathedral
- ♦ BIshop Alan Hopes visited the school and celebrated Mass for the whole school and talked to Y9-11 and visited younger pupils' classrooms.
- ♦ Working towards the Centenary a European Day of Languages was led by Mrs Jane Howarth, joined by European language speakers from amongst the Sisters & students, taught German, Italian, Portuguese and Polish to Year 4 – 11 before Assemblies;
- ♦ A Centenary Garden Fete held on Saturday 7th June, with stallholders from local charities and craft people invited to take part, to coincide with our Open Studios Pupil's Art Exhibition.
- ♦ Poppy seeds, sent by Norfolk County Council, were planted in commemoration of the start of World War I.
- ♦ Book Buddy system restarts with seniors aiding younger pupils.
- ♦ Sacred Heart of Jesus in Norfolk Mosaic made by all pupils and staff with the help of artist Carolyn Ash. Holiday Challenge photographs used for the sides of the triptych. Exhibited in the Forum for Open Studios.
- ♦ Use of Woodland adjacent to the playground. Mrs Penny Peirce was the mastermind behind the project and the Rotary Club donated £5000 in memory

of Louisa Willgrass (nee Cornwall) who was killed in the Thailand tsunami. Opened on Friday 27th June by Little Pedlars, Rotary Club, the Cornwalls and blessed by Fr Gordon. Pupils are able to study & explore in this environment, staff have been supported by a team of hardworking parents. Bushes and trees nutured by Mrs Laban and the Gardening Club will form a boundary.

- **Staff News:**
  - ➢ Miss Helen Harvey, now married, (Assistant Secretary) left;
  - ➢ Mrs Anna Carter rejoined for a year for Y3
  - ➢ Mrs Jackie Cockman completed Level 3 in Teaching & Learning and moved from Kitchen duties to join the Little Pedlars staff to replace Alicia Arthur, temporary staff
  - ➢ Miss Liridona Laska also gained her Level 3

Headgirl: Joanna Simon,
Deputies: Hope Mumford,
Eloise Sorrell

- **Facilities:**
  - ➢ New electric, security gates fitted to the front of the school; area around dustbins smartened
  - ➢ New blue mini bus
  - ➢ Purchased 30 Ipads (PTA)
  - ➢ Smart Heads Office and Reprographics Rooms
  - ➢ Decluttered office and Reception area
- **Senior School Activities:**
  - ➢ Three Senior pupils: Lucy Edwards, Victoria Hill & Lily Wallis Y10 awarded scholarships from CCSS, a Cambridge ISA College to follow a GCSE Computing Programming Course;

- ➢ Houghton Hall to view the exhibition of 'Old Masters' on loan from the Hermitage Museum, Petersburg Y7 - 10;
- ➢ Local shopping survey Y8;
- ➢ Sainsbury Centre to visit the Exhibition 'Master Pieces of East Anglia' & St John's Roman Catholic Cathedral for Mass to welcome our new Bishop, Alan Hopes Y6 - 9;
- ➢ Retreat for Y6/7 to Santon Downham Church and building dens on St Joseph, the Carpenter's Day.
- ➢ Anna Frank exhibition at Ely Cathedral Y8- 10
- ➢ Dalham Hall Stud at the invitation of HH Sheikh Mohammed bin Rashid Al Marktoum at foaling time Y8 & 9
- ➢ Y10's 3 day Geopgraphy Study Trip to Holt Hall
- ➢ In school activities included:
- ➢ Community Service Volunteer talk by Mrs Yvonne Ogden, Y8-11
- ➢ Baton Twirling with Mrs Christian Y7
- ➢ WW1 Remembrance talks on the 'History of the Gurkha regiments in the British Army' by Lt-Col Taylor of the Gurkha Welfare Trust and
- ➢ Trench Warfare by Rev Paul Kinsey Y6 - 9
- ➢ D of E Bronze Award for Years 10 & 11 took place in Suffolk.
- **Lower School Activities:**
  - ➢ Retreat – St Mary's Church, Houghton-on-the-Hill Y4&5
  - ➢ Performance at Norwich Playhouse – 'The Snail & the Whale' and looking at Mother Teresa Exhibition at the RC Cathedral (Y1-3);
  - ➢ Women's World day of Prayer – Y5 /6 play percussion instruments to Egyptian Music
  - ➢ In school activities included:

- Learning about 'pigs' and a visit to Impsons to find out how to make sausages (Little Pedlars);
- Inviting parents to Little Pedlars and Y1's Home Made Soup Day;
- Learning about our teeth with Mrs MacPartlin Y3
- Four pupils from Year 4 were runners up in the Local 'Food & Farming' Competition and won £100 towards the cost of the School's Vice Versa Cookery Book
- **Overseas:** Miss Rachel Wilson organized another very successful Ski Trip to Aosta, Pila

♦ **Charity:**
- As part of the Brecks Food festival, **a** Harvest Festival service was held at St Peter & Paul Church, followed by a picnic lunch in the front courtyard of the school. The Harvest baskets / boxes subsequently formed the basis of a 'Prize Every Time' tombola stall on the market. The £524 raised was divided between St Peter & Paul Church Restoration Appeal and the Swaffham & Litcham Home Hospice;
- Mrs Pat de Swart's Jewellery sales for local disabled child made £354;
- Loose change & 5p collection for the Mission in Rushooka raised £19
- Non-uniform Day – 'Wear it Pink' & a Bake sale for Breast Cancer research (£200+);
- 13 Christmas Shoe Box for the Appeal;
- Sugar collection for BEFA;
- Cake Bake for the Gurhka Trust raised £50;
- Collection made for church missions in Philippines through Action for the Church in Need to support the work in this region so badly hit by recent hurricanes;
- A decorated Christmas Tree was on display at the Parish Church's Festival of Trees; Town Council Bake Off winners – Harry Hunt, Y9, won 1st prize in the Children's section;
- Paper Plane Competition organized by Mrs Laban, with Mr Dowsing as judge. Monies raised went to the Mission in RushookA

♦ **Past pupils**:
- Freya Barlow sadly lost her fight against cancer and died, aged 22, on 5th January 2014. Following a vigil of prayer in the school chapel, her funeral Mass was held at Ely Cathedral, conducted by Fr Michael Johnstone, and was attended by the Sisters, present & past pupils and staff together with many relatives and school and University friends in the congregation of some 500+;
- News of the death of other past pupils Alexandra Dann and Jackie Ollett;
- Victoria Short achieved two distinctions in her assignments at Easton College where she is studying 'Animal Care'.

♦ **Music Drama & Dance:**
- House Music Festival;
- Lower School Christmas & Senior Carol Concerts raised £520, this was split equally between EACH at Quidenham & the Church in Need
- Junior & Senior Choirs (Y5-11) attended & sang at the annual RBL Festival of Remembrance in the Parish church;
- Pupils (Y4-11), together with our cadets force pupils in their uniforms, attended the service & observed the minute silence at the Town's War memorial on 11th November & laid a wreath; Timothy Pennington Y10, sounded the Last Post;

2013/2014 Year Groups

Little Pedlars Assembly. Frozen

Year 2/3 Pink Day

Year 1 Shoe Boxes

Years 5 and 6
Celebrating the
Women's World
Day of Prayer

Year 4

Staff and Pupil Swap day

Years 6 and 7
On Retreat at
Santon
Downham

**Years 8 and 9
At Darley Stud**

**Year 10
Holt Hall**

**Year 11
Pink Day**

- ➢ Younger pupils took part in the Nativity Tableaux as part of the Town Carol Concert;
- ♦ **Sport:**
- ➢ 5-a-side Tournament at Stoke College Y4 - 7
- ➢ Junior & Senior Swimming Galas at Ipswich Crowns Pool. U14 & U16 County Finals at UEA;
- ➢ Two pupils Elise (Y11) & Chloe Sorrell (Y9) selected to represent the County in a Swimming Gala in December;
- ➢ The art of Kick-boxing was demonstrated by Tom of Tom's Kickboxing Academy (Y2-11);
- ♦ The Centenary Weekend on Friday 27th – Sunday 29th June, attracted many past pupils and Sisters to share and join in the many activities with Henchman's Toys and festivities, such as Fashion Through the Ages, Speech and Drama in Decades, Orchestra, past and present pupils, Old Time Music Singing and Victorian School. Mass, celebrated on Saturday by our Bishop, Alan Hopes and on Sunday by past pupil, Father Benedict Bedingfeld (Richard Bedingfeld)
- ♦ The Centenary 'Black Tie' Dinner, with speaker Sir Henry Bedingfeld, and an Auction with Chris Nash on Saturday 28th June.

**Kentwell
A Tudor Experience**

2003 Pilgrimage to Walsingham

2003 Rome

**1995
Science
Competition
at
UEA
in
Norwich**

Chapter 4 A SUMMARY OF THE HISTORY

1989-2007

The real flavour of the last quarter of the Sacred Heart School's Centenary can be found in the annual reports which appeared regularly in the School Magazines covering most of that period. The Head Teacher's report was often bolstered by reports from the Junior School and from the Boarding House.

In 1989 Sister Francis wrote about the new 75th Anniversary Building:

"Our new building coincides with the challenge of a new form of education, the National Curriculum. Physics is included in the Integrated Science Course to GCSE standard, and a programme of interesting and exciting Science Topics commences in the Infants School. The Computer Resource Room provides easy access for classes to use the computers as a tool for all subjects and the Home Economics Centre has seven spacious kitchen areas.

Sincere and heartfelt thanks to so many parents who are always so generous and supportive; paying not only an extra termly levy, but repeatedly donating items for Garden Fêtes, Bazaars, Auctions and Cake Stalls. A particular thank you to the Building Committee who have an incredible drive. They rally everyone to raise money with such apparent ease, and accomplish the tasks with such joviality.

The 75th Anniversary Building will stand as a monument to your efforts, and to your trust and faith:

- to your appreciation of the philosophy of the school;
- to the trust you place in all the Sisters and the Staff;
  and to the faith that you harbour that the school will continue to flourish, under the protection of the Sacred Heart of Jesus.

May God bless you and our school."

1989 also proved a lively year for the Junior School with classroom changes, theatre outings and Anniversary celebrations. There was a special mention of the wonderful weather which had allowed everyone to make full use of the swimming pool – a rare event indeed!

A year later the hard work, generosity and overwhelming support for the school had manifested itself in a remarkable survey of all who had been involved in the new building and general refurbishment of all departments. There is a sense of great pride and satisfaction and enormous team spirit which would drive the school forward to even greater achievements.

In the early nineties the International background of the school became more prominent with the opening up of the former communist countries of Europe which enabled regular contact with Sisters from Poland, Hungary and Slovakia. We were also aware of the immense suffering in the Balkans and one Croatian family in particular sought refuge among us.

The superhuman efforts of the 75th Anniversary fund-raising miracle were kept alive by a regular series of school bazaars, jumble sales and other often ingenious fund-raising efforts for the people of Bangladesh, Brazil, Africa and the Kurdish War. Both Senior and Junior Schools were constantly aware of their own good fortune and of the urgent need to help those in far worse circumstances than their own.

In 1994 the school joined in the celebrations of the centenary of the foundress, Mother Franciska Lechner. Mother General, Sister Nicolina Hendges, visited the school from Rome while everyone was basking in an excellent Inspection Report which led to a newspaper headline, "Convent a rare and special place". There were more male teachers in the Senior School and an energetic and wonderfully supportive PTA added even further to the school's undoubted sporting and academic achievements. The Junior School report of 1994 referred to the hot sunshine which had crowned a truly wonderful year of achievement.

In the summer of 1995 the school paused from its own successes to remember the Second World War with a street party in the lower playground and some interesting visits from grandparents who could bring their personal stories of Britain at War. A new Sports Hall is being planned to relieve pressure on the gymnasium to provide improved all-weather sports facilities, Once again the stalwart and hard-working PTA "courageously embarked" on the new project which received its grand opening in 1997, coinciding with Sister Francis's Silver Jubilee. The school was awarded a National Sportsmark Award recognising its "commitment to and outstanding performance of a wide field of sporting activities".

1997 was a year of several inspections from the Ofsted Nursery Inspection to the ISA (Independent Schools Association). Reports concluded that, "The school offers its pupils an excellent education and prepares them well for the next stage of their lives and education. The SATS and GCSE results bear witness to the high academic standards".

A year later, the retirement of several long-serving members of staff from the School, the Boarding House and the kitchen brought about a reflective mood with the realisation that for all the new technology and facilities, it is indeed the people who gave their love and support, far above the call of duty, that made the Convent the haven of peace and learning that it had become with hearts and minds working in harmony.

The magazine for that year carried a wonderfully detailed Diary of a year in the life of the Junior School. Outings and visits abound and every month is packed with learning activities. Throughout this whole quarter century the Lower School has been providing this solid and commendable foundation for a lifetime of learning.

The last year of the century saw the school looking outwards again with the recognition of the international origins of the Sisters who came from North and South America and from the newly revived European centres from Austria to Albania. Their experiences truly humbled us all. Pupils also avidly followed the adventures of the group of Sisters who began to set up their Convent in Rushooka, Uganda, where more than three hundred orphans lived.

An even more distant prospect was opened up when the School was invited to place a time capsule in the foundations of Shakespeare's Globe Theatre in London. For several years we had supported this beleaguered project with donations and visits, so it was a great honour to be selected for this event and to have "Sacred Heart Swaffham" engraved on a copper plaque in the exhibition hall.

The year 2000 was proclaimed by Pope John Paul II as "a time for forgiveness, sharing, thanks and renewal". Like many people at this time, the school reflected on its growth and achievements throughout the 20th century and began a further expansion with a dedicated Arts centre.

This new project involved the conversion of a listed barn and the Sacred Heart School became the inevitable plaything of the planners. It would be three years of much paperwork, argument, alteration and adjustment before the Art and Music studios and theatre could be fully used. There were echoes of the war years as the blood, sweat, toil and tears eventually came to fruition. The 21st century was indeed proving a challenge, but Sister Francis found solace in the news that more former pupils than ever before were sending their own children to the school, a truly satisfying endorsement.

In 2006 there was a change of leadership at the School when a lay Head was brought in for the first time, but the school continued very much as before. The challenge was to respond to the innovations of the new Millennium – to the great social and political upheavals that were afoot and which were affecting Independent Education.

We hope and trust that our rock solid foundations, achievements and beliefs will continue to equip our pupils for the often disturbing social challenges which swirl around us today.
Written by Valerie Mann, former Head of English and Senior Mistress

2007-2014

Not only were refurbishments to the school's accommodation and the introduction of more technological teaching resources made during the three year tenure of Miss Diana Wynter, the lay head, but the school dropped the word 'Convent' from its name and became simply the Sacred Heart School. Although the Convent and the Sisters remained central to the school's ethos and endeavours, as part of our response to social developments, boys were being admitted to the secondary school for the first time and so the amendment to the school name was considered to be appropriate.

After the anticipated immediate excitement, integration of secondary boys was smooth. For example, additional physical education staff was engaged and the school was able to compete in secondary school football matches, athletics, cross country and swimming events! Similarly, our senior choirs and drama productions have benefited from the masculine dimension.

In 2009, the school's previous long-standing Head Teacher, Sr. Francis, returned from her work at the sister school in Chesterfield, to resume her duties at the Sacred Heart School. Sadly, at the end of her first term back, Sr. Agnes, a much beloved Sister of advanced years, died just before Christmas. She had always loved snowy weather and her death seemed to herald an early fall of thick snow that lasted throughout the Christmas period and it was felt by some that this represented a final message of celebration!

The school was moving forward and in its keenness to maintain standards a Governing Committee was appointed and policies and schemes of work were reviewed. A number of curricular introductions were made, for example, GCSE courses in Theatre Studies, Computing and Spanish. The Reception classes became the Little Pedlars (a play on words with the Pedlar of Swaffham and peddling bicycles) with its own identity and logo. New summer, winter uniforms and sports kit were introduced. As part of the school's commitment to physical health and aided by the PTA, we invested in splendid new playground equipment comprising safe surfaces, a number of wooden climbing and balancing constructions and a wonderful Jungle Gym. Similarly, school lunches were reviewed in consultation with pupils and parents and amendments made. Also, the school has celebrated a number of Sisters' Silver and even Golden jubilees and welcomed young girls as postulants, trainee nuns!

Our links with other countries are strong and every year there are opportunities for pupils to become acquainted with other cultures by travelling abroad. For example, in 2011, the school was proud to be represented by Emily Hill, Rachel Mumford and Hannah Hodges with Mrs Mansfield, Sr Linda and Sr Thomas at the Beatification in Sarajevo of the Five Drina Martyrs, all Daughters of Divine Charity. Our pupils sang for an audience of thousands.

September 2012 marked the 15th Anniversary of Mother Teresa and the Sacred Heart School marked this occasion in two very exciting ways. As part of the school's commitment to promoting lifelong and collaborative learning, the Head Teacher, Sr Francis, had started to provide 'Holiday Challenges'. The challenge for the Easter holiday of 2012, all pupils were given a different rectangular fragment of a larger picture and asked to copy it as

Picasso's Weeping Woman in 144 squares

accurately as possible, using acrylic paints. The pupils were familiar with this unusual request for they had been asked to do something similar the previous Christmas and were impressed to see that all their endeavours collated by the head of Art, who had designed the project, produced a huge and uncannily accurate likeness of Picasso's 'Crying Woman'. This time the assembled picture portrayed Mother Teresa and it was, again, enormously successful.

On the first day of the new school year the entire senior school made a pilgrimage to the Church in Pimlico, which is a Mass Centre for the Albanian community, taking along our beautiful reproduction of the likeness of Mother Teresa. At the end of the previous term, the head of Music and Sr Linda, who is like Mother Teresa, Albanian, had rehearsed us in a number of sacred songs so that the Sacred Heart School could offer its own contribution to this most special Mass.

The school continues to regard as crucial its involvement in the local community and, to this end, has become involved in the annual Food of the Brecks festival. Our pageants and dance, music and displays art and written work have all added to the town's festive air. Our Barn Theatre was even commissioned as a 'Pop Up' restaurant and some of our older students volunteered their services as waiters. Similarly, our Charity work is central to our ethos. The post of Charities Prefect was introduced and the post holder coordinates a number of Charity appeals. Christmas shoe boxes, Pink Days, Rich and Poor lunches, the Rushooka mission: these are only a few of the school's charitable endeavours.

Another feature of the last few years has been the introduction of Enhancement Weeks. Pupils- and staff - have benefited from numerous cross-curricular forays into learning and culture. Insights to Books, Maths, Space, Spanish, PSHEE.for example, have been explored and pupils have benefited from all kinds of visiting speakers such as politician Elizabeth

Truss, the Samaritans, Gurkhas, Counselling/Listening tutors, theatre groups. Trips, some residential, to France, theatres, the Sainsbury Centre, Holt Hall, for example, are an important feature of the curriculum. Opportunities for spiritual reflection have also been developed. Although it has always been the school's tradition to take the departing Year 11 on a day's retreat, the school has extended this so that each school year begins with a pilgrimage for pupils of Year 3 and above and each year group currently benefits from its own annual spiritual retreat. The focus of these days is 'The Three 'F's'! Faith, Food and Fun!

The whole school has benefited from a substantial increase in communication between the Junior and Senior phases. A middle-management committee comprising staff representing both phases has been created in order to promote

Mother Teresa in 88 squares

cohesiveness of the school's policies and development planning. There is more movement of staff between the phases and the school organises a number of whole-school events, such as the celebration of National Poetry Day, when work of every single pupil is displayed in the gymnasium and each class recites a poem to the rest of the school or a Jubilee Street Party, held in the front garden, where we all picnic together. Such events make a significant contribution to our developed sense of community.

Pupils, Sisters, Parents, members of Staff; we are proud of our school and of our individual contribution to its progress. God bless the Sacred Heart School.

Mary Gargett Stringer, Head of English, 2014

Chapter 5 SPIRITUALITY AND CHARITIES

Living the Faith through the School Year
2000 - 2001

Being a Catholic and Christian school is more than just a label. The pupils, parents and staff are given the opportunity to live out the ideals of Gospel values in many ways throughout the school year. This is an enrichment that our pupils absorb from day to day and stays with them for the rest of their lives.

Our school year began with a visit to Walsingham which is an unusual way to start the school year. The pupils go to Mass and can visit the Shrine and light a candle and pray for loved ones. Our school is continuing the wonderful tradition of Pilgrimage in England where things spiritual and social mix in a natural way.

Throughout the year there is weekly Mass in the Convent Chapel and each form takes it in turn to attend. At the end of each term the whole school attends Mass in the Gym to which parents are invited.

The school took part in the annual Remembrance Service held at the War Memorial in Swaffham and the Head Girl laid a wreath. This is a moving ceremony and the presence of young people is important.

The autumn term concludes with a traditional Carol Service with singing supported by the Junior Choir, Senior Choir and School Orchestra. This year a collection was taken to help a teenager who was seriously injured playing soccer.

The Ash Wednesday service was attended in both Swaffham Parish Church and Catholic Church. An important part of Lent is thinking about those who are less fortunate than ourselves and trying to help in some practical way. We joined with other churches in Swaffham to take part in Frugal Lunches. Year 11 organised a rice meal in place of normal school lunch. Some Year 4 children sold potato men that grew real grass hair. This year the money was given to our Sisters in Rushooka, Uganda and to Comic Relief.

Sister Nicolina Hendges, the Mother General of the Congregation visited the school and talked at assembly about education in Rushooka. She told us how eager African children are to learn even though they have few resources.

The summer term saw seven girls confirmed by Bishop Peter Smith. All the pupils and staff had the opportunity to meet the Bishop.

The feast of Corpus Christi was celebrated with Mass and a procession. It was a delight to see younger pupils throwing petals and herbs with such enthusiasm.

The Feast of the Scared Heart is the Feast day of the school and is a chance to celebrate the life of the school. This year it was also Sister Thomas More's Feast day.

As the summer term draws to a close there is one last occasion – the Feast of St Peter and St Paul. The Parish Church in Swaffham is dedicated to these saints.

The school year concludes the way it began, continuing the Christian traditions that are, and will remain, an important part of our children's education.
Mrs Oona Kelly RE Teacher

Who Is Jesus?

The children in Yr 3 were asked how they would answer this question from someone who knew nothing about Jesus. These are their answers:

- Jesus is a loving person and wants peace. *Emily Bell*
- He did miracles like turn water into wine. Jesus is the son of God. He died and rose again. He died for us. *Russell George*
- Jesus was chosen to lead people. Jesus made miracles. Jesus helped other people. Jesus gave his life for us. He saved people. *Francesca Grapes*
- I think Jesus is God's son. He tells people to be good and honest. *Katy Hook*
- Jesus is a leader to all to show people the way to care for others, to show them the way to be good people, to love one another and have peace on earth. He teaches us to pray and serve the Lord in every way. *Louisa Ive*
- Jesus is a friend of the world. Jesus is the light of the world. *Lucy Knights*
- Jesus is one of our best treasures and we are one of Jesus's. *Lucy Lee*
- Jesus is our leader. Jesus guides us wherever we go. *Annabel Lyles*

David Kossoff – The Bible Comes to Life
After a visit to Eccles Hall to listen to a talk by the Jewish Rabbi and author, Francesca Hunt wrote:

Dear God,
How do you manage to create such amazing human beings? Who can actually take one famous, greatly respected book (the Bible) and recreate it in his own style. David Kossof is a marvel, his ability to bring scenes to life, using merely his voice and body action shows genius.
As I sat in the darkened room, waiting for this grand performance, I studied my surroundings. Finding to my amazement, only four bare walls and a small miniature stage placed to the side of the room. 'There must be more,' I thought to myself, 'maybe the colourful array of Biblical characters will jump out from behind the scenes.' But, instead a small quiet elderly man walked placidly onto the stage, turning to the audience he cleared his throat, before saying……'My Lords, Ladies, Gentlemen and Gentlewomen.'
The ride had begun, and for the next two hours, we were taken through the creation of the world, from your point of view, of course God. Lord, I would just like to congratulate you on another great piece of work. Thank you for such a great evening, and thank David Kossoff, for being one of the greatest Jewish storytellers ever to walk this earth. In fact he was so inspiring we did an assembly from one of his books entitled 'Have You Got a Minute Lord!' It was great fun.
Yours gratefully
Miss. F. Hunt 1996

Lent

It has become a school tradition that, come Lent we all put on our thinking caps to come up with the greatest money spinning ideas.

Keeping with the religious theme, many classes gave up things they thought they could not live without. Form 3 made a brave effort to give up their daily injection of carbon dioxide, glucose and additives i.e. fizzy drinks. The other option was that classes provide a service for others; Sister Francis was most pleased with the shiny shoes from Form 1's shoe shining lunchtime. The staff all had polished cars so shiny you could see yourself in them. A variety of competitions were held; one from Form 2 was to design a picture for Mrs Dalton's leg plaster, and Junior 3 and 4 ran a variety of games. Tuck was also sacrificed and sold, as were daffodils.

The Fifth years felt a little sorry for the rest of the school, who were looking decidedly thin and suffering from sugar withdrawal symptoms. We clubbed together and spent a happy hour in the cash and carry deciding which smarties were better value for money. The tubes were distributed among the school and when the contents were eaten they were filled with one pence pieces!

We raised £391.51, and the bank had almost as much fun counting the one pence coins as we did eating the smarties! The money raised is going towards the Sisters in Hungary to help establish Convents and Schools – they may even resemble ours in seventy years' time.
1995

It is our tradition to try to become more pleasing to God and our neighbours by imposing self-discipline on ourselves through prayer, penance and fasting. This is a selection of promises from Years 5 to 11.

Fasting

I will try to cut down on the amount of chocolate and give the money to something more needy.

I will give the money that I normally spend on sweets to charity so that it can be used constructively.

I will give up TV for a week.

Prayer

I will pray for the starving and people in war torn countries and for everyone who needs help.

I will pray more for other people and not always for what I want.

I will pray more and not always talk about my problem but speak to God.

Penance

I am going to keep my room tidy.

I am going to try and be more organised and less grumpy in the morning.

I will start my homework earlier.

I will try to listen to others more and understand people more.

I will make a big effort to help people.
Donna Palmer Year 9 2001

The Sedar Meal

On Friday 18th of March Year 8 were going to have a Passover meal. We watched Sister Francis make the haroset which is made with apple, honey, almonds, walnuts and cinnamon. It was to represent the cement used by the Hebrew slaves when they were working at building for the Egyptians.

The Passover meal is celebrated by the Jews each year and it commemorates when Moses led the Israelites to freedom. Two tables laid out with red mats, small cups with red juice, salt water and haroset. A third table was at the top with only three places set and a plate at the end which is called the sedar dish. On it was a lamb bone, bitter herbs, karpas and a boiled egg. Mrs Kenny, Mrs Mansfield and Sheila as the oldest in the class, sat at that table. The rest sat down at the other two.

2005 The Sedar Meal

To start with we had to eat a herb dipped in salt water – this was to remind us of the tears of suffering. Next we had to eat a small piece of maize, this symbolises the unleavened bread that the Jews had to eat at the Passover. This was followed by 'Haroset'. We also had to eat bitter herbs. These were herbs dipped in a sauce and this symbolised the bitterness of slavery. During the meal we drank four glasses of blackcurrant. The next part of our meal consisted of lamb and vegetables, which is what the Jewish people would have eaten. The shank bone of lamb symbolises the blood on the door; and Elijah's cup- the invitation to the prophet.

During the meal we opened the door in order to let in any poor, hungry children off the streets! We also had to ritually wash our hands to represent the cleanliness of our souls. This meal made us think about the experiences that other people have and the links between Judaism and Christianity.

Amber Dugdale Y8 – 2005, Charlotte Farrier Y8 - 2005, Rebecca Case Y8 – 2006

Our Easter Assembly

- The children cuddled Jesus. The Apostles told them to go but Jesus wanted them to stay. *Mollie Wagstaff*
- The children waved their palm leaves as Jesus rode by. *Georgia Rasmussen*
- Jesus was angry that the temple was used as a place for people lending money. He turned over the table. *Isabel Holmes*
- Jesus and his apostles had the last supper. *Charlotte Riedlinger*
- Jesus asked his apostles to do the same in memory of him. *Rhiannon Emblem*

- They went into the garden of Gethsemane to pray. They fell asleep. *Phillipa Randall*
- The guards led Jesus away to be crucified. *Arjun Bendre*
- When they put Jesus in the tomb they rolled the rock. *Christopher Sutherland*
- Mary Magdalen was surprised when she saw that the stone had been rolled away. *Rachel Wong*
- The guards stayed near the stone. Jesus was in the tomb. *Lucy Pearce*
- Mary Magdalen met Jesus in the garden. She told the others. They were happy. *Talia Archer*
- Three days later Jesus rose again. *Poppy St Lawrence*

Year 1 - -2005

Charities

It has always been a tradition in our school to support local charities and charities associated with the Daughters of Divine Charity. In 2005 the school adopted the motto 'Service before Self', following Jesus's example of service. to the poor and sinners. Our first named Charity Prefect was Eve Pardoe in in 2012. She set about the task of raising the profile of charities within the school.

The following are just a few of the activities thought out by imaginative pupils and staff over 25 years: -

- No sooner had the red noses appeared in Woolworth, ready for 5th March – Comic Relief Day, than the Convent girls decided to take action, by having their own fun and games! Red noses, of course, were included.
- The Fifth Form took part in their traditional trolley race. Last year they dressed up as St.Trinians, this year it was nightwear, ranging from babies to grannies.
- The Fourth Formers did something really original. They somehow persuaded a few members of the staff to partake in a Fashion Show, dressing up from 1960's minis, to an Arab tribe.
- The Third Form decided on a sponsored netball match, but this was no ordinary netball match. The Nappies versus St.Trinians. The nappies obviously were not wet, because they won!
- The Second Form thought that Comic Relief Day should be colourful, and so painted their faces and dressed up as clowns. The red noses came in very useful for this!
- Form One opted for a sponsored cross-country run, for which they would dress up in costume.
- Junior Four had the same idea as Form Five and came in their pyjamas and their nighties.
- Junior Three decided to give their impression of what the future would be like by dressing up in weird and wonderful costumes which they designed themselves.
- The Lower School the pupils and teachers also participated. The children were dressed

in a wide variety of clothes, and had little red noses painted on them.
- The staff of the lower school arrived dressed as nuns, and in return Sister Thomas More arrived in everyday clothes!

Comic Relief Day was very successful for Swaffham Convent. We managed to raise a total of £155.33.

Annabelle Bradshaw and Katie Morris Form 5 - 1989

Form Four's Fashion Show

As Comic Relief day loomed closed, Form Four decided that they had to put on something really spectacular for the big day. Already renowned for such events as 'Blind Date' and the Comic Relief Variety Show from the previous year, we were determined to make 10th March, 1989 a day to remember. We all agreed on our most ambitious project, a fashion show starring members of staff exhibiting their 'trendy' and 'ageless' gear.

This was great fun and all the staff threw themselves into it wholeheartedly. We converted the gym into a fashion house for our budding models and at 30p entrance fee, we packed the hall with enthusiastic, cheering supporters.

Mrs Howarth started the show with a very slinky, silver mini-dress modelled to the music of Down Town by Petula Clark. Time flew by and we saw a Japanese princess, a Chinese peasant and two 'flower power' hippies, a selection of sports gear, an example of an old school uniform, an Arab camel driver, a selection of period costumes bringing us into the 20th century. Mrs Henderson was 'standing up for her love rights' in her Yazz costume.

A couple of items were the talk of the critics the next morning. Mrs Baker looked fantastic doing the 'Hippy Shake' in an incredibly short mini skirt and top, and Mrs Twining in an assortment of black leotards and bin liners that kept on coming unstapled. Every fashion show has to have a wedding dress and we ended with Mrs Howarth in hers complete with hat, gloves and flowers, walking down the aisle to 'Suddenly' the 'Neighbours' wedding theme. The event was a huge success and we made over £60.

PS. When did you say you are opening on the London catwalks?

Sasha Twining Form 4 - 1989

Project For Bolivia

On the 21st January, Donna Palmer, Julia Chapman, Isabel Johnson and Laura Cawthorne woke up bright and early to go to Cambridge. The point of this exercise was to learn three dance sequences and songs for a musical, 'General Mickey'. Our school along with four other Cambridge schools had been invited by Father Dennis Finbow to take part in a musical about the life of St.John Bosco, the young people's saint. This had been written specially to raise money for the street children of Cochabamba in Bolivia. During the next week, every lunchtime we would practise the dances or the songs. We remembered every step and learnt every word, and we couldn't wait until the day.

On 27th January, everyone was heading by coach to Cambridge again. The stage director told us that 1000 tickets had been sold. Well, we did our stuff, the actors and actresses were

great, and the dancers were fabulous too!!! I could tell everyone enjoyed themselves as the audience stood up and sang with us and even joined in with the hand jive. It was a great experience and over £5,000 was raised for Cochabamba.
Suzanne Leckie Form 5 - 1990

Confirmation Classes 1996

It is some time since any pupils of the convent have been confirmed as members of the Church of England. This year is very special as Norwich Cathedral celebrates its nine-hundredth birthday. All the confirmations are to take place there, rather than in large parish churches.

Unfortunately the Vicar of the Parish Church in Swaffham who had been unwell for sometime, was now ill again. This did not bode well for the confirmation classes. Sister Francis was undaunted and told the girls that I could lead the lessons. It was a privilege to encourage and teach the four girls: Sarah Crowdy, Hannah Scott, Kara Goddard, and Franchesca Hunt. The weeks flew by and culminated in the most wonderful and spectacular service.
Mrs Jane Howarth, French Teacher, 1996

I am very pleased that I chose to be Confirmed, and the whole atmosphere in the Cathedral made it an extra special evening which was enjoyed by everyone.
Kara Goddard Year 10 - 1996

Being a Young Catholic

On July 11[th]on a beautiful summer's day, five of us were confirmed. What? Well, according to the Oxford Illustrated Dictionary, to confirm means to:

Provide support for the truth, Encourage,

Make formally valid, Establish more firmly, and Administer the religious rite of confirmation to. So, as a result of the eleventh-of-the-seventh when I was administered with religious rite, I have been supported in the truth, encouraged, made valid formally and been more firmly established.

To have been provided with support for the truth is such a lovely way of putting it don't you think? The universal church has in a sense been witness, that the things I found my hope on – namely Jesus's unfailing love, is truth.

Secondly I've been encouraged. As part of our preparation for this sacrament Sister Francis and Father Michael took us exploring many churches and places of interest. We got to know each other quite well, which means that now we all know at least four other young people with whom we can grumble about our lot in life and ultimately be encouraged by.

Thirdly I've been made 'formally valid' which is not to say that everyone else is formally in-valid but it means that with regards to the church I'm now an adult and all that I do, I take on my own conscience now.

Lastly, I've been established more firmly, which means that I'm better educated in the beliefs of my church, we've openly debated controversial catholic doctrines and I'm now better equipped and more prepared to defend them than ever.

I took a new name when I was confirmed. 'Purity'. I think it sums up everything which inspires our souls, and something that can only be attained in Christ.
God Bless,
Felicity Hemmant Year - 2004

Bishop Earns Certificate

New Roman Catholic Bishop of East Anglia, the Rt Rev Michael Evans took his toy pet lamb along when he visited Swaffham Sacred Heart Convent School last week. He joined the pupils and celebrated the Corpus Christi Mass as part of his programme of visiting schools in the diocese and because of is particular interest in youth. Deputy Headteacher, Diana Wynter said: 'In his sermon the Bishop charmed all, from the youngest to the oldest, with his cuddly pet lamb which reinforced his message – Jesus, the Innocent Sacrifice.' During the offertory procession, many aspects of the life of the school, including a pinhole camera, the letter 'e,' GCSE work and a certificate of attendance, awarded to the Bishop for attendance were presented. The Mass concluded with the orchestra playing the theme tune to Match of the Day. After a tour of the school the Bishop had lunch with a group of pupils including the Head Girl, Victoria Lewis. Miss Wynter said: 'The Bishop's motto for youth is 'faith, fun and food' and at SHCS we fully support this maxim.'
By kind permission of Lynn News, 2002

On Tuesday 11th March we were honoured to welcome the Bishop of East Anglia to our school.
Bishop Alan Hopes is visiting all the parishes and schools in East Anglia and joined us in a celebratory Mass for Lent. We were proud to give him a guided tour of our school and facilities. Having the Bishop lead us in Mass was a spiritually enlightening experience. His heartfelt homily which taught us through the involvement of the younger pupils, showed just how loving of God's children he really is and inspired a sense of holiness and joy in many of us. He taught us how he was an apostle, teacher and shepherd following his vocation from God. He also graciously gave up his time to spend a few moments with every year group and member of staff and was prepared to answer any questions about God, faith and his role. The Bishop's visit gave every pupil and member of staff an opportunity to explore their faith. His wise words and teachings encouraged us to look more closely at the world in a new and faithful light. The whole school will hold this

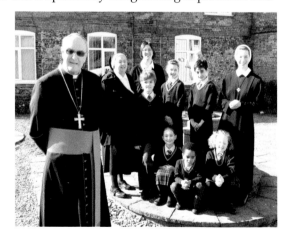

The Bishop of East Anglia
The Rt. Rev Alan Hopes

experience close to their heart. The visit of Bishop Alan will be remembered for a long time. By everyone. His heartfelt homily, which included teaching the whole school through the younger pupils that the Bishop is an apostle, a teacher and a shepherd
Alice Powell Y 11, 2014

Getting Work Experience Right

How can we justify this article being under the Spirituality section? Is all our life a quest for God and the values that cannot be measured? Does our happiness depend on pleasing others or indeed always seeking our own pleasures?

Work experience is, for many, one week of pure fun combining the highlights of adult life with the carefree element which comes from knowing you can leave at the end of the week. However, for some it can be a difficult period, either a banal wave of filing and photocopying, or a nervy experience, with much time spent worrying about making the right impression and whether you are able to make the perfect cup of tea. Having just spent a week at a local solicitors firm, I consider myself something of an authority on the subject. So I have compiled a list of pointers, which, when adhered to, should make work experience enjoyable.

* Foremost excellent tea and coffee making skills are essential. Several weeks beforehand a few evenings should be devoted to the art of tea and coffee preparation. If you suspect your destination has more refined tastes, you may wish to prepare yourself for the risky business of herbal tea making.
* When making a good impression a firm handshake and direct eye contact are vital.
* A neat appearance always goes in your favour. Smart clothes, flat shoes and tied back hair are needed in the adult world.
* If you will be working in an office environment it is guaranteed that at some point you will be asked to do some filing. To ensure you are not caught off guard, I advise that you learn beforehand.
* A variety of conversation is the key to good relationships with your new colleagues. Have a few questions ready.

This guide should aid all intrepid young students with their first experience of working life. When adapted, it should help with even the most dire situations, helping you to impress your temporary boss and to educate others on getting work experience right!
Abigail Daniels Y10 - 2004

Retreats

Retreats have been an important part of school life, and up until 2009 form retreats were mainly conducted for Year 11 leavers. After this date Sr Francis tried to organise a retreat annually for each class and their teachers in one of the holy places in East Anglia such as Walsingham, Norwich RC Cathedral, Clare Monastery, Castle Acre Priory, the church in the woods at Santon Downham and other local churches.

After making crosses from materials they found the pupils made the Stations of the Cross and then travelled to the woods near Mrs Burton's home. As it was the feast day of St

Joseph, the foster father of Jesus and a carpenter we followed his example. Building dens was easy as some people had started some very fine dens in the forest. It is a very interesting place to visit and the training place for the Desert Rats. We all enjoyed our Burton McDonalds round the campfire while listening to Mrs Verne's story of the Lost Soul and finishing with toasting marshmallows. A great day of faith, food and fun was had by all.
Sr Francis, 2014

Year 11 Retreat at Hermitage Hall

Traditionally, Year 11 pupils finish their schooling at the Scared Heart by going on a retreat just before their final exams. It is a time of reflection and friendship. The day started with Mr St Foti talking about his life and faith and a warning about the growing rate of abortions. This was followed by a prayer session in the chapel of the Nativity which is so old that it pre dates the Reformation of the C16th. It was one of the chapels because it was a river crossing on the pilgrims' route to the shrine at Walsingham. We have an unusual 'reflection' during which we lie on the floor and listen to the words of Anthony Mello and moving prayers read by Mrs Howarth.

From today I have realised how much I cherish my class…my friends. We are all so different but together we form the most amazing group of people I have ever known.
Victoria Lewis

I feel today I learned how special each one of my class is. I think that this was possible due to the relaxing place we have spent our day in, I also think that I will never forget anyone and they are an important part of my life. *Kerry Sumner*
There are far too many tomorrows, too many yesterdays but never enough todays.
Emily Nichols

Today has made me realise how precious friends really are and that they should never be taken for granted. A friend is someone who reaches for your hand and touches your heart. Believe in yourself and follow your heart and you will succeed.
Laura Hayes

Our trip to Hermitage Hall made me realise just how much we all care about each other. The strength in the bonds of our friendship really broke through. Leaving is going to be harder than I first thought. My friends made me who I am today.
Chloe Faulkner

After today, I have realised how much my friends have helped me and how when I move on to new schools and friends in the big wide world, that these are the friends I never want to forget.
Heather McCulloch Year 11 – May 2004

Corpus Christi Procession

On 20th June Years 3 -7 went to 'Hermitage Hall in Downham Market for the Corpus Christ

2003 Corpus Christi Procession at Hermitage Hall

procession. We walked along the riverbank following the priest who carried the Body of Christ. We threw rose petals on the road in front of the Blessed Sacrament. There was an altar outside where the Body of Christ was placed and more hymns were sung.

Everybody sat outside to enjoy their lunch. We tucked into a bowl of strawberries with cream or ice cream provided by Mr and Mrs St Foti. Everyone thoroughly enjoyed going around the Dickens Museum and Collectors World. There were strange bits, scary bits, and funny bits and massive collection of old cars, carts and carriages. Finally there was a collection of pretty dolls in national costumes. Before we left to go back to school we had a look in the gift shop and some people had time to see the horses. We really enjoyed the day out at Hermitage Hall. *Sian Smith, Year 7, 2003*

BAFTA Award for Convent Girl
We will give you your heart's desire 'Nothing in life is ever wasted'

Issues! We all have them, at school, at home, with friends, with family....But did you ever consider they could be turned into good? I am privileged to be bought up in a Christian household. Our faith had gone to a new level when we discovered the 'God' channels on 'Sky' satellite television. Eight different channels – all devoted to the way of life that is Christianity. Howard Condor made one programme, 'Revelation', and this became a whole channel. They only have a few full time and paid staff, the rest are volunteers. They make 'live' programmes in the studios! The rest of the air time is bought by churches and ministries from all over the UK.

My mum and I often discuss things in the car on the way home. One discussion was on what we thought prayer was. Mum told me about a painting she had done with Angels and a red phone that went directly to God. This idea finished up with me writing an episode about a girl phoning God and His response.

One day Howard Condor and his wife, Lesley made an appeal for children's sketches on air. We filmed an audition piece in our living room. Six weeks later they called to say that they liked the audition piece and wanted ten episodes by the middle of August! So I set to work and created nine more episodes.

In August we took the train to London and to the studios to film 'The Hotline'. We filmed seven out of the ten episodes. Later when we filmed the other three episodes, I tried my hand at presenting with Bethany, Howard and Lesley's daughter.

I racked my brain for an idea to discuss; then I had a thought – Hallowe'en. Bethany and I survived the hour-long programme, we received lots of calls from children and adults alike, asking more about Hallowe'en and giving us both lots of encouragement. This led to me being offered a 'job' on air advertising the children's programme!

I have to go down to London every other week. We did a live programme from 10.30 - 11.30am, then checked our e-mails for viewers' comments. I still have regular contact from viewers who tell me about their school life and the problems they face, and sometimes we share jokes!

To sum up; If God knew you before you were created, knew your hopes and fears, would he put them to waste? No! He'll use them for His purposes. He will not deprive you of what you love…..He will organise it so you'll be doing what you are called to do….He will give you the desires of your heart.
Rosalind Peters Y9 - 2007

Girls Overwhelmed by 'Thank-you' Letters

Generous school girls have been overwhelmed with letters of gratitude after buying electricity stamps for 52 elderly people living around Swaffham with money from a Christmas collection.

Mrs. Valerie Mann, a senior mistress at Swaffham Convent said: "They are such lovely letters and it's a great example to the children that these people have bothered to sit down and write to us. We never expected it."

One pensioner who received stamps had given the convent an icon to look after.

It had been handed down through her family but Mrs. Mann said how she now wanted to give it to the Convent. "We just thought there were a lot of people living around here who never got thought of."
By kind permission of Watton and Swaffham, Friday 20th January 1989

My Faith

Thoughts and reflections written by each pupil after the annual first day of the school year at Walsingham.

At times when people come together you feel safe and secure that God is near. When I feel lonely I know God helps me to move on and he guides me through my sadness. At difficult times he gives me the strength to be strong and not be afraid. God is there in my life, when I sing and this makes me feel good in my heart, singing brings me close and my faith in God grows stronger. *Hope, Year 8*

I find it hard to remain a good, faithful person all the time. It's hard to have faith in difficult times when there seems like an answer to my prayers will never come. I'm admitting it, as ashamed as I am.

Faith is a hard thing to have: it's belief without proof, and it's a difficult thing to keep. Judging by these two observations, it doesn't take much to realise that to stay faithful, a little help is needed every now and again – and that's what these pilgrimages/retreats give to me – fuel for my faith.

I found so much today; love, faith, spirituality, trust, compassion and I always find that these things intensify within me when I go to highly spiritual places. Hearing tales of the past while standing in the exact place where they happened makes me feel lucky and special, and connected more to God.

I'm not always close to God, but after a pilgrimage or retreat I always feel so much more love for Him, it's a closeness like no other. I know He loves me, and these special trips never fail to remind me just how much. My faith in God is always strong, but sometimes a little push in the right direction is needed, and I get it when I go on these special events. For that, I am forever grateful. *Annabelle, Year 9*

When we go on trips to Walsingham I am filled with a massive sense of faith, mainly for two things. I am one person who has travelled on the pilgrimage out of thousands, this gives a person a sense of awe and shows how small they really are in the grand scheme of things. However everybody still has their part to play, we're all a small cog in a big machine. The other thing that fills me with a sense of faith is how over the last 4 years I have been to Walsingham and seen the changes in my friends and in myself, this is a very reflective experience and makes you realise just how fast you're growing up. The final thing that fills me with faith is that many people have gone on this pilgrimage and therefore Jesus and God must exist for people would not go on pilgrimages, sometimes across thousands of miles, if not.

One thing is clear however from going on these trips, they are a reflective and enjoyable trip and day. *Thomas, Year 10*

I think that school pilgrimages are very spiritually motivating for every student. Going to Walsingham each year gives every pupil of every age an opportunity to find themselves through God. It gives us a chance to be part of the religious community and explore our own faith and beliefs. Faith can be helped to blossom in everyone and being in a peaceful and spiritual environment can bring peace to us and make us able to reflect on everything and how faith can change how we think about life. Attending Mass is also a very important factor because it gives us a chance to pray and sing to Jesus and feel his spirit in and around us. I think it is important to carry on visiting Walsingham because it gives everyone a chance to find God even if they are not one to usually attend church or religious happenings. Faith is in everyone in many different ways so attending these pilgrimages and prayer can lead faith to grow and become a much more important part of our lives by bringing peace to us and causing us to feel closer to God. *Alice, Year 11*

If you find that these thoughts help your faith, the school have produced a book containing all pupil's reflections.

Chapter 6 SCIENCE, ASTRONOMY AND MATHEMATICS

Science is a young department at the Sacred Heart, at only 39 years old. Biology was the first and only science to be taught, by Mrs Baker, between 1974 and 1983, in a lab which is now the RE room in the boarding house. Mrs Black joined the staff in 1983 to teach Chemistry and Physics, at which time a large temporary science building near the tennis courts was provided by the PTA.

The current labs and prep room in the Middle School were built for the 75th anniversary in 1989, the building then being known as the New Technology Block. Science became statutory at GCSE with the introduction of the National Curriculum in 1988 and all pupils currently study for at least one GCSE which includes all three sciences. Most gain two GCSEs in 'Core' and 'Additional' science or take Biology Chemistry and Physics as three separate GCSEs. We currently have specialist science teachers for the three disciplines. Head of Science, Mrs Burton, teaches Biology, Mrs Verne teaches Chemistry and Mr Murphy, our Head of Maths (whose degree includes Rocket Science) teaches Physics. Our practical experiments are enabled by the ever-helpful Mrs Carter, our technician.

We are pleased to note that Pope Francis was formerly a chemistry teacher, and that the patron of scientists St Albert the Great who conducted experiments in physics and chemistry and maintained a collection of plants, insects and chemical compounds was known in the 13th century as 'the teacher of everything there is to know'. St. Albert the Great was convinced that all creation spoke of God and that the tiniest piece of scientific knowledge told us something about Him.

At the Sacred Heart we subscribe to St Albert's conviction and strive to cultivate a love of science for its own sake, to glimpse the sheer cleverness and magnificence of creation through understanding the structure, reactions, and orderliness of life and the universe and the laws that sustain them. We do this by experiment, by deduction, by building on the principles and hypotheses uncovered by pioneering scientists. We also venture into the overlap between science fiction and science fact as with the Year 8 project that investigates the 19 'science fictions' proposed by Jules Verne that have entered everyday use. We see how principles and calculations sometimes have to await new technologies before their uses can be realised. In a Year 10 module on 'materials' we see how science has copied nature to give modern products such as Velcro and Gore-Tex and we see how nano-technology can now put natural processes – such as the antiseptic effect of silver - to our service. At the same time we learn that there are limits to the safe exploitation of natural goods – the safety of nanoparticles in sunscreen and the use of mobile phones are still being researched.

There have been changes in science department personnel over the years but three enduring and endearing members joined us in 2001. These are the much loved Betty Bones, Tommy Torso and Baby Grace who provides simulated lessons in how demanding a baby can be to look after.

In addition to gaining very gratifying GCSE grades, the science department has welcomed visiting speakers, often bringing exciting demonstrations; attended conferences, exhibitions and competitions; contributed to the long-term survey of flora and fauna at the Ecotech and undertaken investigations and projects in school.

Competitions

In seven of the last twenty-one years Sacred Heart has sent teams to compete in a schools' Chemistry Competition at UEA which has been held under different sponsorship and titles, with the format remaining constant. Different experimental challenges are set for each year group. These range from identifying a chemical, to measuring it quantitatively, to adjusting the reaction conditions of an experiment so that it reaches completion in a given time, to building a tower or making a marble run slowly and ring an electric bell to announce its arrival. Each morning of competition was followed by an afternoon demonstration lecture of topical interest. Past school magazines recorded the following details:

- 1993 Helen Downing, Emma Swales, Nicola Compton, Forensic detection
- 1994 Claire and Hannah Morgan (Yr8), Katie Moss and Sarah Skinner (Yr9), Helen Childerhouse and Kate Haigh (Yr10), Emma Scales and Charlotte Blandford-Newson (Yr11), Sacred Heart came 2nd out of 9 schools and enjoyed a lecture on 'Booms and Bangs' after the investigations
- 1995 'Top of the Bench' Chemistry Competition, Katie Coe and Katie Scales (Yr8), Hannah Black and Alice Darkins (Yr9), Lucy Pointer and Hayley Cawthorne (Yr10), Sarah Conway and Abigail Halls (Yr11)
- 1996 'Top of the Bench' Chemistry Competition, Lauren Rix and Emma Peak (Yr8), Helen Ballentyne and Emma Swales (Yr10), Anna Marshall and Sally Pears (Yr11). The Yr8 and Yr11 teams came 2nd out of 10 schools. The afternoon lecture was on 'Pollution and the Ozone Layer'
- 1999 'Top of the Bench' Chemistry Competition, Louise Cartin and Katherine Jennings (Yr8), also teams from Yr9,10 and 11. Yr 9 came 1st, Yrs 8 and 10 were placed 3rd.
- 2005 'Salters Festival of Chemistry' Sophie Willis and Louisa Ive (Yr7), Emily Wright and Sophie Morgan-Short (Yr8)
- 2010 we joined the Plymouth Brethren 'Focus School' in Swaffham for a STEM (science, technology, engineering and mathematics) workshop in which teams competed to build the machine which most efficiently transferred paper clips from one place to another. This was a particularly enjoyable event for us all because of the friendly way our pupils and staff were integrated by our hosts.
- 2012 'Salters Festival of Chemistry' Alice Cooke, Victoria Hill, Thomas Hazel and Lucy Edwards (Yr8) won against 20 other schools and were awarded a very useful set of molecular modelling kits for the school.
- 2012 'Norwich Science Olympiad' Tarn Chamberlain-James, Aaron Blatch, Niamh Hodges, Annabelle Mansell (Yr7); Lilian Wallis, and Charlotte Reidlinger, (placed 2nd)

Henry Perowne, and Cameron Willis (Yr8); Hope Mumford, Elise Sorrell, Mollie Ogden, Joanna Simon (Yr9); Charlotte Fenton, Sash Fountain, Eloise Hunt, Kate Wainer

Visits

- The science department has made a variety of visits over the years to reinforce and supplement curricular learning, to engage with science in research and industry, to undertake novel experiments and simply to enjoy 'thinking like scientists' in contexts outside school.

- In 1997, 1999, 2003, 2006 and 2008 the GCSE groups made visits to the Cavendish Laboratories in Cambridge for 'Physics at Work' Days, at which there were numerous displays and lectures about cutting edge physics research and development delivered by young professional scientists to inspire and encourage pupils towards careers in research and foster awareness of the scientific principles behind modern technology. In 1999 this was combined with a visit to the Botanical Gardens to learn about 'Dry Gardens' and DNA analysis of plants. In 2011 we attended a similar presentation at the John Innes Centre on recent research in plant and medical biology.

- Year 10 visited The Natural History Museum's Earth Gallery in 1997; and as part of National Science week in 2002, Years 10 and 11 visited the Science Museum to see an IMAX film on the Human Body; a lecture on '(UV) Light Relief'; and the Launch Pad and Genetics exhibitions.

Demonstration lectures have been a feature of science department outings.

- In 1995, a 'Faraday Lecture' at Ipswich Theatre linked Faraday's work to modern telecommunications. Kate Haigh, Zoe Hale and Rebecca Collett went up from the audience to assist with some of the demonstrations. In the same year pupils attended a demonstration lecture on Petrochemicals at UEA. In 1997, our department attended a lecture at the Cambridge Corn Exchange given by Helen Sharman the first British woman astronaut in space. It was entitled, 'But What's The Use Of It Mr Faraday?' and explained how his principles of electromagnetic induction are used in modern technology

- In 2002 Years 7-9 attended the 'Bloomin' Science' Show by Johnny Ball at the Theatre Royal to learn about famous scientists and their inventions.

- 2005 Y9 attended an astronomy conference at the Institute of Astronomy in Cambridge lectures on the expanding the universe and careers in astronomy.

- In 2007 pupils visited the British Association Festival of Science series of lectures and discussions. They also took a trip to the Institute of Astronomy in Cambridge to attend lectures on asteroids; the career of an astronomer which can range from exploration of space to work for the Ministry of Defence such as protecting aircraft from missiles and in dealing with landmines; and to undertake a practical activity to calculate acceleration due to gravity

- 2011 Year 7-9 attended a science show at the Corn Exchange in Ipswich, the demonstrations included a hovercraft based on a Flymo.

- In 2008 and 2009 we travelled to London for GCSE conferences at which tips on exam technique were presented along with lectures and demonstrations on topical developments and misconceptions in science.
- Pupils of the Sacred Heart have been climbing the Ecotricity Wind turbine's [300] steps since the year 2000 and experimenting with model wind turbines to maximise efficiency using different numbers of blades and refining their angle to the wind. The wind turbine in Swaffham is the only one in the world with a public viewing platform and we are lucky to have such an interesting resource locally.
- In 2012 we combined a visit to ascend the turbine with some community service, clearing stones and flower beds in the Ecotech gardens, and also participating in the long-term survey of plants, insects and birds. It was particularly peaceful and pleasant to sit in the sunshine and count the birds singing.
- The Inspire Science Centre in Norwich in a former church has a changing range of practical science activities to encourage learning by experiment and our science department enjoyed visits there in 1996 and 2012. In 1996 Year 11 used a vacuum forming technique to make a sign for their classroom.
- Another local venue – Gressenhall Rural Life Museum – was visited by Years 6-8 in 1998 for a Science and Technology day.
- Over many years the Holt Hall Field trip for Year 10 included an exercise in counting species of grasses on the foreshore; and comparing the river quality above and below a sewage treatment works using indicator species. Year 6 visited Holt Hall in 2013 for pond dipping and learned to identify water species.
- We enjoyed a mixed age group visit to Banham Zoo in 2012 with emphasis on animals from different continents, and in 2014 Year 7 made a visit to study adaptation.

Visitors

- In 1997 representatives of British Telecom visited the school and explained the transmission of telephone calls using total internal reflection of light. In the same year a representative from Ford gave a talk on recycling of cars and we learned that cars are made from 75% recycled materials; only 25% of a scrapped car goes to landfill.
- 2001 'Science year' 559,493 people including the Sacred Heart community 'jumped' for one minute at 11am on 7th September to launch the government's Science Year with the world's largest experiment to generate an earthquake. The effect was detected by every seismometer in the country and was about 100th of a serious earthquake.
- he 'BBC Astronomer' Peter Ingram has visited the school twice, in 2003 and 2009, and given exciting lectures to pupils and to parents illustrated with meteorites, a speck of rock from Mars and palm-sized piece of the moon which we were able to pass around.
- We were also visited twice by the Astrodome in 2004 and 2009, an inflatable planetarium inside which we learned about the night sky.
- The Zoolab has been very popular with the whole school bringing a variety of creatures

to see and handle in 2010 and 2012. These ranged from snakes and spiders to giant rabbits and encouraged us to exercise quiet gentleness in our dealings with them.

- In 2012 we were visited by 'A World of Wings' and the whole school enjoyed their flying display of exotic birds in the Sports Hall.

Concern for the environment

Knowledge is intimately linked with responsibility in science as in other fields and so in 1995 Year 7 thought about ways of saving water; and Alex Leeder wrote a piece on addressing global warming called 'If I ruled the World', in which she suggested returning to low technology lifestyles including storytelling and barn dancing instead of television. In 1997, a Yr8 Swaffham Energy Savers Project involved a 6 month campaign in pupils' homes to monitor energy use and take energy saving action.

The Year 8 group of 2008 researched the benefits of reforestation and raised money to plant trees in Israel, contributing the long-term project to reclaim the desert by re-planting biblical species there. They also marked Miss Wynter's leaving by having trees planted in Israel in her name.

In 2012 the Sacred Heart had its first Environmental Prefect, Amy Chandler, who worked closely with Mrs Laban to raise awareness of environmental improvements we could make in school through the co-operation of a committee drawn from all the tutor groups. In 2013 the role evolved into Sustainability Prefect with Luke Watridge appointed to the position.

Science Week and Astronomy Week

In 2002 the Sacred Heart celebrated National Science Week by undertaking 60 second challenges during science lessons. These included: The Rocket, The Pulsemeter; The Cartesian Diver; The Marble Run; The Tower and Morse Code.

A recent highlight in the science department's history was Astronomy Week in 2009. All assemblies and subject lessons had an astronomy theme. A House Competition ran throughout the week amassing star points through quizzes, competitions, performances and the curriculum work. Friday was 'dressing up day' with an astronomy theme.

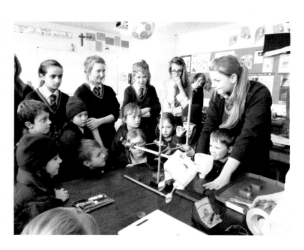

A science demonstration by Senior Pupils

Astronomy Week 2009

Astronomy week started off with a Big Bang! Mrs Verne began with an educational assembly inspiring us all about the week ahead.
There was excitement in the air as we entered the school on Monday morning. The star points board was set up, the competition had begun.

The rest of the week was filled with friendly rivalry between the four houses; Balmoral, Buckingham, Sandringham and Windsor. Star points were awarded in every lesson for the enthusiastic participation, which Mr Stratford tested older pupils on diameters, masses and relative distances from the sun of the planets.

The astrodome was the most unusual of the activities as it informed us about the makeup of our sky as well as the patterns and meanings of the stars.

Awe and Wonder was the theme for Mrs Verne's lessons. Pupils discovered their creative side when describing how they felt about how fantastical and wondrous our universe really is. To sum up in two words: **'It's indescribable'**

Mrs Burton arranged for us all to make rockets in science with the twist of STAR POINTS for the winning rocket. Each house tried and tested different methods of making rockets in order to achieve the best aerodynamics.

P.E is a difficult subject to relate to astronomy, but Miss Foster managed to find out that astronauts do non-weight bearing exercise as they need light bones to float in space. Aerobics was therefore the chosen exercise for the week. Each routine was space themed with many doing moon walks, or making shapes of stars or moons. Some even mimed getting out of their rocket! Seeing smiles on people faces, even those who maybe aren't as sporty as others, was particularly rewarding.

One of the most important parts to the week was the talk from Peter Ingram about space for the parents and older pupils in the barn on Thursday night. Sister Francis came to assembly on Friday morning full of facts about our universe. Mr Ingram was enthusiastic in the way he delivered his presentation and has left us all with a thirst for more knowledge for which we thank him.

Non uniform day was held on Friday and it was great to see everyone dressed in the theme of space. Some came as characters from Star Wars, whilst others dressed as stars and planets.

The week finished off with an assembly and it was lovely to see what the little ones had prepared during the week and performed in the final assembly. Four hilarious sketches were performed by each house in the last bid to gain extra star points. The results were Buckingham 4th, Sandringham 3rd, Windsor 2nd and Balmoral 1". An ecstatic group of Balmorals cheered and congratulated the runners up. Cake was enjoyed by all and it was a fabulous end to an incredible week.

Serena Smith (Head Girl 2009)

Supporting GCSE topics

In 2012 we were pleased to welcome parents and a
former pupil to talk to us about parts of our GCSE syllabus that feature in their work. Dr Felicity Hemmant, a former pupil, gave a presentation on Diabetes, Dr Lisa James gave a presentation on drug trials, and Mr Willis showed us how he processes biofuel.

Year of Faith

2013 was declared by Pope Benedict as the Year of Faith and Year 9 undertook a project on Catholic Scientists to remind us of the 'friendship between science and faith' that St Albert taught. In doing this we renewed our gratitude to Fr Roger Bacon, a 13th Century Franciscan Friar, for the Scientific Method; and the little known Monsigneur Georges Le Maitre the first proponent of the Big Bang Theory which he derived from Einstein's calculations. Fr Le Maitre had called his theory the 'hypothesis of the primeval atom or the "Cosmic Egg"' and 'Big Bang' was a phrase coined by his critics to mock the hypothesis that is now so widely accepted.

The last 39 years have seen many pupils go on to study science at A Level and beyond. We are always very pleased when they return to visit us and encourage present pupils to love science and study it further. Visitors often comment on the familiar smell of a laboratory and say it takes them back to their schooldays. We hope that time in the Science Department contributes to the happy memories of time at the Sacred Heart and to life-long appreciation of the wonders of this world and the principles that govern it.

Frances Verne, Science Teacher April 2014,
taking up the role of Head of Science in September 2014

Maths Challenge Week 2011

The activity week within school for the year 2011 had a mathematical theme — specifically 'Patterns'. This theme was chosen because it is easy to find repeating patterns in the natural world and then see how mathematical ideas can be applied to many everyday phenomena. The pupils certainly rose to the occasion (as always) and there was plenty of enthusiasm and creativity evident in the Maths Relays, fractal drawings, etc. We even had time to find out about the lives of some famous mathematicians.

Fractals

A fractal is "a rough or fragmented geometric shape that can be split into parts, each of which is (at least approximately) a reduced-size copy of the whole".

Although the definition sounds complicated, our pupils were able to learn about real-life examples and create their own fractals during the 'mathematics week'. We saw that however much you magnify a fractal you still maintain the same level of complexity.

  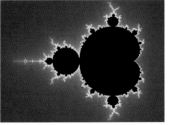

"Wow, that's so cool!"

As we watched a rather hypnotic video zooming in on a fractal, the idea of self-similarity really became apparent. The circle shapes in the first picture (above) kept reappearing at regular intervals.

Real-life Fractals

Whilst originally thought of as a mathematical curiosity, these complex shapes and the associated mathematics can be used to describe a variety of real-life features, from trees to cauliflowers!

Pupil-made fractals

There were some truly inventive designs containing self-similarity e.g. smaller arrows within larger arrows and we were impressed at how quickly pupils understood this complex idea. Many of the fractals made were on display boards during the presentation afternoon.

Mathematics Relay

"Who would have thought we would see pupils running to collect extra maths work!?"

The house relay was staged in the gym and each year group had questions they needed to answer (and have checked) before the next year group could collect and answer their questions. As well as being great fun, this activity demonstrated our pupils' great ability to co-operate and work together as a team.

Pupils of all abilities and ages were able to contribute to their House's points total, with Sandringham narrowly beating Balmoral in this event.

House 'Pattern' Presentations

On the final afternoon, the pupils performed their House presentations. Given the theme of 'Patterns' as a starting point, the Houses were charged with interpreting this word as they saw fit. It was a real exercise in creativity and the diversity of interpretations was very impressive. Most groups chose to focus on topics they had studied during the week, for example; the Fibonacci sequence and Fractals.

Besides the obvious visual links to the theme of patterns, there were interesting musical and dramatic performances which drew deserved applause from the audience. Given that the students had worked to a very tight schedule, we felt they had fulfilled the brief very well.

Balmoral won first place for the Junior Presentation and Buckingham won for the Senior Presentation.

Congratulations to Sandringham, as the overall winners and well done to all the pupils and staff

for their efforts during the week!

Lewis Murphy, Head of Maths 2013 to present and JohnClements, retired Head of Maths 2013

Chapter 7 HUMANITIES

Together we ran the Humanities department from 1991. Mrs Mansfield began working at the Convent, as it was then known, in September 1985 as a part- time teacher of Geography and Mrs Kenny joined in 1991.

When Mrs Mansfield started it was the last year of O Levels and she was teaching a very large group so it was quite a baptism of fire. In 1987 GCSE's were introduced and followed a completely different approach with fieldwork being required for the first time.

2000/01 Year 7 field trip to Hunstanton

Pupils at the Convent were already quite familiar with the concept of fieldwork as Dr Wade Martins, who had previously taught both the Humanities subjects, had set up a course which was called Environmental Studies for the 'first and second' years (Years 7 and 8). We were given a whole afternoon for this and using Dr Wade Martin's immense local knowledge, were able to take the children out, both in Swaffham and the surrounding area. We studied the history of Swaffham finding out about its origins and development by looking at the 'foundation stone' - a glacial erratic which acted as a landmark in the early trading days of the settlement; we examined the Shambles, imagining what it would have been like in the Middle Ages when it was a tightly packed group of butcheries with lanes which often ran red with the slaughtered animals' blood and admired the medieval beams hidden behind the door of the bakery in the town. We did shopping surveys, walked the route of the former railway and examined the brickwork of old buildings to try to establish when they had been built. We also travelled further afield, visiting Saxon churches, medieval castles and Priories as well as Mr Storey's farm at Mileham as an example of a dairy farm

We went to the Broads, particularly Martham and Hickling and the Fens to study drainage and wildlife, we also went to the coast, to study its physical features and the impact of tourism. It was a wonderful opportunity to experience the world rather than just reading about it.

GEOGRAPHY RIVER STUDY

It started out a lovely day,

When we thought things were going our way.

We hustled and bustled, quickened and hastened

To Castle Acre, our destination.

There we saw, to our surprise

(And also through many lies)

For Mrs. Mansfield and Mrs. Kenny

Had told us lies – Oh, so many!

"Deep water!", they said, and "Don't be silly!"

And there it was, both deep and chilly.

Many a frown and woeful expression

Were quickly passed as we started the lesson.

To measure the meander and the straight

Seemed to be our downright fate.

But the splashing and swimming were enjoyed by all

Oh, and of course, the occasional fall

Straight into the river. Oh, what a mess.

From head to toe, yes, no less (Abigail!)

But the day was enjoyed by all.

Sarah Conway, Year 10 2004

Beach Survey. North Norfolk Coast

When GCSE's were introduced coursework and the collection of primary data became a vital part of the syllabus and so 'projects' began to evolve. In the early years, two such pieces of work were required and so we did fieldwork to establish the relevance of Burgess' theory of urban structure to Swaffham and also investigated the suitability of Denver as a site for a nuclear power station, which at that time was part of the structure plan for this area. As time went on, the coursework requirement became one extended piece and so began an investigation into how the behaviour of the River Nar differed at a straight and meander section. This allowed many adventures in Castle Acre, sometimes rain-soaked, sometimes suffering from sunburn, once almost losing a cagoule to a hungry cow and having to overcome pupil rebellion when a water vole was seen in the river. We never told them about the snake once seen swimming there!

Mrs Kenny later instituted a three day residential field trip to Holt Hall which became a highlight of Year 10. The pupils changed their attention from the River Nar to the River Glaven and examined it at several sites. They also were given the opportunity to do some biology studying plant succession in the sand dunes at Holkham or the salt marsh at Stiffkey.

As well as geography, we also taught small groups who opted for GCSE Humanities instead

Humanities Field Trip

of continuing their language studies. This was a modular course which gave pupils the opportunity to look at aspects of History as well as Geography and included the study of a local issue such as the demolition of the fishing quarter of Kings Lynn in the 1960's.

Humanities was replaced by Travel and Tourism which ran between the years 2001 and 2006. This was a more vocational syllabus which looked at jobs in the field as well as the economics of tourism and its impact on different parts of the world. Learning this was a new skill for us as well as the pupils! However, it proved a popular choice and gained some very good results.

Part of this syllabus was coursework comparing two tourist destinations, Cromer and Potter Heigham, followed by work experience in a tourism based company, such as a hotel or a travel agency, which then had to be written up. Sometimes it was a relief the companies didn't read the evaluation of the girls' experiences in the world of work.

Between us, we taught History in the school for many years, with Mrs Mansfield teaching GCSE and Mrs Kenny Key Stage 3.

Key Stage 3 History was taught in chronological order beginning with the Norman invasion and Medieval Britain in Year 7 moving through the Tudors and Stuarts in Year 8 and studying the agricultural, industrial and transport revolutions in Year 9 along with the two world wars.

The syllabus was enriched by numerous visits such as to Norwich Castle and True's Yard Further afield, visits took place to Parliament and the Tower of London.

GRESSENHALL WORKHOUSE

On Friday 24th May, armed with umbrellas, kagouls and various other materials, Year 10 History Group braved the weather to visit the historic buildings at Gressenhall. The trip was to support of our first G.C.S.E. History assignment about the changed made to Gressenhall after the Poor Law Amendment Act of 1834. When we arrived at Gressenhall, we were taken to a small classroom above the cafeteria. This room was our base for the day. Part of the assignment involved studying the outside structure of Gressenhall. The group split into two and went to different locations around Gressenhall, noting the changes. We all met up in our base and each group compared notes on what they saw.

After a brief discussion about the outside of Gressenhall and the possible reasons for these changes, the whole, extremely wet, group went to look around the inside of the building. We saw the room where the inmates waited to hear their punishment and the refractory cell, where the only thing they were fed on was bread and water. The other buildings of interest which we saw in the grounds at Gressenhall were the church, the single mothers' quarters and the master's cottage. The church and the cottage were built some time after the Amendment Act of 1834. The church was designed to reform the inmates and help them reflect on the error of their ways. The Master lived actually inside the workhouse for some years before the cottage was built. The single mothers' quarters were the worst in the grounds because people at that time believed that these women polluted the morals of others and should be kept apart from the rest of the inmates.

After lunch, we covered all the remaining areas of interest. It was possible to see where alterations to the building had been made because of the differences in the brickwork in various areas at Gressenhall. There was just time to take some photographs for our assignments before heading back to school, where we used our historical knowledge and the physical evidence we had gathered at Gressenhall to analyse the information we had found.

Charlotte Jackman, Year 10.

The History syllabus at GCSE abruptly changed in 2010 when British Social and Economic History from the late 18th to the early 20th century was replaced by Modern World History. So, instead of learning about our local heritage by studying the Agricultural revolution (with particular reference to Norfolk when it was a very important place!) The Suffragette movement and the New Poor Law requiring a visit to the workhouse at Gressenhall and we began to study recent history with particular reference to the Cold War.

The school also undertook several trips to the First World War Battlefields in Northern France and Belgium. This proved to be very popular and gave the pupils a real insight into the enormous scale of the war and how it was fought. The visits to the war cemeteries were particularly affecting and were always an opportunity to read from the war poets, to pray and to meditate on the sacrifice of so many.

BELGIUM TRIP

On Thursday 20th June 2013, 50 pupils in the senior school went to Belgium on a trip based on World War I.

We went to the Flanders Museum in Ypres and were given a wrist band which, if placed on a sensor, would show more facts. The museum was on the Western Front side and had been flattened in the war, but had been rebuilt.

Our next stop was the Caterpillar Crater. Caterpillar Crater, It had once been a German trench, but the English had dug under 'no man's land' and put mines underneath. It was said that the blast could be heard in London.

We went to one of the graveyards where the soldiers from World War I were buried. The tombstones were white for purity and when you went up to them, you could see where the soldiers came from; Egypt, Norfolk, Australia and Canada and many more places. Seventeen was the youngest age and 39 the oldest of the few tombstones I read; many were so young.

The trenches were our next stop. Troops and would have been exposed to wind and bad weather. Trenches infested with rats and the troops suffered badly from lice because of the appalling conditions.

This was the end of our trip to Belgium so we started on our trip back to England. This experience has made me more aware of how just one man shooting another man can turn into a disastrous world war and the millions of lives that were destroyed and lost.

Imogen Leader, Year 7 2013

In our time at the Sacred Heart, coursework has come and gone, to be replaced by 'Controlled Assessments', which themselves are due to disappear shortly. We wonder what humanities subjects will be like in another hundred years? At present we seem to be going back to the beginning, where Mrs Mansfield came in, with single academic examinations at the end of a two year course.

When Mrs Wilson joined our 'elite' club she chose to change to the Schools History Project so that pupils now study the World Wars, the American West and surgery.

Have we enjoyed being small cogs in the running of this wonderful school? The answer is, of course, yes! Teaching in this school is an opportunity of a lifetime and we have enjoyed (almost!) every minute.

Long may it prosper.

Hilary Kenny, Head of Geography 2014
Marie Mansfield, Head of History

Chapter 8 TRIPS AND LANGUAGES

'The world is a book and those who do not travel read only a page '- (St Augustine)

My life has been filled with travel since I was a tiny baby and I have been fortunate enough to continue with further exciting adventures whilst at The Sacred Heart School.

I joined the school in September 1987, just two years before the 75th Anniversary of the school and as 1989 hove into view I was preparing to take Forms 1,2 and 3 (as they were known then) to France for a week's language trip. As I was dropped off by my family Sr. Katherine asked them what they would be doing and my son, Duncan, said confidently that they would be going to the pub for lunch whereupon Sister disappeared into the warren that is the convent and re-appeared a short time later with two bags of crisps saying that they could now go straight home!

We travelled to Forges-les-Eaux and stayed in a VVF – a lovely little holiday village with tiny houses to accommodate all the girls – there were no boys in the senior school at the time. This caused me some anxiety but as I had all of the senior staff with me I felt certain that all would be well! Of course, some praying was called for when the local youths discovered that the VVF was full of beautiful English girls. Our outings were fabulous and all necessitated the use of the French language. There were assignments at the station, the market, the picnic assignment, the cheese farm, a day in Rouen, learning about Joan of Arc and visiting both the ossuary and the charnel house where the bones were disposed of during the Black Death, a day in Paris including a trip to the top of the Eiffel Tower and a visit to Les Invalides, the home of Napoleon's famous red marble tomb. It was wonderful and all the girls and staff enjoyed themselves immensely. I neglected to tell you that we had a tutor with us on all the days, except for the visit to Paris, who was to have provided a reasonable amount of language tuition which he did, although he was not ultra-dynamic!

We discovered that Mrs Young is allergic to picnics and flies whilst learning how to make Neufchâtel cheese –a lovely, creamy brie-like cheese which was heart-shaped for the young maidens to give to the English soldiers during the Hundred Years War! Sadly when we had dinner that night one of the lovely heart shaped cheeses was found to contain a dead fly and Mrs Young discovered it – not a great plan as it turned out. There was also a disco to celebrate the end of the trip which showed the dancing skills of the staff! (Or not as the case may be!)

I forgot to tell you that we had so many pupils and staff with us that staff were actually able to have a night off during the week. Mrs Young had persuaded her husband to come so the three of us went out for supper having previously spotted a fabulous restaurant near the VVF. Unfortunately for me there was an enormous Irish wolfhound, called Charlie, who resided there. Those of you who know me would know that I am terrified of all dogs especially large ones. Anyway, on the way there, we were stopped by a Russian lorry driver who needed to know the directions to the abattoir in Forges-les-Eaux. He could barely make himself understood and I tried French, English and finally German. So much for international relations! However, the restaurant was excellent and the food was delicious although the starters turned out to be rather bizarre! We ended up with two 'tomates' which we hoped were 'jus de tomate' but were in actuality grenadine and white wine. The next time we went, a few years later, we had 'perroquets' as a starter – no, not parrots but Crème de menthe combined with fizzy wine.

Forges-les-Eaux 1991

In 1991 we went to Forges-les-Eaux again, I thought it was worth another visit as I had gained so much knowledge of the area and did not want to waste it! We did more or less the same activities and had a wonderful time. No flies in the cheese this time! More crazy dancing though. There was a very nice tutor this time who was interested in the lessons he gave and was on a sabbatical from teaching in New Zealand. He was 'sensass!'

As the 1993 trip was planned, my dear friend and colleague, Mrs Young, suggested that we did not go to Forges-les-Eaux again but to change the venue of the French Trip as she did each year for the ski trip. I bowed to her wish and we set off for Le Grand Bornand, in the Haute Savoie with a clutch of parents, Mrs Abel, Mrs Breach and Mrs Howard. The coach which arrived was the most uncomfortable, cold and decidedly not luxurious coach, however, the drivers were kind and very willing to help. We did some similar activities for this Assignment France as it was called and we had the company of a very experienced tutor who seemed to love red wine. At a cheese cooperative where the locals made the gorgeous Reblochon cheese, Mrs Howard was heard to say "I think Mrs Howarth could do with a bit of help with the translating." The reply came back swiftly "I think she's doing fine!" Then, he promptly disappeared and we next saw him in a bar with a glass of the previously mentioned beverage in hand!

We had fun on the trip and spent a lovely day in Annecy which ended with ice skating at the local rink where one of our girls left her camera. She had been leaving / losing things all over the Haute Savoie and this was the last straw, so I sent her in with the perfectly rehearsed sentence and she retrieved the item! Strangely, she never lost another thing! You know who you are! (Hayley Cawthorne)

On the last day of an extended trip it is usual for the drivers to stay and sleep at the hotel and other arrangements must be made if one is to go somewhere by coach. I had asked the wine drinking tutor if he was willing to book a coach and he said very definitely that this was outside his remit and told me I should go to the phone box in the village and do it myself! Well of course I did just that and for a few moments relived the terror of

1996 1997 Gournay Market

the French oral that the girls were always telling me about. I need not have worried because I am totally capable of performing the exercise... thank goodness.

1995 rolled around and after the cold trip to the Haute Savoie, it was decided to try Rouen as a venue for Assignment France. We stayed in a ghastly youth hostel where the Directeur was very curious and convinced that everyone was doing it! Whatever ' it' was! I received some very colourful, EU sponsored things from him, in spite of saying that I was married, we were a catholic school and that our Headmistress, a religious, was upstairs! This strange encounter made me rush up the stairs to my colleague, and chief linguistic help at the school, Mrs Brandon who served the school from 1978-1998. "Shirley, you will never believe what has just happened, I really need a drink!"

Bank holiday in May 1995 came and Mrs Kenny and I were both invited to go on the PTA trip to Paris for a long weekend. It was great fun and we were delighted to accompany the party. I found a wonderful meal of three courses for 80 francs (£8) – the euro was still a way off! It consisted of a starter, something innocuous, un pavé de viande – literally a slab of meat and chips, followed by apple purée or some such dessert. There were cries of anguish when it appeared that people might have been eating horsemeat! I convinced most people that it was beef but there were a few doubters.

The PTA, intrepid explorers that they were, decided to go to Paris for a second time in 1996. We went too and I think we arrived as Paris St. Germain had just won the cup as the traffic was horrendous that night. There were some awful things being shown on the television channels available to everyone at the hotel. Mrs Kenny and I were both horrified! The rest of the visit was exciting and up to the usual high standard once we had banned the children from watching the TV, although some tried to sneak out to have a bit of night life as we sat by the lift. They were promptly sent back to bed with a flea in their ear! One of the parents was celebrating her 40th birthday that weekend and we had a delicious meal with her to make up for the fact that she had left her husband at home.

In 1997 we dared to visit Rouen again but this time stayed in a hotel in which the Youngs had had to stay during our last visit so that Dr Young didn't run into any of his patients whilst using the communal bathrooms! One of the parents had asked me to reassure him on the safety of his daughter whilst staying there and I think I virtually promised to sleep outside her door. This followed the very awful and tragic murder of an English girl on a school trip in Brittany. You may think I am treating this lightly but I have found that if I ever dwell on the enormity of the responsibility of a school trip I would go completely insane.

That visit included trips to Arromanches, the site of the Mulberry harbour during the Second World War, Bayeux to see la tâpisserie de la Reine Mathilde, a First World War cemetery, Rouen and the treatment of Joan of Arc by the English and the interestingly shaped cliffs at Étretat. These visits confused the perception of the dateline and history of France – perhaps it was all too much to do in a day or two?

There was cross curricular teaching on all of these trips and I heartily thank all the colleagues who put up with my eccentricity whilst in France: these included Mrs Brandon, Mrs Baker, Mrs Mansfield, Mrs Mann, Mrs Kenny, Dr Wade-Martins, Sr. Katherine, Sr. Francis, Mrs Young and Dr Young.

There was a lull in trips after this as there was also a drowning of a child in France on a school trip. It was unfortunate for that school and all the pupils and teachers concerned. It had a definite effect on our parents who entrust their children daily to us and our extended school trips very sadly dropped off.

By 2002, I was itching to take a trip to France again and I had the opportunity to go to London to investigate a new French course for the KS2 pupils where they suggested taking Y5 and Y6 away for four day weekends. I was awestruck – could I take away these tiny children for four days with their parents' permission and ensure they spoke French? Could they be entirely looked after and interested in all these exciting things outside their experience without missing their parents?

Well, surprisingly I was hooked on the idea and the children and their parents were willing for 2003…

**Year 5 and 6
The snail farm**

Whilst on these mini-trips with these pupils we had occasion, several times over the years, to visit Azincourt – known as Agincourt in English – where a very keen Headmaster (and noted historian) of the local primary school and his wife went to the National Archive in Paris and learned early French in order to translate all the documents relating to the battle of 1415. They gave us a talk in their little museum followed by a tour in our coach around all the field of battle. The Headmaster's wife read in French from the diaries and I translated the living history (with a little help from my partner in crime on trips, Mrs Brandon) from the diaries of those who had been there all those years ago. It was a most excellent visit and subsequent visits revealed a fabulous new centre dedicated to the Battle of AZINCOURT, funded largely by the EU, shaped like a longbow!

In 2003, Father Michael, not thinking about his or our carbon footprint, found some very cheap seats on an Irish airline to Rome! We were up and away before we knew it. There were masses of masses and lots of extraordinary sights to see. Mrs Kenny and I looked like the Praetorian Guard on the visit to the catacombs at San Sebastian.   It was a marvellous trip with the Year 9 girls, lots of staff and a sprinkling of Sisters and Fr. Michael.

Our Pilgrimage to Rome

The next day we were on our way to to St Peter's to see the Pope but unfortunately forgot our beloved Yoko and had to turn around to get her. When we finally got to St Peter's Square, there were thousands of people from all different parts of the world. I had an injury so I was put into a wheelchair and was allowed very close to the Pope.

During the ceremony, the Pope spoke in six different languages which was very impressive and when one of the priests called out the Sacred Heart Convent School, the group all stood up to sing our very harmonic Ave Maria.

Later I got to shake hands with the Pope himself (cool – Very Cool!)

Jennie Doran

The Grand Tour – a Buddhist on a Catholic Pilgrim's Tour

I was very pleased with having the opportunity to travel in Italy but it was too short to look round everything. Even though we couldn't go to any famous museums, I had some remarkable experiences of Christian culture. The Holy Father's audience, Basilica di San Pietro, the catacomb beside the Appia Antica, St. Pietro's foot in Domine Quo Vadis … and so on.

When I saw the special sunbeams through the dome of St. Peter's, I felt power, awe and wonder. It was one of the most glorious moments I have ever experienced.

Italian food is very good for Japanese because it has lots of vegetables, rice and sea-foods. Japanese have a variety of original noodles in our culture. I think that most of us are "noodle-eaters" and me too! I absolutely love pasta. I believe good foods teach people history by themselves, for example – Roman gnocchi! We ate it at the convent on the hill in Grottaferrata.   It didn't include potato.   I imagined Roman Emperors eating gnocchi! Actually in their era I don't know if they had some sort of gnocchi or not. But this is the beginning of my new interest or fantasy. Someday I will have an opportunity to research that fact. I am looking forward to it. This is great fun after travelling for me. Viva Italia! Mangiare! Tanto e tanto! Viva gastronomy!

As a Japanese saying describes "Hana – yori Dango! Some sweets are more important than viewing flowers."
Yoko Nakaya, Japanese Student

Grottaferrata

We meet Father Maurice, a Franciscan brother, who has the chair in History down at the University in Rome – he has the gentle accent of a New Zealander.
We visit the Brothers' library and we handled some exquisitely written books from the 13th century – I cannot believe we are doing this and Mrs Kenny wants to cry! MJH
Miss Gooderson thought that Year 9s – teenagers are an exotic species! She wrote : As for the pupils – well my fears proved groundless and all returned safely . Though at what age do they begin to grow mobile phones? They were nowhere near as scary as I had imagined and I was impressed by their behaviour and forbearance in difficult moments. They were interested and good company!"

The 4th of July 2003 marked not Independence Day but the first day of our first Y5 / Y6 trip to Étaples, in Northern France.

Notre visite à Étaples

Sunday 6th July – Today's visit was to a fascinating snail farm which was truly amazing. Madame gave a really informative talk about the half a million snails she and her husband farmed. The children were lucky enough to have a snail crawl up their arms. I will never forget the sight of Miss Wynter with at least trois escargots slithering up her arm and over the lovely gold bracelet she was wearing – I don't think she has worn it since! I must tell you that Mrs Phillips was unfailingly cheerful the whole time and loved all things French – I have another convert.

I am grateful to all those who helped on these trips including Miss Foster who also accompanied us to Northern France and took over the beach games when Mrs Young no longer came, Mrs Chalkley joined us and so did the young new teachers: Mr Murphy and Miss Wilson too. Many thanks to Mrs Jennings who played the role of mother/ nurse / teacher with us also.

During the Whitsun half-term holiday in 2004, we went on our travels again with Fr. Michael to Prague, where we stayed with Sr. Anna in the middle of the beautiful city called Praha. Some of the party had to stay in a hostel, which was less than luxurious by all accounts, some stayed with staff in a kind of dining room and others with the two Australian students in a large dormitory near the kitchen and virtually underground. Mrs Kenny, Mrs Mansfield and I had the privilege of staying on the top floor of a block within the convent complex along with two or three girls. When one looked out of the window very large, imposing buildings reminiscent of the Cold War were visible and made me feel glad to be both British and English and never having to have suffered under such dark regimes.

The visit to Theresienstadt or Terezín was extraordinary and many of us shed tears openly whilst we visited the so-called 'model camp' which the Germans had so proudly used in their Second World War propaganda campaign via the Red Cross.

We made many exciting excursions to places such as the Crystal Fountains and the ballet which was set in the dark and danced by luminous puppets to the story of Doctor Faustus. Much interesting food was consumed and Sr. Anna welcomed us to her English classes too. One night, however, Mrs Kenny, Mrs Mansfield and I were excused by Sr. Francis to go back early to shower at the convent. The building had been cleaned and locked up for the night whilst we were beautifying ourselves. We found that we were marooned in a locked building with what looked like a dead body in a bed at one point which caused screaming, though not with laughter! As we had mobile phones, we rang everyone on the trip. Needless to say, no-one had their phone switched on and we were now in dire straits! I said that I would ring Sr. Thomas More back at school in Swaffham! She called the convent in Prague and someone came to let us out eventually. Of course, Sr. Francis berated us for being late to dinner! Mine consisted of cold peas and potatoes as vegetarians were not catered for! The most curious thing happened at the airport on our way home: I was put down on the aeroplane's manifest as Mrs Johnstone! I don't think Fr. Michael was impressed.

As 2006 rolled on Fr. Michael once again surprised us with the enticement of a trip to Krakow. Luckily we have Sisters in a convent which is handily placed in the city. For me it was to be a strange trip as Sr. Francis announced about two hours before departure that I was to be in charge as she was not well enough to come! Not ideal when there is a new Deputy Head also on the trip.

Of course, we all wanted to go (the staff I mean), the pupils also relished the chance to visit a salt-mine and various other historical places. The most important of these was to be Auschwitz and Auschwitz-Birkenau, the notorious death camp of the Nazis during the Second World War where not only the Jews met their end but also poets, academics, the handicapped, homosexuals, political prisoners and St Maximilian Kolbe, a Polish Franciscan friar, who offered to die in place of a stranger in Auschwitz.

We had an interesting, if rainy, day in the Tatra Mountains at Zakopane where we saw fabulous ski jumps and runs. There we also discovered the delights of 'pierogi' the delicious filled dumplings of unleavened bread. During our visit to Krakow we saw the street on which Oskar Schindler had lived, Ulica Grodzka, and ate supper one evening in that very street. One of the starters would have made my Grandmother Florence laugh as it was meat dripping on bread – the kind of thing many ate during the war years, so I am told. The cloth halls were both enticing and exciting offering as they did many shopping opportunities. Some of us needed to buy the lovely amber of silver jewellery from the artisans there.

A new Sister had come on the trip with Sr. Jacinta, she was a real live-wire and caused me some anguish when she decided to visit the birthplace of Pope John Paul II. There was a massive queue around the house and I could see that there would be no time for her to achieve this particular goal, so I warned her that if she was not at the bus to go back by a certain time she would be left behind. Imagine my surprise when I next saw her, hanging off the balcony of the room where the Pope had been born, shouting 'I told you I could get in.' Like Queen Victoria, I was not amused! (Sr.Linda)

In the autumn of 2006, I arranged a History trip, to the World War One battlefields in Northern France, with Mrs Mansfield. We travelled with a local company from Norwich and stayed in a strange place on a farm which had huge barn conversions which had many bedrooms. Curiously, it also housed very many young boys / men from a local secondary school who stayed there during the week as they were all from the very rural area we were in. It made the life of the staff very interesting although there did not seem to be any real fraternisation. We were given a tour round the farm first and saw many sweet, little farm creatures some of which ended up on our plates for supper! Fortunately many children these days are used to eating duck for dinner. The visit was a great success and we were thrilled to do some cross-curricular teaching and learning once again. Breakfast was typically French, with 'chocolat chaud' in a bowl and 'tartines au beurre ou à la confiture.' Everyone, pupils and staff, loved this shared meal before the visit to the town of Albert. We all remember the story of the falling Madonna on the parish church, she did not actually fall but was slewed at an uncomfortable angle for the majority of the war. I think she was later shot down by the British troops at the end of the war and she has since been re-gilded and put back to her rightful place when the church was re-built.

We met a young French student there who took us to the' Historiale de la Première Guerre Mondiale' which is set in an old castle in Peronne. The exhibits there are displayed in many unusual ways but my favourite was that of an open box in the floor where one looks down on the uniforms and equipment of the different forces of the war. This was followed by a trip to the Lochnagar Crater which is vast and is still a monument to all those brave soldiers who tunnelled under the German lines in such appalling conditions. The crater still measures almost one hundred metres in diameter and seventy-one deep. The cemeteries, which litter the countryside of Northern France and are maintained by the Commonwealth War Graves Commission, are beautiful in their simplicity. The stones look as if they are carved from Caen stone being so white and identical to that of Norwich Cathedral (The Holy and Undivided Trinity). The stones bear the name, rank, number and regiment of the soldier buried there but the most moving inscription I found is that of 'A soldier known only to God.'

Our visits to the battlefields also incorporated a trip to Beaumont-Hamel where there is a beautiful bronze stag commemorating the Canadian army losses. A little further down and also within touching distance of the enemy trenches is a memorial to the soldiers of the 51st Highland Division who fought in their kilts and were known as the 'Devils in Skirts' or 'The Ladies from Hell' by the German troops because of their fierce fighting in the trenches which were so close to each other.

Another visit with this company to the battlefields found our group staying in Arras, a beautiful medieval town known to me from my student days when I had spent time there during my first year of teacher training at an 'École Normale de Garçons.' I had very fond memories of the square where we were actually billeted. This was La Grand' Place an exquisitely decorated, cobbled square almost Flemish in design and architecture. One night a fight took place after some rowdies had been drinking outside. As they lambed into the wooden supports of the building we all felt every single punch!

We visited the Wellington Quarry, which was only re-discovered fairly recently and opened in 2008, it is a magnificent tribute to those soldiers who carefully dug out the wonderfully white chalk seventy metres below the ground and made a hospital as well as hundreds of billets (and latrines) for the soldiers and officers camped there before they went over the top before the Battle of Arras in 1917. The walls have the usual graffiti on them but also some lovely drawings and writings.

Krakow proved to be a favourite with the staff and pupils alike and we decided to go again but this time we stayed in an hotel in the town. This was fine but the top floor of the convent had been beautifully decorated and had rooms with en suite bathrooms so naturally the cost of the trip went up. There were lovely breakfasts which we did not have to provide for ourselves this time. I did not mention, as on the last visit to Krakow, we went to Kazimierz, the Jewish quarter of the town. This was lovely if rather small. Here we saw the home of the famous beautician, Helena Rubinstein, synagogues where men had been slain for just praying and sweet little restaurants. It was so moving. The school which housed the Jewish children and then became offices fascinated us.

The most awful thing happened on the last day, we were walking in a crocodile along the street and the girls were talking to each other very happily when all of a sudden Kate Purkis walked into a lamp-post. There were screams and an enormous egg-shaped lump appeared on her forehead. Sr. Francis or Sr. Danuta made sure we went to the Convent for some aid and then disappeared off for the afternoon visit. Very kindly we were given a bedroom for Kate to lie down in and then some frozen chicken wrapped in a tea-towel to help the swelling go down – frozen peas not being an option! My lack of first aid skills is legendary so I telephoned Mrs Kenny, at school in Swaffham, and said I did not like the situation. Well, eventually we went to the hospital for Kate to have some CAT scans and I was completely terrified as I signed the forms truly 'in loco parentis.' Never had those words had such an effect on me! Fortunately, Kate began to recover and we went back to the convent were we were served with fish for lunch, it being Friday! Then, the most incomprehensible, implausible and incongruous thing occurred, we left for the afternoon visit rather later than planned but arrived at Auschwitz in a taxi. It was most bizarre.

In 2005 and 2007, Years 5 and 6 went to Berck sur Mer and stayed at the fabulous 'Cottage des Dunes' where I made friends with the night watchman – my ability to sleep on these trips occasionally deserts me. Both times we had a wonderful' animatrice' who eased our way around the North of France and the visits went smoothly. Our favourite visit of all was that of the 'Chocolaterie' at Beussent. As we stayed so close to the beach, it meant that we could go there after dinner each night to tire out the children completely before bed time. It was such marvellous fun too when we went to the snail farm.

How to make the perfect croissant

There was a change of venue for the Year 5 and 6 trip in 2009 – we went to Hardelot, a lovely centre to stay in and where there was an equestrian centre which we could see during breakfast. We had the company of Daisy, who was a very small child at the time, her father and Cameron's mother, who was a teacher too. The pupils remember eating lots of apple purée at meal times. There was a castle and a lake nearby which we walked around before bedtime – this was rather scary. The visit was similar to the last trips in that we managed to do all the exciting things we had done before – visiting the market and speaking in French, the visit to the snail farm, the lunch at the 'crêperie' in which we had 'galettes' to start, made of buckwheat flour with savoury fillings, and 'crêpes' with sweet fillings, the supermarket and of course church on Saturday evening too. At the church we were welcomed as normal and Mrs Burton was able to play her flute with the music group and the priest asked if I would translate the gospel reading. This was a great honour and I was thrilled to read about the denial of Peter to the congregation. After the service, one of the pupils asked me in all seriousness 'Did you read that in French or English, Mrs Howarth?' So much for the teaching of French, 'hein?'

2011 rolled round and we found ourselves staying in Berck once again enjoying the beach and the glorious weather. The snail farm was just as much fun as ever and the pupils enjoyed the snail pâté on bread as well as the little pastry shaped like snails filled with garlic butter and a snail. We learned how the slime is used for making cough mixture and also beauty products! I do not think that I will ever be a fan of that!

On a very hot day in the summer of 2013, Mrs Wilson and several members of staff departed for Yprès. The coach left Swaffham in good time to catch the ferry and we finally arrived in the lovely town centre of Yprès in the late morning. I went in with Mrs Wilson to check on the ticket prices and entry times speaking French of course. The lady behind the desk said that she spoke English and there was no need for me to speak French to her. Well, I said that I would continue if she did not mind (practice anywhere is essential) totally forgetting that the people of Belgium felt rather let down by the French during WW1!

The visit was really interesting and almost all of the students enjoyed the exhibits. One was ill and I had to take him out thus missing the most interesting part. The shopping, which mainly consisted of Belgian Chocolate, took place afterwards. Yprès is a delightful place and how some of it survived the shelling it received is a miracle. Next we went to the trenches, although this proved harder to locate than anything else. Eventually we found it set as it was in the middle of an industrial estate!

Our next destination was the Caterpillar Crater, another vast chasm in the ground surrounded by children of all nationalities on their own History trips. Lastly we went to a cemetery, one of thousands all over the southern part of Belgium, to look, listen and pray. The pupils were respectful and so gracious as they read their own part of the prayer. We were all affected by what we had seen that day.

Children at the Sacred Heart School will have no reason ever to be caught up in war, knowing as they do the dreadful consequences of it.

I have not mentioned the enormous fun we had in the language department in 2007 when it was my turn to provide a week of language and activities for all the pupils aged 11-15 (Years 7-10). It was designated 'A Spanish Week.' So I started to plan the kind of days which I had been party to teaching in Austria just before I got married: three hours of language learning in the mornings followed by three activities every afternoon on a carousel – no, not that fab song by the Hollies some of you are remembering but different

Spanish Week

things ensuring that by the end of the week everyone would have completed all of them! So I wracked my brains and found four teachers who would teach vertically grouped children for three hours with five minutes off between the first and second lesson and then break before the third. It was tough going for some of our young linguists but everyone strove valiantly to complete the task in hand. The afternoons were lovely and there were children working on a version of Picasso's Guernica with Mrs Davey in the Art Room, the English Department kindly took up the challenge of some classic Spanish literature, Mrs Heale was a whizz in the H.E. Room preparing tapas, the Humanities Department worked on some Historical and Geographical material and I seemed to just swan around checking all was well. I also employed a fabulous Flamenco dancer and a Spanish guitarist who accompanied her. The dancer whose Spanish name was 'La Espuelita' – the little nail – taught everyone to dance in the Flamenco tradition, even the Lower School children were able to take part. We are lucky that Xavier Navarre and his wife teach in the hall in the evenings and came and taught us all some 'sexy' salsa moves too. It was all such fantastic fun and everyone learned so much about Spain and the Spanish speaking world. Just after this I had my first group of pupils for Spanish lessons.

For the centenary celebrations, we started to learn some of the languages used by our own Sisters, the Daughters of Divine Charity. On the day of European Languages Day in September 2013, a day on which the many languages of the continent are celebrated (not just the ones which are traditionally spoken there) we began our marathon. I planned to teach somehow, with God's help I think, German, Portuguese, Italian and Polish so that when our Sisters arrive to help us celebrate in 2014 all the pupils will be able to converse or at least help to direct the Sisters to the places they wish to get to. The German went well, followed by the Portuguese taught by Sister Eliani who had only stopped off to perfect her English on the way to Rushooka, the Italian went well and the children learned to sing a song in Italian and Sr. Linda and I had strange dialogues with help from Lily Wainer who speaks Italian. The Polish has yet to be taught and I await with bated breath the arrival of the Sisters.

We have had help over the years from students coming from all over the world : Australia, Austria, South Africa, Hungary, Poland, Japan, America, the Czech Republic and very many from France. All of these, including the delightful family who came from Madrid in summer 2013, Maribel Cuenca and three of her five children, who stayed for nearly three weeks and were a joy to have in the language department were welcomed by all staff and students and exposed us to new ways and cultures.

Language, the acquisition of it and its practice and use are essential tools in the global market place and we fail our children if we do not provide them with the ability to use them for harmonious relationships whether at work or at play in the 21st century. Many children in Years 7, 8 and 9 currently are engaged in learning programmes on the internet and I heartily endorse their use we must not be an island nation relying on the relic of an imperial past. The pupils will tell you that I am never without a dictionary or a phrase book on a visit abroad (although these have been superseded lately by a mobile 'phone app or tablet.)

I have been very lucky to have taught so many students here over the years and although my colleagues will attest to my moaning, I am sure they will agree that I have enjoyed teaching languages here and going on foreign trips in particular. I have loved almost every single minute of those and wish to thank all of my colleagues and the Sisters for their support over the years.
Jane Howarth, Head of Languages 2014

Chapter 9 ACTIVITIES

Abseiling
On Saturday 9th December a small group of us gathered together early to do some abseiling. We were greeted by the instructors and shown a huge wall that we had to climb down. We started our courageous journey to the top of the artificial wall. For those who are scared of heights this is not one to be recommended as it is a long way up.
Kate Scales – Year 9 (1996)

Archery Course
At the beginning of the school year, eight members of Form 5 took part in an archery course at Swaffham Leisure Centre.
Against all odds, everybody by the end of the first twenty minutes was able to propel the arrows in the vague direction of the target, some actually being able to hit it.
Over the next four weeks we improved greatly (in our opinion) and were able to play games such as darts – with arrows of course, to see who could pop the balloon in the centre of the target, and who could undo themselves the quickest when wrapped in masking tape!
Olivia Stockwell-Jones (1992)

Assault Course
On 21st June some members of Forms 1, 2, 3 and 4 took part in an assault course at RAF Marham in order to raise money for the people affected by the floods in Bangladesh.
As we arrived most people stared with open mouths and trembling knees at the ten foot walls, thirty foot scramble nets and great pools of water that lay before us. most people managed to stay dry and in one piece and we raised a total of £305.00.
Jemma Hyland (1991)

Athletics
This year we have purchased a wide selection of athletics equipment, which has meant a great deal of practising in leaping, jumping, throwing and springing. We have participated in athletics meetings competing against schools such as Hammonds, Methwold High, Downham Market High and Northgate High.
Amy Landles (1991)

Ballet
We have been running ballet classes at two levels for the past year and a half. All the children in both ballet classes have shown they are enthusiastic and willing to work hard in their class. The two 'taster' sessions in Modern Dance have proved very popular and classes will commence in the new academic year. This is another great opportunity for pupils to benefit from the pleasures of dance.
Miss Michelle AISTQD Dip –
Ballet Mistress (1998)

Barclays Bank

The new school 'Barclays Bank' was opened by Form 3 in June. Every week we collect the money together and Jane Lord, a member of Form 3, takes it all to 'Barclays Bank' in Swaffham.

We have seven people working as clerks at a time and the class is taking turns. Each person who opens an account receives a £10.00 gift voucher for OUR PRICE MUSIC and people under eleven receive a 'Barclay Bill' money box. The minimum amount to open an account with is £1.00.

The idea is to encourage people to save and manage their money efficiently.

Amy Blanch – Form 3 (1992)

Brownies & Guides

Although Units were in the town the opportunity for boarders to join had not been available until September when one of the Units, 1st Swaffham moved to meet in the Sports Hall.

The Guide Company numbers were boosted when several of the Brownie Pack reached the age of transfer to Guides and were joined by a large contingent of boarders.

A mass enrolment of 15 girls took place in November after a considerable amount of work. This candle-lit ceremony was something of a first, normally only four or five would make their Promise together.

Taking advantage of the talents of PE student, Rachel, the girls tackled their Agility Badge and even the faintest hearted got to the top of the ropes in the gym as demanded by one of the sections. All were duly awarded their badges! Also explored were other aspects of Guiding life from the basic knot tying and craft work through to a 'Back to Basics' camp under canvas during the May Bank Holiday when they were part of a camp of 60, 57 of whom had never been under canvas before! Undaunted by the experience some have signed up for another camp during the summer and are eager to venture into the opportunities offered including, an Assault Course, Archery and Abseiling.

The Brownies have enjoyed the facilities offered in the Sports Hall and have taken the opportunity to explore outside as well as inside. They too achieved their Agility Badge under the watchful eye of Mrs Upton and have served tea to parents for their Hostess Badge at an enrolment when six Brownies made their Promise in the Autumn Term.

A survey of security was part of the Crime Prevention Badge and two Brownies listed all the care they gave to their pets and were duly awarded their Friend to Animals Badge. A lot of helping at home and good turns have led to steady progress on their journeys. Father's Day was marked with the production of 'Grass Heads' and sprouting is awaited!

A residential weekend away is planned when the Brownies, together with some of the Guides, will have the opportunity to try Rock Climbing, Abseiling, Canoeing and Archery together with other more traditional pursuits of washing up and making beds – as Brownies are wont to do.

Irene Ranner – Brownie & Guide Guider (1998)

Chess Club

Chess Club was held each Friday lunch time on the balcony of the Sports Hall. There were regularly, about 18 players, the majority from Year 4, but a few from older year groups. Whilst some occasionally played at home, many were complete beginners and had to learn the moves from scratch. To accommodate these we had a Chess Leader, with the weakest players starting at the top and the strongest having to begin their attempt at climbing the ladder from the bottom rung. By the end of the school year, the pupil at the top of the ladder was Katherine Hewkin. So congratulations to her. I am sure that older sister, Samantha, will want to knock Katherine off her perch next term! Thanks must go to Freya Barlow, who came along on a number of occasions to help the more inexperienced players.

John Clements, Mathematics Teacher (2005).

John still continues with his Chess Club, although he now only works one day a week with Mathematics Learning Support (2014)

2007 Chess Club

Country Dancing

On 18th February the Tollhouse Company came to give Forms 1, 4 and 5 an afternoon of Country Dancing. We split up into pairs and then for most of the dances four pairs worked together. We walked through all of the dances once and then danced them.

I think the group that I was with should have been given a prize for enthusiasm, even though our technique was less than perfect. I am sure I speak for everybody when I say I had a brilliant time, if thoroughly exhausting afternoon.

Delwynne Ranner (1992)

Cricket

A big thank you to parents for the encouraging feed-back to this terms cricket coaching, culminating in our little match on the Open Day. With the always excellent attendance's at the practice sessions. I would like to feel that their efforts have been rewarded.

Mark Dewson - PE Coach (1998)

Crime Prevention Quiz

On Monday 11th March the 'Swaffham Crime Prevention Team', namely Catherine Symes, Anna Trett, Delwynne Ranner and Laura Lister, were prepared to take part in a quiz against Hammonds High School.

The second round was held on Wednesday, 13th March at Swaffham Court House. After a frantic revision session, the quiz began. In total there were six rounds. Each question was worth five points, which was varied according to how much or how little we knew.

The score after the first round was 15 all, but slowly Springwood crept ahead, until at the end of all six rounds, the score was 108 to Springwood and 95 to the Convent. We received

consolation prizes of a pen and a pencil. We would like to thank P.C. 'Jacko' Jackson for coaching and encouraging us throughout the quiz.
Delwynne Ranner – Form 3 (1991)

Debating Society

A senior school debating society was set up last year for Years 7 to 11. The founders were Lucy Whigham and Sarah Wright. There was much interest in our first debate, 'Should men be allowed to wear women's clothes, and vice versa? The speakers were Virginia Fitzpatrick-Swallow, Sarah Wright, Gillian Rutter and Sarah Baldry. Lucy Whigham was the Chairman. The debate concluded that men should be allowed to cross-dress.
Unfortunately, this is our first and final debate as interest waned. Thank you to all who helped to start and showed an interest in the debating society and perhaps this may be a challenge for the future.
Lucy Whigham – Year 11 (1996)

First Aid

In the spring term Year 9 participated in a six week first aid course. Our group leader was Irene and her two assistants David and Nigel. They were all from the Red Cross. During the lessons we were taught the recovery position, mouth-to-mouth, artificial respiration. Also we were told how to check if a casualty was breathing and if they had a pulse. Another subject of our lesson was bandaging. We learnt how to bandage hands, ankles and arms and then how to make slings.
At the end of our course we had an exam. During the day before our exam everyone was practising and re-capping on all the things they had learnt during the six weeks.
The exam was better than we expected and we all passed.
Hannah Morgan- Year 9 (1995)

First Aid Course

This began on 21ˢᵗ March 1990 and was to continue for six weeks. In our lessons we learnt how to treat people for shock and how to use bandages. We had a go at putting slings on each other's arms as well. One week our teacher brought in a dummy and we used this to learn artificial resuscitation and heart massage. *Dawn Bellamy Form 3 (1991)*

First Aid

Every Wednesday after school, Year 9 were taught the basics of First Aid. This six week course included resuscitation, bandaging and many other lifesaving techniques. At the end everyone passed the exam which was really hard and we all got a Red Cross Certificate.
Sarah Conway – Year 9 (1993)

Gardening Club

There will always be beautiful grounds at Sacred Heart. They reflect the communal joy in the beauty of God's floral and faunal creations. But, the Garden Club does not take credit for the park like surrounds!
The Sacred Heart Garden Club exists to foster the nurturing skills that all students need to

develop. Through propagating cuttings, germinating seeds, potting up seedlings and marketing the produce students develop confidence and gain a real sense of achievement. They wonder at the life force in living things. Team work, basic maths and social skills feature strongly. Most plants survive, although some may occasionally need replanting!

The current club runs on the model set up by Year 5 teacher, Mrs Rachael Scrafield (retired in 2012). She passed on an ethos of love, support and patience that encapsulates much of the Sacred Heart spirit.

Katherine Laban (Science & Mathematics 2014)

Graphics Club for the Lower School

This club has been started to give the boys in the Lower School an opportunity to discover more about some of the school's graphic programs. It is being run on Wednesday lunchtimes. The software that is being used is:

Serf DrawPlus X3: this is used to create vector graphic drawings and stop frame animations, we will look at creating flash type key frame animations if time allows.

Google Sketchup: this allows us to create three dimensional drawings, render them and put them into real life environments.

This hopefully, will give them a broader understanding of the power of computers and their use in the real world. In addition it will help them with their ICT work in both the lower and upper school.

David Jordan, ICT Teacher 2014)

Latin Club

Nos quattuor puellae linguam Latinam discere incepimus. De vita Pompeiana et de Caecilio qui erat argentarius Pompeianus legebamus. Multus res novas cognovimus, sed-eheu! Difficile est Latinum emendatam scriber.

Translation: We four girls have begun to learn the Latin language. We have been reading about life in Pompeii and about Caecilius who was a Pompeian banker. We have found out many new things, but – Oh dear! It is hard to write correct Latin.

This first year of Latin has helped us with grammar and word meanings in English and French, although not in German. We've found the course quite difficult but interesting.

Katharine Jennings, Phoebe Vincent –Year 7
Kate Edgecombe, Harriet Holmes – Y8 1998)

Lunchtime Activities

Scottish Country Dance

A fun session for girls and boys from Year 2 upwards is designed to introduce some basic dance steps; skip, change of step, pas de basque, slipping step and also some dance terminology. During the spring term the class mastered a dance called 'Popcorn' and have attempted to make up their own dances from the steps learned. Well done everyone – keep practising!

Basketball

This session is designed to introduce the game to boys and girls from Year 2 upwards. Dribbling, passing and shooting for a basket; man to man passing and defensive positions, also some footwork and no-contact rules have been covered. Once the basketball rings are erected progress can be made on the more complicated skills. Michael Jordan watch out!

Volleyball

This introduction to volleyball has attracted boys and girls from Year 2 upwards in two sessions – one for the Lower School and one for the Senior School. All the aspects of the game have been covered – the volley, dig, underarm serve, rotation of players, smash and some basic rules. Both classes have worked hard this year and if enthusiasm won games, we would have Gold.
Carol Price – PE Coach ~(1998)

Paint-a-thon

Another bright idea conjured up by the school council was to raise money for the sports hall by holding a 'Paint-a-thon'. It was designed by Jodie Wick and Charlotte Widdowson, but was available for the whole school to participate in the painting. It ran very well and the finished piece is now successfully completed and displayed as a 'rose window' in the gymnasium. Thank you to all who helped.
Charlotte Widdowson 1996)

Photography

For our Duke of Edinburgh Award Scheme seven members of Year 10 took part in a photography course which would cover the skill section of the award. During our course we learnt how to take better pictures, develop the film and to print our own pictures in the dark room.

Our course lasted ten weeks and we produced several masterpieces. Vaughn, our tutor, gave us the option of taking pictures of either pets or children for our final pieces, which we had good fun taking.

The course was enjoyable and I am sure that Year 10 would recommend the Duke of Edinburgh Award scheme to anyone in the future.
Helen Downing – Year 10 1996)

Pop Mime '97 - 'Stars in their Eyes'

The room was filled with a buzzing anticipation. Two young girls stepped out from behind a small screen. Attired in full 1960's costume, their eyes twinkled with excitement as they prepared to address the crowd. 'Ladies and gentlemen, welcome to this live event at the Walsingham Centre in Swaffham, and to our very own Stars in their Eyes'.

No, this wasn't a broadcast by the studios of ITV, but a modest performance by a group of talented young people who under their own direction managed to produce one and a half hours of musical entertainment and raised over £100 for the Sports Hall Fund.

Adorned in colourful costumes, and prepared to shock, amuse and amaze their audience, the groups ranged from Sixties Classics – such as 'Leader of the Pack' – which was performed on tricycles, to present day pop-bands including 'The Spicettes' and the cast of 'The Rocky Horror Show'.
Franchesca Hunt – Year 11 (1997)

Pottery

As part of the Duke of Edinburgh Course, twelve members of Year 10 had to participate in several activities in order to gain the Bronze Award. For the craft section we were given a choice between pottery and photography. Nine of the twelve chose the photography classes. The remaining three people decided on pottery. The course was to be run every week for around four months. In the first lesson we were given an introduction to our new teacher Meg and got to grips with the clay. As it was a whole new experience for all of us we started on something simple – a bowl. Even this proved too much for me, and the end result was far from a bowl. During these pottery sessions Sister Francis and Sister Jacinta frequently accompanied us and their creations included a candle holder made by Sr. Francis and Sr. Jacinta made a wonderful pot for future use in the Sister's garden.

Over the weeks, we all made good progress and our hard work soon started to show itself. Decorating tiles, bowl-making, plate decorating, moulding, designing and making a wall plaque were just a few of the many objects we made and still we have to make our final piece and colour and glaze all our other pieces. So far the pottery course has been much enjoyed and all our works will be on display when we have finished.

Louisa Jones – Year 10 (1996)

Safety First

Year 10 had a visit from a CLO (Community Liaison Officer). He came to talk to us about safety and to tell us how important it is to look after ourselves and what to do if we were ever in trouble.

* Shout for help
* Carry a personal alarm to set off
* Put a speed dial number on your phone to someone who can help or 999
* Make sure people know where you are and what time you are getting back
* Stay in crowded areas
* Stick with your friends, if one is ill never leave them
* Never leave a drink unattended

He also spoke to us about calling for help, he said that it is more effective if you call FIRE than if you call HELP because children shout help all of the time but no one shouts fire unless there is a fire.

Michelle Lane – Year 10 (2005)

School Council

The original aim of the Council was to encourage pupils to put forward suggestions and new ideas for the school. Everybody who was approached about it was enthusiastic and we agreed that we would go ahead with the 'Swaffham School Council'.

Elections were held within Year 11 and Sarah Skinner was elected Chairman, Hayley Cawthorne Vice-Chairman and Lisa Tansley Secretary. Each Year elected two representatives, and we held our first meeting on October 20th, 1995.

We had many ideas put forward, such as the Paint-a-thon, bike-sheds and new cookery hats, and I am pleased to say that many of them have been accepted and put into practice.

I have enjoyed my role as Secretary, which included writing and typing up the minutes of each meeting. I hope that Year 10 will now go on and carry further ideas forward through the school and that the Council will continue in years to come.
Lisa Tansley – Year 11 (1996)

Self Defence

Self Defence – the dictionary says and I quote: - "Protecting one's self by means of force" which is basically what it means. So as most of year 8 sat on the black mat one Thursday after school, we waited for our victims, PC Canfor and colleague.

As the weeks progressed we learnt all kinds of different and wonderful skills, such as how to break someone's leg as well as their neck.

We all passed and gained our certificates. Clare Gammell was awarded a special cup for being the outstanding student of the year and Hannah Scott was a very close second.
Rachael Bryan – Year 8 (1995)

Self-Defence Skills

BEWARE all attackers, mad loony killers and muggers! That is what all the Convent kids will be saying to their attacker just as he is about to grab them! If the shouting doesn't work, then PC Jackson's self-defence method is bound to!!

A certain member of the school, mentioning no names… found a unique way of fighting off your attacker, and trying it out on Jacko, found that it worked. Unfortunately, this person doesn't wish to have her name revealed!!
Louise Hammond, Form 4 (1989)

Team Building with the Army

It was a cold morning. I arrived at school and was promptly told to change into my PE kit and go outside, all that the class knew was that we were doing a team building exercise with a few men from the Army, but none of us knew what it entailed.

We had to line up and were divided into three groups of seven; the three groups went off to three different activities. All the different activities were based on a scenario which the Army may have to face. For each activity we had eight minutes.

For the first activity we had to get the whole group and a pretend ammunition box across an imaginary river, we could stand on the three stepping stones but you couldn't jump from one to the next, you had to use two planks of wood to get from one stepping stone to the other. It was even harder due to the fact that we could only fit five people maximum on each stepping stone.

The second activity was a barrel of toxic waste which had spilt and was upside down in a mine field and we had to turn it over the right way. All we had to use was a long piece of rope and no one could step on the minefield. The idea was that, you wrapped the rope around the barrel, twisted it until the rope was securely around it and then you could lift it out! We had the right idea of twisting the rope around the barrel, but we ran out of time.

For the third activity we were blindfolded and one person from the group had to guide the whole group through a minefield to a pretend ammunition box. We all took turns to guide the group. I thoroughly enjoyed my morning with the Army, despite when we failed or

someone 'died', or when we had to go for a run and do ten press-ups, and when we got very muddy!
Becky Nichols – Year 11 (2005)

The Clothes Show Live '96

The bright lights swirled around the giant stadium, the music pumped out the speakers as the voices of Jeff Banks and co. were heard over the cries of excitement. The models strutted their stuff in outfits designed by people such as Betty Jackson and Ben de Lisi. The line up even included Dalmatians and their male model owners! This

2005 Team Building with the Army

was the Clothes Show Live '96 and Years 10 and 11 were just a fraction of the many eager faces looking out from the audience. This was the event that we had all been waiting for and finally it was here and we were not just going to see the 'non-stop catwalk shows'. Shopping fever had seized everyone as stripy flares to cheap designer flares were snapped up by the bargain hunters.

Various modelling agencies also had their stalls and this is one reason that I have been asked to write this article because I was scouted by the international modelling agencies 'Storm'. A huge surprise considering I have braces, ginger hair and was wearing an overlarge jumper; hardly the pinnacle of the fashion world! I was asked various questions filled in a form and had a Polaroid taken. I was also given a leaflet to take home which was greeted by my mum with "they will never ring." The next day they rang asking me to come down to Sloane Square, London the HQ of Storm so they could tell me more about the agency. So, on a snowy morning about a week before Christmas I travelled down to London where I found myself sitting on a comfortable settee looking at pictures of Kate Moss in Vogue! I was told the ins and outs of the agency and compared to an already working model. I was sent a Christmas card from the agency and have been waiting for a call to do some test photos since but GCSE's are the priority for anyone in Year 11, as many people know, so I am still waiting! I have not been forgotten though and I am described as the one with the ginger hair and freckles. So ginger hair does have some advantages!

We all thoroughly enjoyed going to the Clothes Show and what I have written is just one aspect of it. Many of us have decided to go next year and I urge anyone who has the chance to go to this event – it's great fun. The only advice I would give you is to be prepared to fight the crowds for the best bargains!
Nicola Compton – Year 11 (1996)

The House Theatre Company Presents..........

At the beginning of the autumn term, a drama group was formed with Mr Steven Andrews at the helm. We were split up into two groups the 'little ones' and the 'big ones'. . The

Senior Branch decided on a farce called 'Three Bags Full' and the Junior Branch decided on a pantomime, the all original 'Cinderella'. The 'Three Bags Full' cast worked extremely hard on their performance and the end result was very good. Although, surprisingly for the first performance, the company decided to do the most difficult kind of play – a farce performed in the round.

The cast was as follows:

Mrs Rigby, .	Sara Davies;
Sylvie,	Louise Hammond;
Myra Hanson,	Caroline Sutton;
Daphne Vaughn,	Katie Mindham;
Dora Bell,	Susan Titcombe;
Mrs Treddinick,	Jessica Aistrup
Audrey Gregg,	Hayley Archer;
Mrs Smith,	Sarah Nurse

With special thanks to all who helped behind the scenes and all those who helped in the front of the House.

After many weeks and one postponement, finally, on Friday 10th February we performed. We raised £45 from the evening, which went to charity. Everyone had a great time, on and off stage and everyone was sad that it was all over.

Katie Mindham – Form 5 (1989)

The Norfolk Show

On 26th June, instead of playing games, Forms 3 and 4 spent the afternoon at the Royal Norfolk Show.

Once we got there we could see the clouds looming and had been warned that we might need Cagoules and wellies, but we had faith in the weather and ignored this advice. Halfway through the afternoon the heavens opened and where were the wellies? On the coach.

While we were at the Show, we saw a number of stalls including ones showing hundreds of different types of cheeses and their names (which I'm not even going to try to spell!) and stalls that displayed a selection of sausages with names such as Aunt Bertha or Sizzling Sizzler.

After a couple of hours, by which time we had completed our surveys, we met back at the gate, ready to return to school. So with soaking feet, stuffing sweets, holding balloons, wearing paper caps and covered with stickers, we boarded the coach and set off back to school.

Caroline Morton – Form 4 (1991)

The Riding Course

On the Thursday after the Easter holidays, 14 children rushed out of school and onto the little red bus. It was the beginning of another 6 week course at North Runcton Riding Stables. At 4 o'clock we arrived and the little children jumped off the bus and ran straight up to the rather surprised looking ponies.

The younger group learnt to walk, trot, canter, bend in and out of poles and the most important thing…they learnt to stop.

The older group had a great time walking, trotting, cantering and jumping

On the last week, both of the groups had a competition. The younger group played musical chairs on ponies and the older group 'Handy Pony'. Both groups thoroughly enjoyed this and were very pleased with the rosettes everyone received.

Alex Dalton and Ruth Paterson (1991)

The Tollhouse Company

On Wednesday, 6th February we all trooped into the gym, kitted out in our PE gear, ready to do a workshop. This was led by the Tollhouse Company.

We took partners, and after several demonstrations from the experts, we eventually managed to get ourselves into the starting positions. The music was very fast and lively, and we charged around tripping over everyone else's feet. We were very exhausted and that was only the first dance. Luckily it was time for some songs. These were very good, helping also to rest our weary bodies at the same time.

Deborah Bircham – Form 3 (1991)

Theatre Studies

When Sister Francis suggested a possible Theatre Studies course earlier this term, there was a great rush of enthusiasm. So much enthusiasm, that the pupils had to be divided into three large groups, to be taught by our new member of staff- Mrs Pickering.

So far we have only had a few lessons, but each one has been incredibly enjoyable, developing our imaginations, acting and miming skills. .

Helen Payne (1995)

Tuck Cupboard

The tuck cupboard was an idea put forward by various members of Year 11. The idea was to have sweets and chocolates available at school during break times. Sarah-Jane Cartin and Sarah Beales took on the role of Tuck Cupboard Managers and Mrs Cartin kindly went to the Cash and Carry each week to buy our stock. The cupboard now produces enough money each week to buy the stock for the next week

Rebecca Collett – Year 11 (1996)

Walking in the sun

On Friday, 4th May, the time came once again for the school sponsored walk and eager for a day without lessons, everyone arrived at school promptly. It was a very hot day, and the sun was beating down, therefore everyone turned up in shorts. That morning a multi-coloured procession of people marched out of school and into the country. With cups dangling from our belts, a lot of laughter and the sound of plodding feet, we reached the first checkpoint, nearly dying of thirst. However, still in high spirits we marched on at a quick pace, eager to reach the lunch stop.

After lunch it was time to get up and go again. No-one rose from the ground as quickly as they had sat down, but with the end of the walk only a few hours away, we plodded on, enduring the pain and smiling, despite the aching legs. .

There comes a time when you regret the fact that Swaffham is on a hill, and that is at the end of the sponsored walk. It is really disheartening when your legs are killing you, after nineteen miles, to find that the last mile is all uphill! With encouragement from Mrs Dalton, we all completed the long climb and arrived at school with smiles on our faces.

It was the time to put our cheesy feet up while we contemplated whether the effort had all been worthwhile.

Emma Reed – Form 5 (1990)

Windsurfing!

On Saturday, 9th June fifteen people from our school went down to Denver Sailing Club to go (I mean attempt to go) windsurfing!

Firstly, we had to fit on wetsuits to see what we would be wearing. This was one of the hardest parts to overcome! It felt like we were dislocating every part of our body, trying to get them on! What would it be like getting them off when they were wet!

Next we were split into three groups of five. The first group went on the simulator (which is a surfboard and sail on a type of turntable) we learnt how to turn the board and control the sail. So then the first group were allowed in the water, while we chose to watch before having a go on the simulator. The first group were allowed to have a go at balancing on their boards without the sail. They waded into the mucky water and we waited for them to fall in!

I managed to fall in a hundred times, or it seemed, windsurf into the reeds and get stuck, do seven turns and to be pleased with myself. I got back on to land and struggled out of my wetsuit, got dry and put some warm clothes on. We thanked the instructor for a great day. Next came the rush for putting our names down for the next course!

Lucy Reed – Form 2 (1990)

Year 10 Duke of Edinburgh Award

This year's, Year 10 have been an active Duke of Edinburgh group, with the majority of the class taking the award. To achieve the skills section six people took pottery, all passing. The shooting course has recently started, on Saturday mornings. The girls who took neither shooting nor pottery are half way through Theatre Studies. After we all passed the physical test, we all had to

**1991-1992 Year 10
Duke of Edinburgh Award**

prepare for the mock expedition. All went well, after we recovered from the weight of our rucksack and all the excess food and clothes we took. The practice went well. The real expedition was taken by Sarah Beales and Zoe Hale. At the same time, some of the girls did their practice. This was a record D of E year with all but one member of year 11 taking part and passing the Bronze Award.

Zoe Hale – Year 10 (1995)

PSHEE

For the third consecutive year, we suspended the timetable for a few days in order to focus on a curriculum subject. PSHEE is a subject in its own right and also over-arches the whole school experience. It supports our commitment to holistic education of the whole person and encouraging students to be self aware in their personal development. As a Catholic School we encourage students to be themselves but to make sure that self is the one God would have them be.

We invited in a number of outside speakers to share their professional experience with the school; and encouraged further, individual, high order thinking on the topics through the use of worksheets at the end of each half day. The listening, discussing and thinking were off-set by activities for well-being, undertaken in large groups to foster solidarity within the school community.

Collective reflection was a key feature of the educational experience which began with the school gathered for assembly, individually reflecting on self-image; and ended with the school gathered to reflect individually on their evaluation of all that they had participated in.

Many students expressed a great experience of community and we are very proud of this. In the world of Catholic education there is a move to explore the use of 'communion' where we have been wont to say 'community'. This is because 'community' has become somewhat diluted through wide application and use, and no longer conveys some of the sense of union beyond our own institution, and partaking in the fruits and benefits of our work and ethos that is still conveyed by 'communion'. (This is not to be confused with the Holy Communion received at mass.) As a school we will be looking at how we might develop beyond what we have experienced as community towards the experience of communion.

Frances Verne Head of PSHEE

AUTUMN 2001 PSHEE WEEK

Drill

Dancing under the Buttercross in Swaffham

Chapter 10 Physical Education

Physical Education over the years has changed dramatically, from formal drills on the field, to taster sessions for kickboxing and speed cup stacking! Girls are now expected and even encouraged to perspire! Competitive sport became more important from the late 80's and has developed into a very important part of the school curriculum. It has given all the pupils the opportunity to test their self-esteem and to challenge their physical ability. The House system was first introduced to encourage the pupil's academic ability but soon it was realised that the introduction of house sports competitions encouraged the

Drill

organisational skills of the most senior pupils, as well as promoting loyalty within the houses. One house captain describes the winter term House sporting events in his final assembly speech:

"To set the scene, Sports Hall 10:00am, the smell of fear wafts through the air. We see eagerness in the eyes of the opposition, they want to win-but so do we! We shoot, we pass, we dodge and we succeed. At this moment, I am unaware of the final score but like Tom Daley's mum, watching her son nail a triple flip backwards into the watery depths, I was proud!"

Harvey Jones Sandringham House Captain 2013-2014.

House Sport Competitions have altered over the years. The first sports day took the format from the TV programme 'It's a Knock Out'. House captains like today, had to organise their best players to suit the activity. In recent years it has been encouraged that as many pupils as possible should take part, for example in house rounders a pupil from year 5 to year 10 must be included in the team of nine.

Winter sports

Netball

Netball has always featured as a key sport in the school. Over the past three decades the netball teams have played to a high standard and have been the area winners for the U14

House Netball

and U16 age categories for many consecutive years. All girls from year 5 to year 11 play in regular fixtures against both state and independent schools, with more success stories then defeats.

Hockey

This sport has always been played with great enthusiasm, being a harder game to learn our successes over the years has been mixed. However, we have had an U16 team in 1999 win the area competition and go through to play in the final at Norwich, being the only team who drew against the county winners.

Football

With the school gaining more boys, football has appeared on the curriculum and in extracurricular activities. The U11 squad have had plenty of success against local teams and in the ISA regional tournament, Sacred Heart School narrowly missed a slot in the semi finals. History was made in March 2014. The long awaited House Football tournament was held on a lovely sunny afternoon. Sandringham took the senior trophy whilst Windsor were awarded the junior trophy.

Football

Cross Country

The sport everyone thinks they dislike but it does bring out the pupils individual determination to improve their times and stamina. The first success the school had in cross country, was when we were invited to a year 7 cross country competition at Necton Middle School. Everyone enjoyed this run with its warm and friendly atmosphere. We won the trophy over several years and were the eventual final winners at the very last race, when they presented the trophy to us to keep. Now we enter the area and ISA competitions with some amazing individual results.

Gymnastics

All pupils, particularly in the junior and lower senior school have gymnastic lessons. The pupils are always keen to meet the mental and physical demands of the sport. Back in the

1990's and 2000's, a Norfolk competition was held which we regularly attended; a nerve racking occasion especially when leaping over the high box, or not making a single mistake when performing the floor routines.

Ski Trips

It is difficult to believe that there have now been 12 amazing ski trips visiting 11 different resorts.

The first ski trip was organised in 1990, when we went to Löfer in Austria, (37 pupils and 13 adults made up the party). Sr Francis had very kindly allowed us to go in February! The holiday was jam packed with activities, obviously a lot of skiing but lots more too: visits to Salzburg, quiz night, bingo, tenpin bowling and of course Tyrolean dancing. This format

was followed in the next 3 ski trips, Valloire 1992, Folgarida 1994 and Tonale 1996.

It was then suggested that perhaps it would be easier to go by coach. This appealed as the queuing at the airport was always a nightmare. So off we went in 1998 to Montgenèvre by coach but as we started to climb the mountains, the coach began to heat up and one member of the party said her shoes were melting! We also

The Ski Trip

encountered an avalanche just after that. As you can imagine the journey was not as restful as we had hoped, so on the next trip to Le Corbier 2000, we went back to flying, which continued until the last trip organised by Mrs Young to Bormio in 2006.

Miss Foster was keen to continue the biennial ski trip but decided that the only way to travel was by coach, coaches had improved by then and we arrived at St Gervais, France, in no time. She also organised the next trip in 2010 to Alpe d'Huez. Finally, Miss Wilson arrived; also very keen to continue the ski trip, she found a perfect resort in the Aosta Valley, Italy, called Pila. Again the trips have been action packed but with the added advantage of a fantastic town, both historical and great for shopping!

Mrs Young said "I have enjoyed all the trips, all very different, with amazing pupils; it's always great to see how they all improve during the week. I have been very privileged to have been able to take part in all 12 trips and I would like to thank the school for allowing them take place. However, I need to say a big thank you to all the staff who supported me when I was responsible for the trip. They would not have taken place without you. Thank you!"

Mazoe Young Former Head of PE

Summer Sports

During the summer there never seems to be enough time to enjoy all the activities that are available to the pupils. Everyone loves playing rounders, splashing in the pool, speeding around the track and playing a leisurely game of tennis. Due to the summer sports being a more individual competitions, the senior boys have been able to compete.

Tennis

Tennis has always been an important game with pupils not only playing against local schools but having in the past the opportunity to play at Queenswood. Due to our involvement over the years in tennis, we have been given the opportunity to go to Wimbledon, to experience the wonderful play and general atmosphere of the whole day. What a wonderful experience, and last year we saw ANDY MURRAY!

Athletics

What a wonderful sport for all. You hear pupils saying "Oh Miss I can't run" but they soon realise there is an event for everyone. Athletics has become very popular from year 4 to 11, especially with the opportunity to take part in the ISA Athletic competitions each summer. Since the London Olympics, Athletics has really become exciting and the pupils love competing for a chance to be on the podium. At the last ISA Athletic event the senior team brought home 22 medals, a fantastic achievement! Those that do not get selected for the athletics teams, still get a chance to compete for their house in the annual House Sports Day. This is a mixture of serious and light heated events, a great day for competitors and spectators alike.

Rounders

This is perhaps the favourite activity, in the summer there is nothing better than hitting the ball over your peers heads and then running as fast as you can from post to post, watching of course, for the fielders doing their best to try and get you out, not this time! Rounder to Sacred Heart! It is not only a social game but also is very important in developing team spirit, learning to work and relying on other players. Competitions are also played against local schools and many times we have returned with smiley faces.

Swimming

How lucky we are to have our own pool. All the pupils have been able to take, sometimes daily, a dip in the well heated pool. Over the past years there must have been hundreds of pupils taking their first strokes, before coming real water babies. The swimming gala has always been the highlight of the end of the summer term events and I am sure you could hear the shouts of encouragements from afar.

The Annual Swimming Gala

Games Captains

Each year a games captain has been selected to assist the PE Department run practices, select teams, and inspire the pupils at Sacred Heart School. Thank you to all those who have taken on the responsibility and led the school to so many great successful sporting achievements.

For many years, the pupils of Sacred Heart School have proven that with hard work, determination and team work great results can be produced. Every child that has entered the Sacred Heart Changing rooms has had the opportunity and experience to belong to a team, whether it be the school netball, cross country or a house sports team. The rules, tactics and kit may have changed throughout the years, but one thing has always remained the same, and will always remain, Sacred Heart pupils know how to win and lose with grace and dignity.
Rachel Wilson Head of P.E. 2014

House Sports

Year	Games Captain	Year	Games Captain
2013-2014	Phoebe Dent Richard Keating	2000-2001	Laura Larwood
2012-2013	Olivia Ruppert Aimee Shaw	1999-2000	Rebecca Keane Gorgina Newling
2011-2012	Naomi Coates	1998-1999	Poppy Thompson
2010-2011	Sophie Newby	1997-1998	Alexa Hastings
2009-2010	Francesca Grapes	1996-1997	Helen Downing
2008-2009	Rebecca Newby	1995-1996	Hannah Howard
2007-2008	Amber Dugdale	1994-1995	Elissa Hyland
2006-2007	Megan Coombes	1993-1994	Laura Bloomfield
2005-2006	Nell Forbes-Robertson	1992-1993	Anna Marie Clifford
2004-2005	Kerry Sumner Tara Dugdale	1991-1992	Olivia Stockwell Jones
2003-2004	Charlotte Hankins Julia Chapman	1990-1991	Catherine Symes
2002-2003	Harriet Maule	1989-1990	Ineke Bell
2001-2002	Jonquil Rix	1988-1989	4 House Games Captains

Chapter 11 ART

The Art Department's ethos is that every child has the ability to be creative in some way.

The Sacred Heart in Norfolk Triptych

created to celebrate our centenary

Over and above our regular lessons, pupils are taught a wide range of skills enabling them to produce interesting and creative work, using a range of different techniques. We have introduced holiday challenges, where pupils are encouraged to show their imaginative and creative abilities in any way they wish, on a given subject. This has produced some truly outstanding responses, from subjects as diverse, as Sardine cans to Angels.

Another innovation has been the introduction of several projects involving the whole school, to produce very large pieces of art work. Picasso's Weeping Woman in 144 squares, Mother Theresa in 88 squares, which travelled to London for an exhibition to commemorate her death. Our most recent work is a mosaic triptych of the Sacred Heart of Jesus in Norfolk, to celebrate our centenary year this year.

Over the years the Art department has been fortunate to develop strong links with the Sainsbury centre at the UEA. We regularly take groups of children to see and respond to their wonderful exhibitions, most notably those of the Surreal friends, Hedsor and Mary Webb. Inspired by these we in turn put on two full scale exhibitions of our own, where we have invited the gallery organisers and guides to visit. These were a great success and raised funds for the Swaffham Home Hospice from refreshments and card sales of our work. Most recently we have been lucky enough to see the Great Masterpieces of East Anglia, a wonderful confection of art and artefacts with strong connections to East Anglia. We were also given the opportunity to see the Houghton Revisited exhibition, another once in a lifetime bringing together of great masterpieces under one roof. A great privilege.

In addition to these enterprises, we exhibit pupils work as part of the Norfolk Open Studios initiative, during the summer term, where all pupils have an opportunity to showcase their achievements to their families and the general public. Selected pupils work is also entered in the annual ISA Art competition, as well as other local and national competitions when appropriate, with very good results.
Meg Heale Art, Pottery and HE teacher 2014

Chapter 12 MUSIC

On researching events in the Music Department since the 75th anniversary in 1989, one "constant" became immediately apparent - Sr Thomas More. Since then, and before, she has consistently participated in, or helped support the many and varied activities, whether on a weekly, annually or "one off" basis.

In 1992, together with peripatetic teacher Mr Eddie Seales, Sr Thomas More helped reform the orchestra from existing smaller groups. The very same year they participated in the Swaffham Festival of Youth and won the first prize. Since then the orchestra has endured with ever changing size and instrumentation, taking a leading role in concerts, carol services and masses. The Senior Choir has also been very active, taking part in numerous concerts and festivals both at school and in the wider community. They appear to have become a "fixture" at the Royal British Legion's annual Festival of Remembrance.

In1997 singers from years 4 to 6 took part in the Junior Proms at the Royal Albert Hall. In 2000 the Junior Choir was formed for children in years 2 to

Sr Thomas More

4. In the same year the Junior Music Group expanded into a Junior Training Orchestra to accommodate the numerous Lower School pupils studying with the growing group of peripatetic teachers.

2006 The School Orchestra

In 2003 the Music Department moved into its impressive new accommodation in the Barn Arts Centre. This enabled class lessons, orchestra and choir practices, individual lessons and even concerts to take place in the same building, bringing an even greater unity.

GCSE Music was first offered to pupils in 2000 as an optional, after school activity. It soon proved

The Band

popular and has subsequently been a timetabled option choice for Year 10 and 11 pupils. A huge part of GCSE Music is composing. This has been received with great enthusiasm. Pupils as young as Year 3 undertake creative activities and gradually build on their acquired composing skills over the years. There have been many masterful pieces composed with examples being performed at concerts both at home and abroad! Sasha Fountain stunned pupils and staff at the Convent in Prague in 2012 by performing one of her moving compositions.

The House Music Festival was first introduced during the academic year 1986/87 with pupils competing for the Constable Music Shield. Since then this has grown into an ever increasingly popular annual event with independent, visiting adjudicators and a wider variety of solos and ensembles. The "Mystery Item" was introduced in 2002, initially for that festival only, but has been included by popular demand in every successive year. An original composition class has also been included for both individuals and small groups. It has been a pleasure to welcome back former musical pupils Sarah Skinner, Alicia Eldridge, Felicity Jemmett, Helen Harvey and Sarah Inman as adjudicators.

On occasions there has been the opportunity to participate in extra activities. These include Douglas Coombes workshops, African drumming and Spoons workshops, Music Technology seminars, a concert performance of Joseph and the Amazing Technicolour Dreamcoat in Cambridge, a stage performance of General Mickey at the Corn Exchange in Kings Lynn and Back to Broadway Musical Summer School.

Many individual pupils have achieved great musical success, gaining impressive ABRSM examination results and high grades at GCSE. Chloe Faulkener has forged a career in music technology. Tiffany Rivett, who delighted audiences with her accomplished violin solos, is studying at the Royal Welsh College of Music. Hannah Hodges auditioned and gained a place at Trinity College Saturday School in 2012. In 2007 Francesca Grapes was selected as a chorister at Norwich Cathedral.

Music at the Sacred Heart is alive and well. Who knows what achievements we will witness in the future?

Jane Harvey (Head of Music 2014)

Chapter 13 ICT

Commodores, BBC Bs, Acorns, Laptops and Ipads

My introduction to computers came about because I discovered one lurking in the Year 6 classroom. I had no idea how it worked but luckily there were some 10 year olds who were much more clued up than I was. We spent a lot of time playing a game which was like tennis and I decided that I had better get up to speed on this new technology.

2013/2014 ICT

With the new Middle School building came an IT room which housed our first network, with BBC B computers and a dot matrix printer which clattered away happily when commanded to print. Technology didn't move quite so fast in those days and the BBC computers served us well until we were able to upgrade to Acorns and colour printing.

Our next stop was Windows, 'Dos is dead', I was told and the new desktop icons which launched the software certainly made life easier for the users. Large floppy disks became small floppy disks, which didn't actually flop and the dot matrix printer was banished as inkjets and colour printing became more affordable. The school office had a computer and so did Sister Catherine; the technology was spreading. Other classrooms had standalone machines and printers however, the future was a network.

As the number of computers grew Sister Francis decided that we needed help to keep everything working, enter Mr Philip Riedlinger and Mr John Sorrell. The two of them were brilliant at sorting out problems and they made sure that things ran as smoothly as possible. Technology always seems to sense when you are in a hurry to complete a task and we were finding that the old network was struggling. Mr Sorrell to the rescue, he is an electrician and also a Lion, who just happened to know the right person. Mr Peter Young, who I had never met, volunteered to give up some evenings and start the rewiring of our computer system which would enable us to have a school wide network. Mr John Williamson also arrived to get the internet set up. For a while the two of them were a bit like the characters in the fairy story, 'The Elves and the Shoemaker', they came at night, things happened and I came into school next morning to discover what new delights had been installed. Mr Young of course is still with us and when we did meet I soon discovered that I would be set to work during the holidays, drilling holes, taking computers apart and standing on the top of ladders hanging on to cables.

The last 25 years have been tremendous fun and I have learnt such a lot. Mr Young has made it possible to have over 100 computers in the school, pupils and staff are able to use laptops on the system. Projectors are in many classrooms, quiet colour laser printers print our work and most of the time everything works. In our centenary year iPads will be coming into classrooms as a mobile resource and as the internet in Swaffham is upgraded to fibre, download speeds should improve dramatically. The future for technology is both exciting and challenging. 'What's not to like!'

Vivienne Phillips IT teacher (1987 to the present)

Chapter 14 ENGLISH AND DRAMA DEPARTMENT

Over the years, Sacred Heart pupils have turned their hand to many a literary and dramatic endeavour, from declaiming Wordsworth and performing the works of The Bard, to selecting the nation's favourite read and excelling in L.A.M.D.A. examinations. Throwing themselves enthusiastically into all that they do, our young people never fail to demonstrate their many talents and discover the joy that is to be derived from rising to a challenge!

Theatre visits have been an important part of the pupils' curriculum enrichment programme and while William Shakespeare has formed a valuable core of their theatrical experience, pupils have also seen 'Hobson's Choice', 'The Woman In Black', 'War Horse', 'The Caucasian Chalk Circle', 'A Lion In Winter', 'The Crucible', 'An Inspector Calls', 'Carrie's War' and 'All My Sons' in recent years at both local and national venues. In addition, we have enjoyed visits from touring theatrical companies such as 'Black Cat' and more recently, from King's Lynn with 'The Tempest' workshop.

Back in 1990, *Grace Chambers* wrote about Form Three's visit to the Theatre Royal, Norwich, to see The Royal Shakespeare Company's production of 'A Midsummer Night's Dream',

> This play was fantastic. It was humorous nearly all the way through. The actors
>
> had a good relationship with the audience, making them laugh, young and old.
>
> The scenery and costumes were mediaeval gothic. The fairies weren't dainty
>
> but naughty, living in a 'rubbish tip land'.

The pupils were fortunate enough to be watching Kenneth Brannagh's production in which Emma Thompson and Richard Briers were performing and this is what raised *Glenys Russell's* expectations.

> I immediately expected a humorous performance and was particularly interested,
>
> having seen them both perform on television, to see how they acted on stage.
>
> All the human Athenians were dressed in traditional Greek, almost 'statue'-like
>
> clothing – whereas the very comical workmen were dressed in contrasting present
>
> day wardrobe. This gave an abstract effect when both groups were on stage together'.

In 1992, George Bernard Shaw's 'Pygmalion' was greatly enjoyed by Forms Three and Four at The National Theatre. Following a backstage tour, pupils watched an 'excellent' production in which Frances Barber, whom today's pupils might recognise from 'Doctor Who', gave a 'very believable and well-portrayed' performance as Eliza Doolittle. *Emma Marie Clifford* ended her school magazine piece writing, 'I advise anyone who is visiting London to go and see it at The National'.

roles. Presentations have included 'Romeo and Juliet', 'The Taming of the Shrew', 'Much Ado About Nothing', 'Macbeth', Twelfth Night' and 'A Midsummer Night's Dream'. One year pupils engaged in a pageant, dressed in approximations of Elizabethan costume and playing appropriate instruments as strolling players. Several scenes were enacted in the Buttercross to a large and appreciative audience of parents and passers-by. Undaunted by the problems of traffic noise, our pupils sang and 'strutted' their 'hour upon the stage' but unlike the Scottish King who lamented life's toils, *their* efforts were triumphant! 'I am happy to do it because I'll never have another chance to take part in a performance of Shakespeare in public in the street!' (*Naomi Coates*, Year 10, 2011).

Dramatising set texts enables students to explore language and nuance more closely; to experiment with different interpretations of lines and scenes and to arrive at an interpretation of the playwright's ideas and attitudes which might otherwise prove elusive. They can then analyse and discuss these scenes with far greater familiarity and understanding.

The Shakespeare Experience has fostered some backstage talents among the staff in areas such as lighting and sound, costume, scenery and music. Additionally, a number of us learned to apply stage make up; this was harder than it looked! In the early days of The Bard in the Barn, Mrs. Payne (*Melody Payne's* mother) very kindly assisted the staff with

make-up, passing on professional tips and bringing her expertise to bear on the more elaborate requirements of a range of protagonists, sprites and witches! Parents, Mrs. Webster and Mrs. Hopkinson and, former pupil, *Emma Nickerson*, also generously gave up their time to apply the greasepaint and soothe pre performance nerves! Similarly, Year 8 pupils have been given the opportunity to apply for the position of Stage Hand and successful applicants also supported the performance as prompts, lighting assistants and scenery movers, learning a great deal in the process.

The Bard in The Barn

Such is the commitment of the pupils that one even arrived in a neck brace following a horse riding accident, and another with a broken arm, to perform their parts! Pupils speak fondly and wryly of collisions with trees and crosses; squashed feet and twisted ankles and yet the overwhelming memories appear to be of evenings of 'great success…where the comical situations made the whole experience enjoyable and memorable', (*Freya Barlow*, Year 10, 2006) but also of the disappointment 'because it was over' (*Gemma Mott*, Year 9, 2005). 'After months of practising, weeks of sleepless nights, well for the staff, we finally finished. Now we can reflect on all the fun and laughter that we had'. (*Claire Morgan*, Year 10, 2006). 'After the performance as I lay in bed that night, I felt excited and proud of the whole class as they had done so well. Now I just want to do the whole performance again!' (*Megan Combes*, Year 9, 2005).

Much the same might have been said by pupils in 2008, when the entire Senior school returned to the South Bank to visit a variety of venues, including The Globe Theatre, followed by a backstage tour at the National. Here, we were introduced to some of the life-size horse puppets which featured in the ground-breaking production of 'War Horse'. This extraordinary play, an adaptation of a Michael Morpurgo novel, left us tremendously moved and astonished at some of the spectacular effects – the drum revolve which was used to create an eerie no man's land and an enormous replica of a German tank which, when pitted against a single horse, brought into sharp focus, the scale of the task faced by our forces in the Great War.

Another gripping production was Stephen Mallatratt's dramatization of the Susan Hill novel, 'The Woman In Black' which was the final stop of the 2007 London visit.
Ellie Shergold wrote,

> Like every London trip, it was an early start and a late finish. Years Ten and Eleven went to London for Drama and Art. This included watching a performance at the Fortune Theatre of 'The Woman In Black' before which we took part in a workshop In the Theatre Museum (Covent Garden)

National Poetry Day is now an established fixture in the school calendar, delighting pupils, parents, teachers and visitors alike with the extraordinary inventiveness of those involved. The topics, which have included Stars, The Future and Dreams, are selected by The Poetry Society and then responded to by schools across the country in ways of their choosing. The value of learning poetry by heart has been recognised once again both pedagogically and psychologically. At the Sacred Heart, contemporary poems are balanced with works from our literary heritage for pupils to learn, helping to cement the importance of this skill in a young person's psyche; we also hope to foster a love of the language and rhythms of the poetic voice in its many forms.

 The event provides an opportunity to bring the whole school together and observe the ways in which the children progress in knowledge and understanding as they employ a range of methods to present their poems, sometimes serious, sometimes humorous, to an appreciative audience. One notable highlight included a whole school community recitation of William Wordsworth's 'I wandered lonely as a cloud…' as each person wore a daffodil brooch in support of the Marie Curie charity which was aiming to break the record for the largest number of people reciting a poem at once as part of its publicity. Ancillary staff and parents joined us on this occasion!

 The Bard In The Barn has become a firm favourite in the school's calendar. We have been delighted by the excitement and anticipation which the event always generates. The considerable achievements of Sacred Heart pupils in mastering some of the most powerful and technically demanding lines in English Literature in order to bring them to life on stage as part of their Key Stage Three and Four work have not only enhanced their understanding of their set texts but created some wonderful memories to treasure. It has been the department's philosophy to present scenes from the chosen plays rather than whole plays in order to provide all students with the opportunity to master substantial

175

Year Nine pupils wrote most feelingly about their experiences of our 2013 double bill, 'Romeo and Juliet' and 'Macbeth'. 'I felt as if the stage made everyone and broke no one. We all shone!' wrote *Victoria Hill* (Year 9). **Lilly Wallis** continues, 'In Act One, Scene Five, I could sense the whole class felt totally united in the atmosphere… everyone cooperated beautifully and was proud that the scene impressed and entertained the audience. It felt particularly satisfying to hear the audience's laughter when it was intended'. She also spoke of the 'unity and friendship' between Years Nine and Ten. *Fionnuala Lewis* explained, 'I proved to myself that I can learn long duologues…I found that by having such a large part in a scene, I could overcome my fear of acting in front of other people'. *Antony Clark* summed it up simply by saying, 'I loved every minute of it and I want to do it again'.

After superb performances from both casts of Year Nine and Ten pupils, the performance to the school took place the next day on a themed 'own clothes' day. We had unfortunately failed to anticipate that footwear might prove an issue but ultimately, we thought that the Capulets and Montagues cut a sartorial dash in their capes, 'hose' and… Converse baseball boots! Another Shakespearian first!

Our pupils have also had notable successes in writing competitions such as the Independent Schools' Association Essay and Creative Writing Competitions (*Emily Wright*, Year 8; *Rosalind Peters*, Year 10) and Sophie Willis' (Year 9) haiku sequence was the winning poem in Swaffham's lottery bid for a sensory garden. In 2007, Francesca Grapes won a place as a judge on the Booktrust Teenage Prize panel with her winning short story. *Hannah Lacy* and *Rosalind Peters* progressed to the regional heats for the BBC's 'Hardspell' competition and in the Ottaker's Bookshop Poetry Competition (2006), held in conjunction with National Poetry Day, we had many successful entrants. *Eleanor Steinfeldt* and *Daisy Stonach* (Year 6), *Emily Wright* (Year 7), *Phillippa Hood* (Year 8)**,** *Emma Goldsney***,** *Michelle Lane* and *Colleen Whittred* (Year 10) were all shortlisted and received prizes whilst Daisy and Colleen received additional honours and their entries were submitted to the next stage of the competition.

Drama has had a long and lively history at the Sacred Heart School. It encompasses Speech and Drama lessons which culminate for most pupils in L.A.M.D.A. examinations and successes, Drama lessons up to Key Stage Three and Drama as a G.C.S.E. option.

Catherine Hill, Speech and Drama teacher and Mrs. Valerie Pickering's predecessor, enjoyed many excellent results amongst her pupils at all levels from Grade One to Gold Medal as we do today. Drama Evenings were also held to showcase the pupils' work and entertain parents and friends. *Victoria Osler* **and** *Isabelle Retzlaff* of Form Five described one such extravaganza in 1992,

> Shakespearian characters met Mole and Ratty; dulcet tones overlapped with the
>
> searing sound of violins in a hairdressing salon…what could we be describing? A
>
> Music and Drama Evening, of course! The brain-child of Mrs. Hill and Mr. Carter

flowed with class and style despite one red-faced pupil who forgot her words.

Nowadays, we enjoy watching Mrs. Pickering and her daughter, Mrs. Alexandra Bhundia's L.A.M.D.A. pupils take to the stage to share with us their examination pieces every year. It is a delight to witness the confidence with which some of our very youngest pupils give dramatic readings of humorous poems and perform much-loved pieces from musical theatre. We are then just as likely to be plunged into serious and challenging texts, requiring our older pupils to exhibit a range of dramatic skills and knowledge that can only leave us feeling impressed by the maturity of their understanding and their sense of purpose. The award of *Rachel Mumford's* Speech and Drama teaching Diploma from Trinity College, London, at the age of sixteen in 2012, was a notable achievement.

Judging by Mrs. Hill's yearly reports, it became fraught around examination time with 'extra lessons in the lunch hour, after school and even extra days...the adrenalin flows high'. She might indeed be describing the situation *today* as examinations loom, for little changes both in Speech and Drama and with the current G.C.S.E. performance examination, the culmination of two years' work and 40 % of pupils' total mark. The latter has changed considerably over the years and now requires twelve hours of filmed workshops and practical performance examinations for which the theme is set by the examination board. As always, the Sacred Heart pupils have met those challenges with creativity and imagination. With workshops on subjects as diverse as 'Tomorrow's World', Oppression and 'A View From The Bridge', pupils have gone on to produce their own devised performances on a range of topics from great women of history, slavery, and the future, to 'plays [which] must make the audience stop and think', the brief for 2013. This was the first year in which boys had taken the G.C.S.E. and coincidentally, the first time a performer had had to be pushed on in a wheel chair after an accident just ten days before the examination! Undaunted, the show went on, as it must!

In addition, Adrian Connell, Musical Director and Producer for the Norfolk Youth Theatre has staged two productions over the years, 'Vackees' a World War Two drama and family favourite, 'Oliver!' The latter took place in July 2006 after months of Sunday rehearsals during the Spring and Summer terms. Pockets were picked, more gruel was begged and complex dance and vocal numbers were learnt as the production slowly came together. The pupils showed great dedication, attending weekend after weekend , whilst a small band of willing parents turned their hands to acting, costume sourcing, wardrobe and backstage duties. The final performances were warmly received and the skill of the pupils admired. I wonder if Mr. Hodges still remembers his lines and his time in the spot light?

The Book Buddies reading scheme is one of which the English Department is very proud. Its ability to build bridges between the Junior and Senior School is vitally important, both socially and educationally. Senior school pupils now volunteer to partner pupils in Years 3 to listen to them read each week. The initiative creates a sense of responsibility in the older pupils and an understanding of the part they play as role models. The juniors enjoy the experience of reading to the older pupils and look forward to their weekly sessions. In turn, the Senior students learn much about how to listen sensitively and ask pertinent questions. They also experience the satisfaction of watching their book buddies' reading skills and confidence develop during the course of the year.

Past pupils have commented:

Book Buddies is fun and I like getting a sticker! I enjoy reading longer books and working on my expression. *Aaron Blatch* (Year 2)

Book Buddies

I like reading to new people. *Olivia Howard* (Year 2)

I enjoyed Book Buddies because it was nice to be the person who was read to rather than being the reader! I gained a lot of patience in waiting for my Book Buddy to figure out a new or difficult word. *Abbey Morgan-Short* (Year 7)

I have learnt from being a Book Buddy that if you want children to listen and learn, you have to make reading fun. *Hannah Dolman* (Year 7)

Literature encourages us to look outside ourselves, providing a window through which to view the lives of others. Consequently, it can also foster empathy, that most vital of senses. Literature can delight and transport; it can comfort, enlighten and teach us. It is one of the keys to opening the door to the belief in 'service before self'. Encouraging reading in the Senior School is, therefore, vitally important and Library lessons help to achieve this at Key Stage Three. Pupils have enjoyed completing Reading Awards in addition, over the years, to participating in book fairs and listening to visiting authors and actors giving dramatised readings of their own or classic works of literature. A number of year groups have established reading groups, selecting a range of modern texts to read and discuss and we have regularly shadowed the CILIP Carnegie Prize for Children's Literature. This last venture has proved popular over the years as we try, between April and June, to race our way through a shortlist of up to eight contemporary novels and then predict which text will win the coveted prize. We are often accurate in our predictions and the meetings are an opportunity for the lively exchange of views and ideas and the consumption of much fruit and cake! Whether, in the twenty-first century, we choose to digest fiction via electronic devices or more old fashioned paper methods, our young people still relish a good story! Long may it continue!

Wendy Padley (English and Drama 2014)

Chapter 15 BOARDING HOUSE

While the last quarter of our Centenary has seen so many additions and innovations in every aspect of the school, there has been one distinct casualty, as the Boarding House fell victim to the social and political changes that have come about.

In 1989 the Boarders' annual magazine report was still reflecting the special relationship that boarding brought to the school. Often a third of a senior school class would consist of boarders who would regale the day girls with their adventures. The fact that the boarders were a close-knit community from ages 11 to 16 made for a cohesive atmosphere throughout the school.

Parties, barbecues and outings were reported on with great enthusiasm throughout the period and regular tribute was paid to matron, Mrs Wilding, and her successor, Mrs Phemister, who ruled with a kindly, but firm, hand.

A regular army of foreign Sisters and students brought a breath of fresh air to the Boarding Experience; but, with the social upheavals of the 21st century, there is little call for boarding today.

Reporting in 2005, on a Hawaiian Night, a Year 7 boarder wrote, "We all paraded in Hawaiian costumes before going for cocktails in the dining room. Mally had prepared an exotic meal which we all very much enjoyed. Afterwards we really had fun when we all took turns to walk down the catwalk while Miss Dixon commentated. Then each dormitory presented a Hawaiian performance and St Mary's won.
It was all topped off by a team quiz run by Freya. This was a fun night and we all hope we have many more times like this."
The real flavour of the last quarter of the Sacred Heart School's Centenary can be found in the annual reports which appeared regularly in the School Magazines covering most of that period. The Head Teacher's report was often bolstered by reports from the Junior School and from the Boarding House. *Summary by Valerie Mann*

Life in the Boarding House 1989
"CINDERELLA"
On 10th February, 1989, the House Theatre Company consisting of Boarders performed a play titled "Cinderella". The cast was as follows:

Buttons	Laura Traylon
The Ugly Sisters	Clare Jones , Jessica Hilton
Cinderella	Lucy Williams
Baron Hard-up.	Sophie Goodale
Fairy Godmother	Alex Dalton
The King	Dawn Bellamy
The Queen .	Simone Grafton
The Prince	Danielle Churchill
The Rabbit/ Messenger	Karina Vandamere

We all practised for weeks on end, working very hard, and gradually the play began to take shape. Then on the big day, we performed in front of a large audience, we did very well and Mr Andrews, our director, was very pleased with us. Altogether, we raised £45, a great success. ... We all enjoyed doing this play and are looking forward to the next production.

Alex Dalton Junior 4

1990

The first party to take place this year was the Halloween party. We had a mixed selection of Frankensteins, witches, wizards, ghosts, ghouls and goblins! We thought that it was necessary to play the legendary chocolate game. We also had people sticking their bare feet into eyeballs, tendons and human livers! I think that this party was thoroughly enjoyed by everybody who took part.

The second party of the year was the Christmas party. Again this was a huge success, we gave it a theme of Hollywood Boulevard where everybody had to dress up as their favourite Hollywood character. We had everybody from James Dean and Marilyn Monroe to Roger Rabbit and Rambo. Yet again we played the chocolate game but instead of using the traditional two furry dice we used ... Charlotte! Who after being rolled around on the floor screamed a number, depending on how hard she had been pushed. After sharing out the presents from underneath the tree nobody went away empty-handed. Good luck to next years' organisers, it's hard work, especially trying to convince Woolworths that we needed their Halloween window displays more than they did!!!

Some of the younger members of the boarding house made their own production of 'Alice in Wonderland'. After weeks of practice it was finally performed in front of families and friends at a Music and Drama evening in the gym at school. Everybody who took part enjoyed themselves very much.

Sophia Root Form 5

1991 Junior Boarders' Activities

This year there are seventeen junior boarders. The first exciting event we had was a Halloween party, where we all dressed up in Medieval clothes and Sarah Goddard won the competition. We had a lovely party, and after that we came in and had hot dogs.

Next came the Christmas party. After prep we had a lovely tea, with crackers and a bag of sweets. Then we went to the activity room in the Infant school and we played lots of games. We played Ladders, Musical Statues, Musical Bumps and we had a dancing competition. The Juniors went to bed later than usual and everybody really enjoyed themselves.

In March there was a Festival of Youth. Most of the Juniors took part in the singing competition against other schools. At the end we all got a certificate.

Now it is the summer term, and all the boarders are allowed to go swimming after tea. Sometimes on special occasions we are allowed to play tennis on the courts.

We have both enjoyed being boarders this year very much.

Kara Goddard and Joanna Aitken, Junior 3

1994 Memories of Boarding

Well, what a year it has been.

I began Year 11, thinking how slowly my last year was starting to go. But how wrong I was.

What, with lots and lots of hard work, hard play, and coping with little boarders, time was passing by very quickly. (As they say, "time flies when you're having fun" – or not as the case may be!!)

Sister Thomas More began the year again as Provincial Superior.

Sister Catharine is the Superior again, and Sister Agnes has returned being her usual busy self.

While Yvonne was ill Sister Jacinta was our gallant cook and discussed menus with us.

Unfortunately Mrs Wilding and Mrs Beardsall have both had operations on their eyes. I hope it was nothing to do with looking after us, because Sister Emilia took over!

Last year, Sister Vedrana exchanged places with Sister Gabriella (now called Sister Danica) and works at the Croatian / Bosnian Mission in London. The Mission sends medicines and food to their war-torn country, and Sister Vedrana was fortunate enough to travel with the UN Convoy, thus enabling her to visit her mother, who lives in the village where so many were massacred.

Aurore de Rochefort, a French student from Orleans, came to stay with us for the Autumn Term. And, I'm sure that Aurore found her stay here very useful. I hope that she has learnt as much English as we did French!

The Christmas holidays were soon upon us, after the usual rigmarole of the Halloween and Christmas parties – successfully organised by myself and Alex!!

The beginning of the Spring Term saw all the boarders spending most of their time talking about their Christmas pressies, and the all-night wild parties which had been attended! Tension in the house began to grow as "Emma and Alex were becoming intolerable over their mock GCSEs." However, we survived them, and then enjoyed a fun-packed half term. The remainder of the term was jam-packed with visits to drama evenings and playing basketball with our very own Michael Jordan – Sister Danica!!

Although Alex and I have been working "very hard" for our exams, this Summer Term has definitely been the best.

We were joined by three French students, Edwige Delcroix, Sophie Lemaignen and Colombine Ribault-Menetiere. They have livened up the boarding house, and I'm sure that they have benefitted from their stay.

The boarders' free time during the last few weeks of the term has been used up by playing tennis and swimming. But while they were slaving away during prep, Alex and I relaxed to watch Wimbledon, or to cheer on Ireland in the World Cup.

All there is left to say is "Goodbye to the Sisters and staff, and thanks for all their help." And of course thanks to the boarders – what an experience this year has been. –

I'll miss you all!

Emma Thompson, Boarders Prefect

1995
The Boarders Report

The initial problem for the present Year 10 boarders was to organise the annual Halloween party. This involved preparation for the 'chocolate game' and 'apple bobbing', a game in which Sister Francis played an active part. The boarders all participated in dressing up as the 'Adams Family' and other spooky characters....

As Christmas drew near, there were requests for a Christmas performance. Sister Francis produced the script, to be directed by Mrs Morgan. This was then successfully acted out by the boarders. After many rehearsals we decided that what we needed was to have a rehearsal in the actual place of performance – Hermitage Hall, where we were able to use the swimming pool and other fitness facilities available. The night finally arrived and all seemed to go well.

The next event on the calendar was the Christmas Party! Santa surprised our youngest boarder, Nadia Mullins, aged six, with an unexpected appearance. Small presents were handed out from Santa's sack to all the boarders, including Year 10. The party was thoroughly enjoyed by all.

Over the past year there have been several arrivals and departures from and to various countries. Kazuko, from Japan, fascinated us with her Origami and Japanese cuisine. Her visit sparked off a number of activities such as Japanese dancing. To do this you need to be graceful and delicate, which we were not, but it was very relaxing. A Japanese evening was arranged and was a great success with some of the boarders helping Kazuko and Mrs Racey prepare the delicious food....

Other arrivals included Lucija from Croatia and Virginie from France, who came to join us for a few weeks to learn English. Our foreign friends who left us were Vesna, Snyezena and Valentina, all citizens of Croatia, and during their stay they helped us to understand the suffering of their country.

During the Winter and Spring terms, Sister Francis kept the younger boarders amused by creating activities for them to participate in. These included the making of dough figures and masks.

Mrs Acton taught us how to make Chinese spring rolls which we all enjoyed and later in the year we sampled a full Chinese meal. An Indian evening was also arranged with Mr and Mrs Doran hosting the event with a collection of slides and interesting artefacts on display.

..... The weekend of the 13th of May saw some of the boarders in Paris, walking down the Champs Elysee and climbing up the Eiffel Tower. The unfortunates who couldn't go, were given full details, on all the views, more than once, so that made up for our disappointment of not going. During the summer term tennis and swimming after supper were the 'in' thing as was Wimbledon on TV. The entire year has been very successful and has passed by rapidly. We are looking forward to doing it all over again.

Emily Fitzpatrick Swallow and Lucy Whigham, Y10

1996

This year was my best so far. New rules were made to make the boarding better for us. Much of the long winter was spent doing art and craft with Sr Francis or going to local drama productions... Boarding is like belonging to a second family, even if we don't always get along, and it's great being a part of that special family. *Franchesca Hunt, Yr8*

The Boarding Inspector's visit

Year 11 decided to ask the inspector, Mrs Docherty some questions. She works for the Department of Social Security., and we asked her what aspects of her job she enjoys.

A: I enjoy meeting members of staff and children. It is a worthwhile job which gives me great satisfaction. I feel that I am ensuring that children receive the care that they should.

Q: Do you feel that the atmosphere at the Convent is different to that of other school?

A: First of all, let me just say that generally the atmosphere of small schools is different to the atmosphere in larger schools. I say this because small boarding houses have a more homely feel to them. The teachers and boarding house staff seem to know the children better and it is more like a family. I find that the Convent is always warm and welcoming to visitors, staff and children, and above all the children seem very happy to be here........

Emma Thompson and Sophie Whigham, Year 11

1999

Refurbishment has commenced, old carpets have been rolled out and new carpets rolled in. This has created a more homely and warm lifestyle for the Boarders. Storage space has been renewed and updated. But improvisation has been the watchword in the boarding house, a fine example being that the old broom cupboard is the new home for the telephone!

My nearly nine years at the Convent and Boarding House have seen many pupils and Staff come and go. My first experience of a member leaving us would be Sr. Madeleine. I'll always remember her kindness and constant support around the Boarding House. She would often be seen in the company of 'Jet', Mrs Dalton's sheepdog.

Mrs Beardsall and Mrs Wilding also had a very kind and supportive input through their services to the School and the Boarding House, and they are sorely missed. Mrs Beardsall used to be in charge of the little one's Prep session and Mrs Wilding kept tight control over the older pupils.

In my last two years or so Mrs Woodwards helped us. She would arrange tea for us, with plenty of chocolate biscuits. Then later Mrs Smith arrived, and she now continues in Mrs Woodwards' position, looking after the little ones at prep time.

Since September of this year, there has been a touch of the Irish with the arrival of Mr and Mrs Kelly. Mr Kelly has taken the Boarders out on various occasions, including an outing to our Head Girl's performance of 'Snow White and the Seven Dwarfs' held in Fakenham. They have both arrived with great gusto and enthusiasm for after school activities.

The School's Catering system has improved immensely. There is now a bigger emphasis on healthy eating, fresh salads and hot vegetables have made eating more enjoyable at School, especially for the Boarders.

In the Spring term I had the privilege, as Boarders' Prefect, of showing the Inspectors round the School. Throughout my years as a Boarder there has always been the presence of Sr Francis. We have shared our thoughts and opinions, and created a good friendship.
Georgina Newling, Year 11
(Georgina was a little rascal when she was younger, but when she was a Boarder's Prefect she knew the exact turn of phrase to use with the Boarders and sounded just like Sr Francis)

2002
Being in the boarding house for four years has been an experience that we will never forget. It has taught us a lot of valuable lessons; our experiences have been vast and we have made lots of friends who we will always remember.

Living here has made us very independent and grown up. We have had good times and bad times and had many friends whom we won't forget.... A thank you to Mrs Phimister, who we will all miss as she retires this year. She always listened to us and was very fair.
Danni & Steph

2005 The Boarders Year

This year has been, to say at the least, an eventful one full of a wonderful variety of activities – creating memories to be shared by everyone involved. These have involved such things as regular visits to West Acre where we have had much fun paddling in the water and enjoyed many a 'Bacon Butty' supper. Other evenings have involved things such as being educated in beauty therapies where many of the girls enjoyed a facial. The Gap year students, Alison and Lucy returned to Australia, and sadly Mrs Barton, Sr Francis's sister also had to leave after kindly volunteering to stand in as House Mistress until a permanent replacement could be found. Mrs Woodwards arrived, a bright new light about the Boarding House with many new and fresh ideas; introducing such things as the 'reward box' and helping Rosie Cross develop a new supper menu. Due to her wonderful connections with other schools, a link between Sacred Heart and Eccles Hall School. With them we have had some lovely evenings of entertainment such as a Connect Four Championship and a Concert followed by dinner. ..
Callie Oatridge, Yr10

Clautilde

On Tuesday 7th June we had a student visitor called Clautilde, from France, who came to the Convent to spend some time with us boarders for a week, in the hope of improving her English. While she was staying Years 9 and 10 visited Eccles Hall School, an invitation for a meal. Tthis allowed her to extend her opportunity of practising her English and experiencing some English hospitality. We thoroughly enjoyed her staying with us. We had a great time with her, enjoying her company and hope she enjoyed ours.
Rebekah Page Y7

Jacqueline Wilson

The Boarders had the pleasure and honour to go to Cromer Pier Theatre and see Jacqueline Wilson, organised by our Librarian, Mrs Heaver. We were privileged enough to be able to buy some of her books, if we so wished, and have them autographed. We then sat in the theatre where she told us a little bit about how she first became interested in writing and how she went about making a career of it. Did you know the magazine 'Jackie' was named after Jacqueline Wilson, as she was the youngest member of the team?
It was a wonderful night to inspire you to write as it could lead to a much fulfilled career that you love and we learnt lots in regard to her writing processes, which some of us found very useful for when we write our own creative pieces in English. We also learnt of new upcoming books of hers.
Callie Oatridge Y10

Mrs Lane's Farm!

This year on Wednesdays, some of the younger pupils in the Boarding House went to Mrs Lane's farm. We planted lettuce, cabbages, potatoes, cauliflower, and pumpkins. On the farm there were chickens, geese, cows, roosters, sheep, horses and a rabbit. We helped with some of the animals – such as having a laugh trying to herd sheep in the dark! Whilst we were walking around, Abbey and I had a close encounter with some geese. We also went on walks in the woods, picking bluebells and lots of other beautiful flowers. It was very nice of Mrs Lane to invite us to her farm and we thank her very much, as we really enjoyed it.

Games with Miss Foster

On Monday nights Miss Foster has the Years 5-8 from 4.15 to 5.15pm and the older ones, Year 9 upwards, from 5.30 to 6.30pm to play games. We played many things, such as badminton, netball and rounders. I particularly like badminton and netball best, because I am improving with the extra practice and now I am getting good enough to be entered in tournaments. It is fun and we hope Miss Foster continues to offer us this extra help.

Hollywood Legends

After an interesting trip to Church Farm we went to a dinner in Swaffham at a place called Hollywood Legends. It is full of pictures of famous people from the past and present. It was a really great place to be. There was a great atmosphere, with friendly staff and a '70's music' jukebox that everyone could choose songs from! We all had a sing-along to songs such as "Greased Lightning" and "Kung-Fu Fighting", but what really got us dancing was the "YMCA". As you can probably imagine, a set of girls dancing around at a diner was pretty funny! Especially as we were not the only people there! Soon enough we all got what we came for: the food! There was a wide variety of food to choose from, though most of the people on my table chose pizza. I really enjoyed myself, the food was great and I would recommend it to everyone. *Charlotte Farrier, Y8*

St Raphael Club

Once a month some Senior Citizens, able and disabled, meet at our school for Social Evenings. Some of us, from the Boarding House meet with the elderly ladies and gentlemen to ensure they get the best from their meeting and merely to enjoy the pleasure of their company. Whilst there, we do a variety of duties ranging from tea making to simply talking to them.

Among the entertainment offered this year we had a group of Swaffham Players who performed numbers from their recent shows, a talk on Home Security and a Flower Arranging demonstration – all of which the members have thoroughly enjoyed. Members have also enjoyed a Strawberry Tea, a Fish and Chip supper and a Christmas dinner, the latter held at the George Hotel. Another outing was made to Sandringham. Other evening activities saw everyone playing Bingo and taking part in Quizzes.

To sum up, this club enables the members not only to have regular contact with one another, but gives Anne, Victoria, Alicia and myself the chance to contribute to community life. *Hanora Carroll, Y9*

2006-2007 Art & Craft

Mrs Lane gave us some pumpkins that we had grown, so we turned these into lanterns for Halloween and the firework party. It was hard work but they looked very nice when the candles were lit inside them. *Summer McCall, Y3*

The younger boarders made binca mats as Christmas presents. They took a long time but looked lovely when they were finished. We also decorated little boxes using glitter and stick-on tiny shapes.
Whitney Hurst, Y7

The knitting craze hit the Boarding House. Even those who had never knitted produced long, long scarves, despite the sighing and dropping of stitches! At Easter we had to 'dress a wooden spoon'. Some of the creations included a dog, a bride and a rabbit!
Rebekah Page, Y7

For Spring we decorated flower pots and put crocus bulbs in them, they all grew. Mine has purple and yellow flowers. We made Valentine cards too. *Henrietta Colborne, Y3*

Not to be outdone the younger ones also made bread for the Harvest Festival and extra loaves that we ate with lemon curd! With the prospect of Mothering Sunday we made Kit-Kat biscuits and peppermint creams under the supervision of Sr Linda and the GAP year students. We all enjoyed the elderflower water ice, the Kitchen and Dining Room were fragrant all evening as it cooled! They also made Easter chickens for the upcoming holiday.
Callie Oatridge, Y11

Bulgarian State Circus

On Wednesday, 5th October, after an early supper, twenty-three of us from the Boarding House travelled by mini-bus to the recreation ground in Swaffham, where the Bulgarian

State Circus had set up their tent. We found our seats and, after a delay, the show began. The lights came up and a Miss Amanda entered the ring where she then did tricks in a hoop up in the air. Next came two boys who juggled, after Rusty, the clown, and his stereo, gave us a disco – he was very funny.

After the break, we saw Rusty again. This time with his comedy car, this made us laugh all the way through the act. Last of all, and the very best part of the show, were the amazing jugglers who even had amazing glow in the dark juggling balls. We had a great evening and wish to thank Sr Francis for the treat.

Whitney Hurst, Y7

Castle Acre and West Acre

On some fine nights the boarders went to Castle Acre or West Acre. At Castle Acre we climbed the castle and rolled down the hills screaming! We played lots of cricket there and the Polish and Czech students came with us. At West Acre we went walking through the river where Claire said there were crocodiles! …

Alice Goldsney, Yr6

The first of the half-termly suppers took place and Miss Wynter joined the girls for supper, which had been prepared by two of Year 11 pupils with help from Mrs Doreste, (Mally). It was a rather festive occasion with pink table cloths and napkins and the food was delicious. The starter of ham was followed by chicken kebabs and scrummy chocolate fudge cake. Year 10 entertained her with lively conversation. She is reported to have enjoyed the meal very much and congratulated Victoria and Emily on cooking and serving such a splendid supper.

Alicia Eldridge, Year 11

Eccles Hall School came for supper.

This was followed by some hysterical entertainment which was provided by them and some of the Sacred Heart girls. We were split into groups and had to act, mime, sing or dance to their piece of separate music. One performance was a Hawaiian wedding and another was a mad man knocking out women who wanted a cup of tea! What seemed wrong, though, was that the BOYS dressed up as ladies and the GIRLS dressed up as boys! But overall we had a lovely evening with lots of laughs.

Alice Goldsney, Y6

Hawaiian Night

We all paraded in Hawaiian costumes before going for cocktails in the Dining Room. Mally had prepared an exotic meal which we all very much enjoyed. Afterwards we really had fun when we all took turns to walk down the catwalk while Miss Dixon commentated. Then each dormitory presented a Hawaiian performance and St. Mary's won. It was all topped by a team quiz run by Freya. This was a fun night and we all hope we have many more times like this.

Kate Purkis, Y7

Rounders match versus the Air Cadets.

This was organised by Claire and Hanora. We won 20 – 13. A special thanks to Miss Foster for staying behind late after school to umpire and well done to everyone who participated for playing excellently. Later that evening we played 'Unihock' against the cadets, which we won of course. Now they want a return match!

Charlotte Farrier, Y9

Favourite Things

Sr Francis's Ice Cream Parlour is very popular with the Boarders. Having to choose between strawberry and vanilla ice-cream with pink wafers, jewel sweets, marshmallows, chocolate sauce, strawberry sauce, maple syrup, jellies, mint chocolate sticks, chocolate wafers, lemonade and surprise toppings too is very difficult. Our favourites are the vanilla wiggly worms and the pink marshmallows!

Summer McCall & Emily Gostling, Y3

Boarding House Inspection 9ᵗʰ - 11ᵗʰ October 2006

It was reported that the atmosphere is very good. The pupils were found to know who to ask for help, the food is varied and good, they enjoy the activities offered. Praise for all the Staff, especially for the Boarding House Mistress, Mrs Woodwards, who it was reported 'has brought life to the Boarding House with her energy, kindness and affection for the pupils.'

BOARDERS REPORT prepared by Charlotte Farrier, Year 10, with additional contributions.

September 2006

Since the boarders have been back we have been doing different activities involving food, for example bread making. We went blackberrying and apparently great fun was had by all.

We had a boarders' quiz which was exciting and interesting, especially when a certain Year 9 thought 36 divided by 3 was 6. So far we are having plenty of fun making the most of the pool in whatever sun is left from the summer.

This month we have made lemon curd; had a visit from the beautician at Cape Amethyst and learnt about skin care. Michelle Oatridge was the 'guinea pig' for a make over! We also enjoyed a movie evening, watched the school's recent production of 'Oliver' and helped at the St Raphael's Harvest Auction.

The regular suppers prepared by Year 11, which have become a feature in the Boarding House, were in the hands of Michelle and Claire Morgan under the guiding eye of our wonderful cook, Mally. Claire taught the younger boarders some dancing and mobile phone holders were made.

We had a visit from Cape Amethyst in October. We were shown how to cleanse our faces properly; what and what not to use. We were advised to use alcohol free products so as not to damage our skin! We were told that our daily routine, morning and evening should be Cleanse, Tone and Moisturise. Kate and I were used as models and by the end of the evening our faces were glowing.

Alice Goldsney, Year 7

We have done lots of cooking this year. We have baked bread, which we ate with the lemon curd we had made. We also made cakes and biscuits. I liked it when we made sweets for Mothers Day. We made four different sorts of marzipan, vanilla fudge, chocolate truffles and chocolate fudge. I liked the marzipan best, but I did save some for Mummy.

Rosie Pollock, Y4

November saw us making pumpkin masks ready for our boarders' Halloween party. Thanks go to Ellie, Elle, Miki and Hanora for helping to organise it. At the party we played games such as Musical Statues and had our very own Simon Cowell for a dance competition. Miki and I later developed a technique for pass the apple. What a great Halloween!

January the younger ones presented a Fashion Show, with what to wear for different occasions, this was very entertaining

February We had a bingo night that was enjoyed by all who played. We made Melting Moments which were eaten very quickly. Anne Doran and Ellie Fisher entertained us with a concert, they demonstrated six pieces of musical talent and we were waiting for an encore.

We have made Valentine's Day cards for that special someone and Chocolate Buns, which our Brownie boarders used towards gaining their Hostess badge; we also made Mother's Day cards and we had another Boarders' quiz. Those taking part in this event used their common sense to ask those doing work on the computer to look up the answers! …

April and May As the nights are getting lighter, we are able to get out and about, making the most of the sun and nice weather. We went to the Park in Swaffham where Claire showed off how great she was at football, proving that girls are just as good as boys. We have also visited Castle Acre, where some climbed the walls, and where one of us got stuck climbing down! We have also played various sports, such as tennis, in the school grounds. We said 'goodbye' to the Year 11 boarders – officially they were on study leave but were still around the House. To mark their hard work and the fun that they have given us, we had an 'Ice Cream' Leaving Party and Awards ceremony! There were knickerbocker glories all round; Anne's team were the best of the year, because they washed up to music from her MP3 which meant it was more fun and quickly finished, even the Staff danced round!

Other events

We all went to West Acre to watch The Wizard of Oz. We recognised several of the performers as they were pupils from our school. The Lion was my favourite character because he was so nervous. The Witches were the funniest and the Munchkins were very lively and excited. I thought the way that they expressed the story made it feel as if it really happened. In the interval we had the chance to buy a drink and some delicious sweets. I really enjoyed it all.
Summer McCall, Y4

Arts and Crafts

We have made and decorated a number of things including glass painting, making cards, bookmarks, decoupage boxes, decorating candles and yo-yos. Those of us who took part in these Arts and Crafts had a fantastic time.
The thing that I enjoyed most was the glass painting. Mrs Woodwards brought in some glass jars which we decorated with glass paints, in our own designs, then we put a candle inside them.
Anna Stevenson, Y7

BOARDERS' LIFE 2009-2014

In September 2009 I succeeded Mrs Woodwards as the Boarding House Mistress. At that time, due to some leg injury, Mrs Woodwards had to wear an enormous cosmic-style boot, which did not prevent her, however, from hopping cheerfully around the school. Her inexhaustible energy, good humour and kindness were always mentioned with great appreciation and fondness by the Boarders.
We continued to engage in a variety of activities, both indoors and outdoors – weather permitting. Our favourite trips were usually those to Castle Acre, where we could play 'Hide and Seek', roll down the grassy hills (not me, though!), and to West Acre. The latter has been a perfect place for BBQ and paddling in the creek, organising duck races and making sure that I got as much soaked by the little darlings (not mentioning any names) as possible. Sr Francis has been always willing to assist as a minibus driver. A couple of times we also went to the cinema in Dereham, circus in Swaffham and the Bonfire Night in Marham. The outcome of one of those visits to was two goldfish chosen as a prize at the Marham fair by Izzie and Georgie. Thus the long lasting tradition of keeping the boarding

house as a non-animal zone has been broken, much to the Boarders' delight. Sr Francis herself provided a capacious tank and a couple of other fish to keep the Marham fish's company.

Thanks to Mrs Mumfords' hospitality, we had another animal-related experience. Invited to her farm, we enjoyed running among cute newly born lambs and even feeding them with milk! Izzie, who had always wanted to be a vet, proved herself quite skilful, and others also did rather well.

One of our recent venues has been Hillborough House, where we were kindly invited by Mrs Van Cutsem. The House, chapel and the garden are truly impressive. We tried our best singing in the chapel.

Back in Swaffham, we have been jogging, playing rounders, tennis and other games on our premises or in the Park. Whenever possible, the Boarders use the swimming pool as well – such a good exercise before bedtime!

As befits a Convent School, an inseparable part of the bedtime routine has been night prayer. Typically led by a Sister, it is a valuable time for reflection after an active day. I am impressed how the Boarders have been always keen to add spontaneously their own prayer intentions, praying for each other, for theirs families and friends as well as for those in any kind of need. The list would be rather long sometimes! And I soon discovered that we *had to* pray for Kate's hamster as well, otherwise she would get very upset. I also learnt that there was no point trying to explain that animals do not have souls… Anyway, at times our night prayers would turn into mini-theological debates about the spiritual world, about God, creation, free will, Heaven and angels. And Verity would invariably ask me afterwards: 'Are you going to say your Rosemary now?' (she meant Rosary, of course). Personally, I was very moved when Verity and Jasmine asked to be prepared for their First Holy Communion, which was finally celebrated in June 2012, coinciding with Verity's Birthday.

Talking of Birthdays, we always like to celebrate them with a party, followed by some games. Recently the funniest (and most confusing ones!) have been led by Lucia, our Postulant. Remember 'The Sound of Music'? So … who can make a party like Lucia?! Anyway, I am truly grateful for all the wonderful help and input we have had over these years from our Sisters, Postulants, (Gap) students from different countries and the indispensable Ms Wookey, always eager to assist Boarders with their cooking, swimming, Prep and other activities. I want to mention also Mrs Smith, a lady of many talents, who used to do arts and crafts activities with the Boarders. Especially the youngest ones enjoyed making cards for Christmas and other occasions, sewing felt Christmas decorations, trying knitting and embroidery etc. We also tried our hands at painting Christmas stained-glass decorations, sowing Chinese style cushions, creating embroidery floss Easter eggs and origami folding. Some of the origami butterflies are on display in our wonderfully pink Drama Room, along with the motto: LIFE IS BEAUTIFUL!

Sr Danuta FDC

Gap Year Students

1991
Zrinka (Ziggy) Beno(Croatian)
1995
Kazuko Sekiguchi (Japanese)
Vesna Krasjinovic, (Croatian)
Snjezana Martinovic (Croatian)
Valentina Palosika (Croatian)
1998
Kyoko Takasuki (Japanese)
Rie Shiroto (Japanese)
Rani Jayasinge, Candidate
2000
Morne de Plessis (South African)
Daniela Vaglietti (South African)
2001
Julie Clampettt (South African)
Andrea Hickman (South African)
Anne-Cecile Jeannoit (French)
2002
Yuri Taskahasi (Japanese)
Yoko Nakaya (Japanese)
Anna Bradshaw (Australian)
Helga Oneida (Hungarian)
2003
Minnie Seward (Australian)
2004
Miheala Baltoiu (Romanian)
2005
Alison Dowling (Australian)
Lucy Troup (Australian)
Anna Szetna (Polish))
2006
Anna Dixon (Australian)
Sharne Montgomery (Australian)
Weronika Nowak (Polish)
Simone Freiling (German)
Ingrid Clohessy (South African)
former pupil, short stay)
2007
Veronica Buchanon (Australian)
Jade Parkes (Australian)
Martina Calusic (Croatian)
Fljorina Koljic (Croatian)
2008
Olga Koprowska (Poland)
Christina Rapatz (Austria)
Stefanie Koboltschrig (Austria)
Anna Szfner
2009
Monika Szlagor (Polish)
Miriam Brendt (German)

All helpers in
the

Boarding
House and
School

2010
Chantal O'Brien (Australia)
Rebecca Williams (Australia)
Sara Haynes (England)
Claire Ainsworth, candidate, (English)
Hanna Obrusnikova, candidate
(Czech)
Adele Coy, Aspirant FDC

Chapter 16 HEAD GIRLS' REPORT

It has been the custom for Head Girls to write about their experiences for the magazines and also to give speeches at Prize Giving or Carol Concerts. Here is a flavour of their writings:-

Hannah's Bow

As the end of the term draws close and the resident Form 5 prepare to leave, the school's attention turns to the forthcoming election of the new Head Girl. The class was forced to squirm under the close scrutiny of the rest of the school as bets were laid and a few favourites began to emerge. It was a real shock to be chosen, but a great honour, and I think I can safely say that Victoria Brett and I have had a lot of fun this year.

For the benefit of my successor, I have decided to write a list of the duties expected of a Head Girl, but which until now have never been explained. So here begins the Ten Commandments for all the Head Girls of the future.

1. Thou shalt make the Appeals at the Carol Concerts in a loud, clear voice so that none shall escape.
2. Thou shalt make presentations throughout the year to all visiting dignitaries.
3. Thou shalt collect all monies from the members of the class and invoke the wrath of Mrs Ranner if the totals are incorrect.
4. Thou shall take the class register in the event of the absence of Mrs Baker.
5. Thou shalt organise the staff party and the Christmas party.
6. Thou shalt attempt to organise an outing for Form 5 at the end of the year – despite everyone having very different opinions on what they would like to do!
7. Thou shalt organise a fund raising scheme for Lent – trying to persuade Form 5 to give up something …anything!
8. Thou shalt make all class announcements in Assembly.
9. Thou shalt be the staff's dogs-body, at the beck and call of everyone.
10. Thou shalt be Form 5's spokesman, allowing them to air all their views without risk of punishment.

I would also like to take this opportunity to remind the new Head Girl that throughout the year she must take the blame for everything that Form 5 do , and often seemingly the things that most of the rest of the school do wrong (sometimes this includes the staff!)
Hannah Reynolds Form 5, Head Girl – 1990

The Curtain Falls

With only a week to go before we leave, it seems appropriate to say on behalf of Form 5, Goodbye and Good luck'. The past five years seem to have flown by with many good and bad times, especially so, this last year with each one of us involved in matters of great responsibility. The job of Head Girl has been very enjoyable. However, it has also been very frustrating at times, and it is mostly during these moments when you certainly need the backing of the rest of the class, especially Hannah Hunt as Deputy.

The time has come to give a little message to Form 4, and in particular the new Head Girl: I would like to remind you of the great importance of being 'grown up' and responsible, and I hope that you will be. All that remains to say is good luck in the future.
Clare Kelly, Head Girl, Form 5 – 1991

Keeping all the plates in the air at once

It was not until the last day of the Summer Term that Form 5's responsibilities were announced. When Sr Francis told all the Senior School both Joanna Moss and I were delighted. I felt that it was a great honour, and realised that although it would be a fulfilling job, it would not always be easy.

It took me several weeks to come to feel at one with my position. The balance between my work, which seemed to be piling up at the beginning of the term and all my responsibilities to the school, and still being able to feel happy within myself and with all my friends and family, was not an easy path to find. After a while, I seemed to manage to keep all the plates in the air at once.

I thought that as Head Girl, I should take my responsibilities very seriously, but I wanted to keep my place as a pupil. It was important to me that I knew everyone in the school and maintain my friendships with all the pupils. Throughout the year I believe that I have grown in confidence. Originally when addressing the school my self-confidence was low; but I have improved, and now I am happier to speak in public.

Joanna Moss, my Deputy has been very supportive; she has helped me with all my jobs and the organising of events. I know that without her I would not have managed. Form 5 has worked well together to organise different events. All the class have been co-operative and most occasions went smoothly, and were enjoyed by us all I hope that the next Head Girl will enjoy her position as much as I have at this lovely school.
Grace Chambers, Head Girl, Form 5 – 1992

Were we going to get the school to dress up in red or pink?

I have to say that I have thoroughly enjoyed being Head Girl. When I was first given the position I was a bit flabbergasted at the thought of all the tasks that I would have to endure over the course of a year. However, over the summer, past Head Girls gave me plenty of handy tips, mainly about how to keep calm, and they also told me that I should enjoy the experience.

I soon realised that I was by no means alone; indeed I had the whole class behind me. We all listened to each other's ideas and soon began to work together.

Our first task was non-uniform day. Were we going to get the school to dress up in red or pink? Or should that be yellow or purple? No, we settled for the plain old non-uniform day, and decided to hold it on Children in Need day. We raised £82.71 for Quidenhams Children's Hospice.

During December we all had our fair share of panicking at the thought of getting the Houses organised enough to bring in goods for the Christmas Bazaar. As I was not involved too much, I was able to sit back and tell everyone to calm down. Soon the

Christmas Party was upon us, and I do not know quite know to describe how I felt on the morning of the party. I was very energetic and pleasantly surprised, for the whole class merged together as one to form the best team I could ever have imagined. The party went off smoothly and everyone enjoyed it.

Yet again, after the mock exams I was able to sit back and mutter sympathetic words whilst watching my friends organise the House Music Festival.

After a very enjoyable skiing holiday in Italy there were only ten weeks left before the end of term, and it was time to write my final report. With exams these last few weeks have been very hectic, with our day trip out to Chessington which turned out to be far better than any of us imagined; our retreat to Mr Foti's – courtesy of Sr Francis was a relaxing and enjoyable day; the staff party which brought back all those crazy memories of the Christmas party and finally Year 11 struggling to produce the school magazine.

For me, being Head Girl has been an experience that I will never forget. The most nerve wracking moment was during the Carol Concert when I had to deliver the Head Girl's speech. *Alex Dalton, Head Girl, Year 11 – 1994*

The room with the padded seats

Sr Francis asked me if I would be prepared to be Head Girl. I was honoured but also apprehensive. What exactly would the job involve? I had all summer to work this out but it was not until September that I began to get some answers. Returning from the summer holidays as Year 11 felt strange. We finally found ourselves in the room with the padded seats. It wasn't long before we discovered that their main function was somewhere to collapse as the year flew past. This year has seen us trying out our powers of organisation. Over its course we have organised two non-uniform days; one raising money for Romania and one raising money for Comic Relief. I don't think that we will forget the teachers' nice green outfits in a hurry! As well as school events we have also had to run House events. We must have looked funny at times, as we rushed about, trying to get people to play in teams, play a musical instrument in the Music Festival or bring in something in House colours for the Christmas Bazaar.

As with all fifth years, exams have been the main focus, with the mocks in January and now we have just finished the real things. Only time will tell how we have done! The year has gone quickly. The most nerve racking thing that I have done as Head Girl was to deliver a speech at the Carol Concert and I shook like a jelly. Over the last few weeks I've had to organise the end-of-term trip and the staff party. Both events went well. I would like to thank the class and staff for being there when I needed support.
Helen Childerhouse, Head Girl, Year 11 – 1995

Interview with Sarah Skinner, Head Girl

How did you feel when you were told that you had been chosen as Head Girl?
Well, to sum it up in one word….ecstatic! I mean, it is not every day that you hear news like that. If I remember rightly, my words were - wicked!

Over the summer holidays I had great ideas about what I would do with my time as Head Girl. I feel that I have achieved the main part of what I have to do. However, with extra time, I am sure that I could have fitted in more.

What new things have you introduced to the school?

Here I must give a mention to year 11 as a whole. I really do feel that we have worked extremely well together and have introduced some really great things like the Tuck Cupboard and the School Council, where pupils can tell us what they really think about the school. Also Year 11 now has a Common Room where they can socialise over a game of table tennis or a cup of tea! Other events that we have organised have been a non-uniform day based on the theme of colours, and a 'Paintathon' to raise money for the Sports Hall.

How have you found working with the staff?

I have found it both fun and challenging. Overall, everyone has been enthusiastic. Also, there has been a real family spirit within the school which I will greatly miss.

How will you look on your days at the Convent?

Not without tears welling up in my eyes, I can tell you! I have absolutely loved my time here and I shall never forget it.

What advice can you give to your successor?

I could honestly go on for hours, but the main thing is to get in there and start organising straight away because time will pass by and you will soon be doing your GCSE's.

Finally, do you have anything to say to the school as a whole?

First of all, I would like to thank everyone for making my year as Head Girl so great and I hope it has been as much fun for you as it has been for me. Secondly, I want to wish you all the best for the future. We are all very lucky to have had the opportunity to be part of the school and each one of you has the ability to make this a real solid starting block from which you can launch into the rest of your lives. I believe that everyone is special in their own right. Each one of you pupils, staff and nuns, will remain in my fondest memories always and I hope that I have managed to bring a little smile into your lives too!

Laura Harcourt, Interviewer, Year 7 – 1996

Sarah Pickard (nee Skinner) has a daughter attending the Little Pedlars and in September when her son starts at the school she will be teaching music to the Lower School.

Looking back, looking forward

The nervous young girl walked down the corridor, her heart beating wildly inside her chest. Butterflies had vigorously taken flight inside her stomach and her knuckles were white as she gripped tightly to the handle of her small brown satchel....'

Six years later, after having left the Convent, memories of my first day there still remain prominent in my mind. Recollections of boarding provide me with colourful visions of secret feasts, shared troubles and lazy summer evenings spent by the swimming pool or on the tennis courts. It may not resemble Enid Blyton's version of events, but life in the Boarding House was never dull. I shall never forget the time a certain close friend of mine was taking a bath during fire practice and was forced to flee from the building with just a towel wrapped tightly around her!

I would say that it was an advantage having such a large 'family' on site, but as you can imagine there can also be a down-side to having twenty girls all under the same roof. The arguments, or as many of my fellow boarders would call them, 'disagreements', tended to start over something rather trivial and quickly erupt into a full scale battle, by which time any sane person would have left the room. Boarding, however, has been good for me; I believe it has helped to strengthen my bond with the school and has helped me mix more freely with other age groups.

There have been many times throughout my six years at the Convent when I was persuaded to contribute, under rather bizarre conditions, to fetes and other events run by the school. For those of you who don't already know, I was the great, all-knowing Madame Mystic Meg' at the Christmas bazaar two years ago. Although I did not have any previous experience and appeared to have no obvious knowledge of the art of fortune telling, Sr Francis still believed I was the perfect person for the job. Unlike some of my younger clients who found it amusing to ask, "What will be the winning numbers for this week's Lottery, Mystic Meg?" Eventually I managed to explain that important information, such as the winning Lottery numbers, could not be revealed to the general public for fear of losing my licence. Fortunately most of the children seemed happy with my reply, although one small boy returned to his mother and said, "Sorry mum, I didn't get a chance to ask her where the toilet was, she was too busy fork –tuning!" The mother gave her son a puzzled look before approaching a nearby pupil for directions to the nearest cloakroom. This was just one eventful moment during the numerous occasions I attended, where images of costumed characters, bunting and prizes remind me of this small, individual school.

Memories of my last year at school are probably my most treasured, as I felt our class grew even closer at the prospect of separation. We have always been close and I know that the antics of Hannah Black and company were guaranteed to cheer me up when I was feeling low. I would like to thank every member of my class, especially Helen Ballantyne, who all supported me during my time as Head Girl. I would like to thank all those members of staff who helped me cope with the responsibility.

As the last page is written and another chapter in life's long book lies complete, I look to the uncertainty of the future, wishing for the security of the past. My time at this school has helped me to discover who I really am, and has given me the confidence to be an individual. I am proud to have been a member of this school, a community based on trust and commitment, where all of its members strive to achieve the same goal: to give opportunities through education.

Franchesca Hunt, Head Girl, Year 11 – 1997

A Head Girl with very long arms

The last few months I have been so busy that I don't think I even realised that I am soon to leave. Looking back I remember how incredibly scared I was when I first entered Miss Gooderson's classroom desperately searching for a familiar face. I soon settled into Junior

School life and all the usual trials and tribulations of a young girl, were all I had to worry me. The prospect of the 'big school' where there were only 'big girls' always seemed very glamorous. Changing classrooms for different lessons and carrying my text books around with me sounded incredibly grown up, well, that was then, and this is now. A Head Girl with very long arms!

When I joined Year 7 I thought that it would be a very long time before I got to year 11. Yet the last few years have really flown by. I have been on many educational visits. I have been to ballets, the Globe Theatre, the Houses of Parliament, art galleries, the Tower of London, - the list is endless. Through 'Take your Daughters to work day' I have been able to have work experience with Radio Norfolk, the Eastern daily Press newspaper and a local veterinary surgery. I particularly recall the French trip to Rouen which was lots of fun. There are many stories I could tell from smelly cheeses to the art of tearing a baguette!

Whilst at the school I have completed my Bronze Duke of Edinburgh Award. The expeditions were immense fun, even if we were either soaking wet or boiling hot. One thing we did learn was how to know when we were lost; we had a lot of practice at that! I have also been on four of the ski trips and have enjoyed myself immensely each time.

At the start of Year 11 when Sr Francis asked me to be Head Girl I was astounded. But after the initial shock I could not help beaming – I was so proud. My first real opportunity to make decisions as Head Girl came with non-uniform day. Mrs Black gave us the idea of 'Jeans for genes' Day', and after I had organised this I felt that I had established myself in the position. My scariest moment was giving my speech at the Carol Concert. As I stood in front of the audience, my hands were shaking so much that I thought that I might drop my speech. My legs were trembling too, making it look as though I was simultaneously giving my speech and doing the river dance! The event that I had looked forward to organising was the Christmas Party. This year we decided to have a change from the usual discos and we chose to have a 'fun and games' afternoon. I was really delighted how the afternoon turned out; everyone joined in the 'Feel the Teacher' in which one of the female teachers was accused of being Mr Blackwell.

Whilst at the school I have been very involved in the annual Music and Drama Evenings and this year was no exception. I have played a wide variety of characters including a Daffodil, a very convincing witch from 'Macbeth', a naughty little girl, and a Punk version of the fairy Mustard-Seed from ' A Midsummer Night's Dream'. I have followed through my interest in Drama by taking all the LAMDA Awards and I was able to take my Theatre Studies GCSE in Year 10. I shall always remember my little chats with Mrs Pickering; she is a very inspiring lady.

The Staff Tea Party is my penultimate task as Head Girl and there is a kind of sweet sorrow in organising it. Our aim this year is to talk to the teachers and to thank them for all the time, effort and patience they have devoted to us over the years. The closeness we share, especially that with our closest friends, is due to the familiarity the Convent instils in each individual. We have all shared something special at the Convent.

Now the time has come to sign off I would like to thank Sr Francis for all her advice support and guidance over this past year. Good Luck to the new Year 11 and especially the next head Girl – you will soon find that those tempting green cushioned chairs are not for lounging in but for collapsing in when you have so many things to organise. I have been lucky to have been given responsibility at this lovely little school and I hope that my successor appreciates this at the beginning of her year rather than the end is now looming. No doubt at our final assembly there will be a few tears shed, and I shall be hugging everybody and everything. I should like to say goodbye and good luck to all my classmates. I hope you all fulfil your ambitions, be they shepherding or working in a high powered law firm.

Kate Scales, Head Girl, Year 11 – 1998

The Diary of a Head Girl

*   9th July. 12.00pm I find out that I am Head Girl: mixture of emotions – worry, joy, surprise…A huge burden of responsibility has just been thrust upon me. How will I cope? Thank God, I have Natasha to help. 2.30pm – end of year Assembly. Wait for the gasps of horror as my new role is announced. 2.32pm – No gasps of or screams. School seems quite happy with the decision. 3.45pm – go home and tell Mum.
*   9th Sept. Holidays nearly over. Pack bag for school and finish homework.
*   10th Sept. Back to school. Small children seem to be under the impression that my name is 'Head Girl'.
*   14th Sept. All day trip to Walsingham. Go to church, pray, have picnic. No Earth shattering responsibilities yet.
*   16th Sept. Announce my first Council Meeting – 1.00pm in the Sports Hall. Beg half the class to come in case no one else does. 1.00pm – quite a good turn out and some good ideas. Surprised? You bet!
*   22nd Sept. Science Trip to Cambridge. Listen to lots of lectures. Very educational!
*   12th Oct. Announce Non-Uniform Day for 23rd of the month to raise money for Addenbrookes. Need 50p from everyone.
*   16th Oct. Only got half of the money. Start to get frantic. Ask those in question a b o u t whereabouts of money. Bombarded by queries of what non-uniform day? Ahh! Am I invisible?
*   19th Oct. Announce Non-uniform Day again!
*   20th Oct. Find those still in debt and scrawl 'I owe Rebecca 50p1' on the backs of their hands.
*   23rd Oct. Get all the wretched 50p's! Day is a success. Half term at last!
*   26th Oct. Sleep in until about 2.00pm.
*   2nd Nov. Back again
*   9th Nov. Parents Evening. Have ridiculously high predicted grades. How can I e v e r live up to these expectations?
*   11th Nov. Hand in Maths coursework. One subject down!
*   28th Nov. Christmas Bazaar. Help Sandringham (my house) with their stall. Eat delicious cakes from the kind PTA.
*   1st Dec. First mock exam. Remember GCSE'S are next year – how could I forget.

* 7th Dec. Mock job interviews with Mr Eddie Doran to prepare us for life after school. Whole experience is totally daunting as I realise that I am growing up   a n n o y i n g l y fast.
* 9th Dec. I am asked if my speech for the younger pupil's Christmas Concert is ready. When is it? TOMORROW! Beg Mrs Rizza to help me with it.
* 10th Dec. Deliver speech. Seems to go down quite well.
* 15th Dec. Adapt speech for senior School Concert. Read speech again. Don't know what I would have done without Mrs Rizza!
* 17th Dec. Break up for Christmas. A well-deserved treat I think.
* 25th Dec. Happy Christmas! Have almost forgotten about the horrors before me – Mock GCSE'S I'll start revising after Boxing Day!
* 31st Dec. 12.00pm – Happy New Year! OK, I'll start revising tomorrow.
* 11th Jan . 1999 Back again. Alright, so I didn't revise as much as I wanted, but I promise I will for the real things.
* 16th Mar. I know I haven't written for a while, but you would not believe the amount of coursework we have to do. 8.00pm time to relax – St Patrick's Day Party is in the Sports Hall. Congratulations Mr Kelly, it was a huge success. Possibly the most fun I have had at school. 12.00am – Happy St Patrick's day to one   and all!
* 25th Mar. House Music festival. Experienced a twisted sense of satisfaction watching the House Captains running round frantically, like I have been for the last seven months.
* 26th Mar. Break for Easter. Why call it a holiday? All I'll be doing is revising! That's not what I call a holiday.
* 19th Apr. Back for the last term of my school life. My brain is full of pointless information after a holiday of intense revision. Hopefully, it will pay off next month.
* 24th Apr. My sixteenth birthday party. Try to put the stress of exams behind me and enjoy the night.
* 14th May. French oral exam. A total disaster. Sorry Mrs Howarth.
* 19th May. GCSE'S officially start. This year has gone by annoyingly fast.
* 21st May.   Go to Mr Eric St Foti's at Hermitage hall for a day of relaxation, meditating, eating and swimming. I could get used to this. Shame, I won't have a chance.
* 10th Jun. Right in the middle of the awful exams. Good job I have plenty of hair to compensate for the load I am losing.
* 22nd Jun. Last exam! No more exams. Exams are over! Hasn't quite sunk in yet. 8.00pm go to Eleanor's for a celebratory 'No more exams party'. Most fun I've had in ages!
* 1st July. Go to Cambridge for the Year 11 'Leaving Treat' have an 'all you can eat lunch' at Pizza Hut. 1.30pm – go punting. Possibly the most terrifying and difficult experience of my life. I'm quite surprised we didn't sink. Must just take time here to thank Mrs Howarth for her help in the steering of our punt – Yes, I am being sarcastic!
* 2nd July. To wake up feeling totally thrilled at the prospect of leaving after eight long

years. Actually I felt quite depressed. 11.45 – leaving Assembly. Keep telling   myself I will not cry. What did I do the minute the first hymn starts? Start blubbing! Natasha has to finish off the reading for me. Seems like I am more   emotional   than   I   first thought. Whole class starts howling. It's not supposed to be like this. 2.00pm – look back and walk away from that friendly building for the last time as a Convent girl. I think I'll miss this place….

Rebecca Keane, Head Girl, Year 11 - 1999

Been there, done that, got the uniform

When I was asked to be Head Girl by Sr Francis, it was the most rewarding and proudest moment in my school career, even more important than playing the role of Jesus in the Passion Play. Not only was I being given the responsibility of being the representative of all the pupils at the Convent, but also to follow in the footsteps of past Head Girls, that I frequently gazed up to on the plaque with its gold lettering.

I returned to school in September with all my emotions running high (try to remember being a sixteen year old), for this was to be the crucial year of GCSE'S and the last year we will have together, so we made sure that it was not wasted and made a pact to make it a year to remember for all of us.

Over the next three terms of my appointment, occasions such as Feast Days, Non- uniform Days and fund raising for different charities filled year 11's with collecting and raising money, as well as the smooth running of events. Thank you to the school pupils for their co -operation with ideas for the School Council Meetings and the welcoming lack of complaints about frugal lunches.. The Christmas Party was by far the grandest event to be organised. Competing against previous Year 11's parties, I can quite confidently say that ours is officially top of the league. Year 10, you have a hard act to follow.

Over the last five years that I have been at the Convent, some members of my class have left and others have joined. We have all developed and matured into young ladies, and even though we have come together as a class we are all still individuals. The convent has taught us determination, given us valuable encouragement and advice to pursue the path we have chosen. I don't just see eighteen students, but eighteen strong characters with such a broad spectrum of qualities; all together as a class, we shine. This only could have been achieved because of the Staff and Sisters, who have guided us throughout the years. Only now do I realise how incredible it is to do, year after year.

A special thank you on behalf of Year 11 to our Form Tutors Mrs Leonard, Mrs Kenny and Sr Francis for supporting us. I look forward to the future with excitement, in the knowledge that I have been taught to face anything that is thrown at me in the future; though this thought is tinged with regret for leaving the securities of such a special school.

Looking back, I can remember being in Year 7, in crisp new uniform and boater and envious of the 'big girls' in Year 11, as soon they could do what they pleased when they left. I was mistaken in this belief. I now have a slight yearning to be that little girl again, as never again will I experience such a content school life.

Harriet West, Head Girl, Year 11 – 2002

Juliet, summed up our ethos and work ethic at our 2012 Prizegiving when she said:

This school is extremely special and unlike any other, offering what I believe to be a priceless education. Each student is treated as an individual and given many opportunities to increase their independence and confidence, something which would not be achieved in a larger school.

The small class sizes allow students to study subjects in great depth and at a pace they are comfortable with, providing optimum learning for everyone.

The unique quality of attention given to each student as an individual is reflected in the diversity of students who receive awards. Every student is given the tools and opportunities to reach the high ideals set by the school and are rewarded when they do so. The diversity of awards, not only for achievement but also for effort, provides a great insight into two of the main aims of the school, 'To value, appreciate and enjoy learning' and 'To further curiosity and creativity.'

The awards show it is not always the end result that defines whether they are recognised as prized students but, sometimes, by the obstacles they overcome to achieve the best they can.

The variety of subjects the school provides, which includes both academic and practical activities, also gives each student the opportunity to excel.

More active-minded students are just as able to progress as those who are more scientifically minded; students who may not be able to achieve the highest grades are rewarded if they have applied themselves to the best of their ability.

The annual House music and sports events give students an opportunity to try something new and may even reveal hidden talents. The holiday challenge is one example of the school encouraging everyone to develop their own creative talents, whether it's through art, poetry or music.

This school may only be a stepping stone on a long road ahead but it is one which students can look back on and fully appreciate as a once in a lifetime education.

Juliet Fenton, Headgirl, 2013

A truly loving and caring family environment

In June 2014 the school will be celebrating its centenary, something of which we are all very proud. For the past hundred years thousands of girls and boys have been privileged enough to pass through the doors of this unique school.

As Head Girl and a pupil of thirteen years I know only too well how life-changing the Sacred Heart School can be. During this time, I have felt that what some may see as a mere collection of buildings, has in fact become a second home for me. A place where I feel safe and secure, a place with the same Christian principles I strive to live by, a place where I belong. This is what the school hopes to inspire in all of its students.

At a previous open day, I was asked to explain my school experience to a prospective parent. I had to pause a minute to call on a bank of memories compiled over my time here. Did I describe whole school events, such as drills on the school field displaying the youngest and oldest students as equals? Or the way that somewhat delicate matters are always handled with the utmost care; or the feeling that someone was always there, whichever way I turned, waiting to help me find my path again. How could I choose when they have all had such a great impact on me? I told them not only this, but about my second family, people who I have grown up with by my side, those who have taught me important life lessons when I needed them most and the ones who have contributed greatly to the last thirteen years of my life. I chose to say these things, as this what the school and my time here mean to me.

At this school, a pupil is not punished by their peers for raising their hand in response, but admired, a student is not challenged when achieving an outstanding mark, but congratulated, no child goes unnoticed or is overlooked, but is cherished.

It is a fact, that daily life will often present hurdles, whether this is encountering difficulties in a particular subject, or something perhaps more emotionally straining. Whatever the obstacle, it is how we deal with it that defines our situation. 'How we fair in the fight', you could say. This, perhaps, is the greatest lesson taught here, advice and guidance that prepares us for life outside the classroom. This is what sends the children with once crooked ties, out into the world as well rounded, young ladies and gentlemen.

I speak for generations, including my own mother, cousins and sister when I say these things, and when I say that this school, and all the Sisters and staff have made a truly loving and caring family environment for me and all of my fellow students.

Joanna Simon, Year 11, Headgirl, 2014

GCSE Results

We are proud to say that our school has had consistently high results for GCSE subjects.

We are not a selective school, so these results are excellent and show the dedication and support of the staff who encourage each pupil to give their best. Pupils respond to the atmosphere of learning, small classes and individual attention. The following is a list of A – C passes for the last 25 years:

1989	85%	2002	83%
1990	82%	2003	92%
1991	86%	2004	100%
1992	81%	2005	89%
1993	73%	2006	95%
1994	78%	2007	83%
1995	76%	2008	100%
1996	86%	2009	100%
1997	94%	2010	100%
1998	78%	2011	90%
1999	84%	2012	73%
2000	81%	2013	90%
2001	100%		

2004 Head Girl
Victoria Lewis
Celebrating her GCSE results

The school will always occupy a special place in my heart

The Fountain family have been in association with the Sacred Heart School for over 21 years, and even though my 13 years as a pupil at the school has come to an end, my relationship with the school has not, and I hope, will not come to a close. After spending most of my childhood as a proud pupil of this school, it has always felt like a home away from home and no matter how long I wait before I return to walk through the gates of the Sacred Heart School, I know I will never feel out of place or unwelcome. This school is unique to say the least, which still remains its most wonderful quality.

I've found that my fondest memories are the events which I distinctly remember having strong objections to when I was participating in them.

These events include the countless trips up to the Buttercross, in Swaffham town centre, one of which being dressed up supposedly to resemble a character from Shakespeare, however with a curtain around my neck and a drawn on beard I doubt I was highly convincing, while fearlessly clutching a banner and shaking a maraca to no obvious rhythm. The performance of Shakespeare that followed I'm sure would not have won many awards however, I know that a smile never left my face as I tried to comprehend the situation I had found myself in. As a 15 year old girl, this was not a preferred hobby of mine. Experiences like this that the school gave me have taught me so many lessons which I know I would never have learnt anywhere else.

Thanks to these fantastic, but strange and slightly humiliating situations the school presented to me I am an extremely confident public speaker, I find meeting new people, and unexpected circumstances not a challenge, or something to be feared but as an opportunity and something to embrace.

The school has shown me that it is better, not to overthink but to do, and has given me a philosophy to which I plan always to adhere; every opportunity can only have two potential outcomes, either that it will be a great success, or it will be very funny, and a wonderful story to pass on so you might as well try!

When I look back at my time at the school I know I have a completely unique set of memories that others would not have the pleasure to acquire, and the main question raised by looking over these memories is; where else is like this? The answer; nowhere, or at least not to me as the school will always occupy a special place in my heart.

Sasha Fountain, Deputy Head Girl and Music Prefect ,Year 11 2013

Chapter 17 STAFF MEMORIES

something to be proud of. I will always remember with love and affection the many boarders I have helped to care for, especially during the years I 'lived in'. It was like being part of a big family; so I have had almost a life time of involvement with the Sisters and the School.

I hope to still keep in touch and attend the various school functions.
Monica Wilding (nee Baldry) 1939 - 1998

ANN BAKER'S RETIREMENT - FAREWELL

Twenty years ago when Mrs Baker joined the School she spent all her time teaching Biology in a small, but perfectly formed, lab which fitted into what is now the R.K. room!

Of course, we learn in History lessons that people have grown over the generations, but in our case it has been pupil numbers and the National Curriculum that have burgeoned.

Staff over the years have been persuaded to write their memories for school magazines, and occasionally their stories have been written by others. This is just a flavour.

Thoughts From the kitchen

I started work at the Convent in 1972 when Sister Margaret was the Sister Superior. My position was to work alongside Sister Mary Joseph, who was the Head Cook. We worked together for 14 very happy years. She was a lovely lady and I am sorry to say that she is no longer with us.

Yvonne came to work at the Convent in 1986 as Head Cook and I was Assistant Cook. We worked together very well, but she also will be leaving soon to have a baby. I wish her well. I have seen many changes at the Convent and have had the pleasure of meeting lots of Sisters and making friends with them. They were very good to me when my husband died, and with great compassion helped me through my loss. The same goes for all the ladies - we have had lots of fun and laughs together and I will miss them all - that and their company. Last year Sister Thomas More, the Sister Superior and the Sisters gave a Dinner Party for all the Staff. It turned out also to be a surprise party for my working at the Convent for 25 years. It was wonderful and I will never forget it. I have seen many children come and go. They come in as very small children - the boys leaving at eleven and the girls at sixteen as young ladies.

Lastly I would like to thank you all for putting up with me for 26 years. I am taking very happy memories away with me and my time at the Convent will always have a special place in my heart.
Lily Cleaver - 1972 to 1998

A record association

It will be a sad day indeed when I retire at the end of this school year, but I will take with me many happy memories.

I believe my long association with the Convent must be something of a record, spanning well over half a century - I can hardly believe it myself.

It all began, when my father took command of the troops here a few months before the war broke out.

It was in September of that year my sisters, Valerie and Margaret and I started at the school. It consisted of a long hut that was very cold in winter and very hot in summer. There were only three classes - Senior, Junior and Infants, about 75 pupils in total. We had five Sisters teaching and one lay-person, Miss O'Kelly. I can truly say I loved every minute of my school days, so much so, I even spent time with the Sisters during the holidays, also my best friend, Trudi, an Austrian refugee was cared for by the Sisters until she left school, when, like me she worked in Barclays Bank in London. She now lives in Canada, we still keep in touch. After about four years in London, I returned to Swaffham, married with a baby son, it was a great joy to me that my four children also received their education at 'my school'. Looking back over the years of our school what a great success story it is; thanks to the hard work and dedication of the Sisters and Staff the school has gone from strength to strength. The high standards and the academic achievements are something to be proud of.

Mrs Ann Baker

I will always remember with love and affection the many boarders I have helped to care for, especially during the years I 'lived in'. It was like being part of a big family; so I have had almost a life time of involvement with the Sisters and the School.

I hope to still keep in touch and attend the various school functions.

Monica Wilding (nee Baldry) 1939 - 1998

Ann Baker's retirement-farewell

Twenty years ago when Mrs Baker joined the School she spent all her time teaching Biology in a small, but perfectly formed, lab which fitted into what is now the R.K. room! Of course, we learn in History lessons that people have grown over the generations, but in our case it has been pupil numbers and the National Curriculum that have burgeoned.

In 1983 Mrs Baker was joined by Mrs Black and the new Science department moved into a large, temporary building which the P.T.A. had sited by the tennis courts. Physics and Chemistry joined Biology on our curriculum.

It soon became clear that even more space was needed and in 1989, our 75th anniversary celebrated the opening of two new purpose-built labs and a prep room in the New Technology Block. Sciences became statutory subjects for GCSE. so all pupils spent much more time in the labs than ever before.

In the years since Mrs Baker replaced Mrs Gribbon as Deputy Head in 1986, the frequent Government changes in education have increased the burden of administration to remorseless levels and, more recently, Sister Francis' absence made it necessary for Mrs

Baker to give up teaching to be Acting Head of both Junior and Senior Schools; a task she fulfilled with universal compassion and efficiency. Hers has been a calm and capable presence throughout both schools which will be sorely missed by us all.

Valerie Mann Senior Mistress 1994

Retirement reflections

A whole year has passed since I last wrote in the magazine and quite a different year too. I decided to retire when my husband, on his retirement, started to go away and enjoy himself too much for my liking! When I started to think about joining him, I did not realise that the end of this school year marked my twentieth at the Convent, so "what better date to mark my retirement" I thought!

I shall miss everything so much, I am sure, but I intend to keep myself really busy. I want to emphasise what I have said to pupils before though. Remember, you are very lucky to be in a small caring environment where everyone knows you and you are someone. Keep this in mind whatever befalls you, you will always find a person at the Convent willing to listen and help you. It does not happen at all schools I can assure you. I shall miss the familiar faces at assembly every morning, but I promise I shall be back - if you will have me and circumstances allow - at the Christmas concert. I hope people will keep in touch and then the break will not seem so hard. I wish all the staff and pupils a fond farewell sending them my best wishes for the future. I also thank the parents for their tolerance, kindness and understanding - and for producing some of the nicest children I have met in 25 years' teaching (no swollen heads please amongst the pupils)! I shall think of everyone frequently.

Ann Baker, Deputy Head and Acting Head, 1974 - 1994

By divine chance?

My working at the School came about more or less by chance and, as it turned out, was one of the luckiest chance encounters that could have happened.

It was the Spring of 1973 and my husband, Colin, was teaching the then Headmistress, Sister Margaret, to drive. Never one to miss an opportunity to advertise, Sister mentioned that the School was having a Summer Fete so Colin and I went along with our three children then aged 9, 7 and 4 years. We liked what we saw and had a further look around with a view to the children starting there the following school year.

In September 1973, our children, Joanne, Patricia and Roger duly started their school life at the Convent. However, the 'school run' proved to be a rather difficult problem having to transport the children to and from Swaffham. I realised with all three children now at school I would be free to consider some suitable work to fit in with school hours so I mentioned that I would be interested in a job at the school / house / office should a vacancy arise.

My prayers were answered when in the following January Sister Margaret phoned to ask if I would be interested in starting as an assistant in Infants 1 and thus it all began! I worked

with two different temporary teachers initially, until the Easter Term when Jill Williamson joined the Staff and our long and successful working partnership began. What wonderful, fulfilling years these proved to be, giving me so many happy memories. My home is full of mementoes given to me over the years and each one evokes little memories of the pupils. For example, I remember twin boys that could only be told apart by a large freckle on one brother's nose; one very deaf little boy who, with our help and his own determination learned to read. Perhaps some of my most special memories will be how proud I have felt at School Concerts and performances, to see young people standing in front of an audience confidently reading, and knowing that I had some part in that. I can say that on these occasions many a tear has welled in my eyes. I had only really intended to work while my children attended the school but somehow stayed 15 years longer!
Barbara Wade 1974 – 1998

Twenty years on

When I moved to Swaffham in 1976 I didn't know what the future would hold. As it happens, it has turned out to be some of the happiest years of my life.

Mrs Brandon, Sister Francis, as Headmistress. and I as School Secretary, all started on the same day. In theory I worked mornings but trying to cram everything in meant the reality was quite different. Records had to be kept of the cost of each book every child had with the total amount to be charged on parents' accounts. I was responsible for the payment of books, stationery etc., invoiced to the School, in addition to the Secretarial work. A stencil had to be made for school letters, exams etc., and then copies run off. Now it seems like the dark ages! Life was equally as hectic then as Mrs Ranner finds it now.

Classes were so full that, if a child didn't start in Pre Infants', it was difficult to get them into the Lower School. After a couple of years there was a vacancy in the Boarding House and I remember Sister Francis' amazement when I asked to change my job. I arrived in the Boarding House to over fifty girls. Junior Prep was taken in the same room as now with many girls trying to tuck legs under tiny tables still to be seen in the back of the Dining Room. No carpet on the floor in those days! The room was the Pre Infants classroom during the day. Many things have changed over the years in the Boarding House but although the girls change there are always some who seem to be in trouble! I have always loved children and whilst working with them never lost sight of how I was as a child and so didn't expect them to be perfect. Unfortunately, at the time, children don't realise that when they are disruptive you don't love them any the less, but they have to be disciplined! It was always a great pleasure when boarders came back to see us and their first words were usually 'I'm sorry I was so naughty'. I don't remember them like that. The Boarding House is their home during the week and is a place in which to be themselves, to learn and grow and, hopefully, to find the right values in life. Each girl is very special to me.

I am still very much in touch with the Convent, the Sisters and, of course, with Mrs Wilding and Mrs Phimister whose friendship I found invaluable in working in the Boarding House.

I certainly haven't gone into retirement as I seem to be busier than ever working in the voluntary sector which keeps me happy, although I do miss the boarders and day children who came into my care.

The Crocodile

I think this has to be confession time. I've often found it difficult to keep my sense of humour under control with the boarders when I knew I shouldn't be laughing. Also I've often had to tell them off for things I did or didn't do as a child. In particular I was always in trouble for not doing my music practice - a thing I really regret now! God Bless....
Mrs Pat Beardsall - 1976 -1998

Travels with a crocodile

I have travelled extensively since first joining the Convent School in January 1978. Year 5 and I started life together in the Mobile - Eskimo boots in winter, lessons alfresco in the shade of the big tree in the summer.

A few years later we moved to half of the present Art Room - a strange year, then down to the Music Room. All that space! But oh, those freezing cold Monday mornings in winter! Damart shares rocketed as we kitted ourselves out with thermal underwear. Later we had a cramped but cosy year upstairs in the Senior Common Room, with uninterrupted views of the traffic on the A47, while the Lower School was being constructed. Then back to the Music Room, followed by another session in the Mobile before our caravan finally came to rest in the new Middle School. All the moves were carried out with the invaluable help of a faithful 'crocodile' of small persons carrying large boxes.

Many Christmas drama productions saw the 'crocodile' plodding up and down to the Gym for rehearsals, our emotions moving from hope to despair and then to panic as the performance date drew near. Would someone fall off the stage at the crucial moment? Would somebody burst out of a costume or would the safety pins hold? The relief when it was all over and everything had gone well!

Some of my travels have taken me further afield and I have interesting memories of my visits to France - the colourful markets where the girls made their first tentative efforts to speak French, the excitement of the visits to Paris with everyone dressed to kill, the beauty of the Bayeux Tapestry and the fascination of the displays in the D-Day Museum at Arromanches to someone of my generation. The 'crocodile' in France is more of a friendly group, but it is still close behind you, as I found out to my cost when I entered a bank, the girls hot on my heels, and we promptly found ourselves trapped and squashed between two security doors, waiting for the time-delay mechanism to release us! Some of my fondest memories are of the visits I have made with Years 5 and 6 to various regions of the country. All those magnificent castles and cathedrals and the marvellous historical treasures we have seen in York, Canterbury and Stratford.

There have been funny experiences as well. Did I really cross a white water river in Wales upside down on a rope, at an age when I should have known better, in order to maintain some teacher cred. With Year 5? What about the time when Sr Victoria went AWOL in Whitby and Mrs Zelos ran up and down the prom calling ' Has anybody seen a nun? I'm looking for a nun.' The startled onlookers were expecting Jeremy Beadle to jump out from behind a convenient deckchair at any moment. What a cheer went up from the children when shortly afterwards Mrs Zelos returned with Sr Victoria safe and sound! Now I am starting a new chapter in my travels, accompanied not by the children but by the video camera which I was delighted to receive as your parting gift but I know that for evermore, from time to time, I shall still be looking over my shoulder to see if the 'crocodile' is keeping up.

Mrs Shirley A Brandon 1978 – 1998

Years 5 & 6
Stratford Upon Avon

Are we there yet?

Some years ago, Mrs Phillips and I decided that we would take Years 5 and 6 on a biennial field trip. An exploratory visit by the two of us was essential to check out visitor attractions and, of course, to find suitable accommodation for fifty plus children with supervising adults.

Once the basic building blocks were in place, an itinerary needed to be planned. Numerous toilet stops were essential when taking young children out and these were factored into each day's programme. This always caused amusement amongst the colleagues who accompanied us. One remarked,"I don't think I can go to the toilet that number of times in one day!"

Another essential item was food. Breakfasts and evening meals were catered for, but supplies for picnic lunches and snacks needed to be bought. This task was ably taken care of by Mrs. Phillips, who ensured that no child would go hungry while we were away! With the coach booked and children, adults, luggage and supplies on board, we were ready for the off!

A visit to Stratford on Avon with its many Shakespeare connections speaks for itself, and on the final day a visit to Warwick Castle, just a few miles away, completed our trip.

Yorkshire provided enough material for two trips, once to York to see the Minster and Jorvik Museum, and on another occasion we centred our visit on Whitby with its Captain Cook connections, not forgetting Bram Stoker's "Dracula"!

The south coast offered us many opportunities. On one occasion we spent a fascinating morning at the Channel Tunnel Exhibition, while the tunnel itself was under construction. Here we discovered exactly what was happening out there under the sea. Later, we made an interesting discovery about the White Cliffs of Dover - you can actually go inside them! They have a maze of tunnels, constructed during the Napoleonic Wars, and used again as a communication centre during World War 2. Finally, the Royal Dockyard in Portsmouth, with its three historic ships, proved a valuable hunting ground for us. When we visited H.M.S. Victory a young sailor was our guide, and when he was asked if it were considered an honour to serve on such a famous ship, he thought for a moment then replied, "The Captain says it is." What a diplomat!

These are just some of the many places that we visited. To the children it was an adventure, and for us an excellent opportunity to extend their educational experience, and, much to our relief, we never lost a child, though we did lose Sister Victoria in Whitby, but only briefly.

Shirley Brandon, Year 5 Class Teacher (Written in 2014)

Mrs Catherine Hill

Farewell To You All

Yes! I'm afraid it is farewell from me.

Last year on Monday 15th September I was standing in my kitchen looking out of the window as I was eating a piece of toast for breakfast, I said to myself out loud. 'Back to school on Wednesday'. The summer had been a good one weatherwise, and I had enjoyed myself, but the sudden rather horrid death of Diana took me by surprise, I had almost been holding my breath in disbelief since I heard the news.

About to sit and watch another programme on the Princess I decided to take some clean linen upstairs first and that was it! I just made it to the bedroom, but I didn't make it to the Convent two days later; I was in hospital having suffered a mild heart attack. Now I am writing this 'Good Bye' letter and not quite sure what to say. You see, I thought I would never leave; the work had become part of my life.

Oh yes, I got fed up at times and some days were horrendous, but it's the same for all of us, isn't it?

Its twenty years next year since I started at the Convent.

Sister Francis was in a spot, the Drama Teacher had just died. There was a plea for help in the newsletter; my own daughter had just become a pupil, the stage had been my profession so I thought, why not! To my surprise Sister took me on, and I have been grateful ever since. What an experience, all those wonderful children. To be in thencompany was a privilege and to be one of those directly influencing their future a task of great responsibility, not always easy, but such a joy. Often I would drive home after a day at the Convent really happy with my work and loving every minute of it. That is why I thought I would never leave. But leave I must.

My husband has been ill with cancer and other problems for the last three years - he even managed to fall down the stairs and break his hip a couple of weeks after my heart attack - he won't mind me telling you this, we often have a good laugh about it. So, for both of us, now is the time to slow down a bit, we may look for a house with a smaller garden though neither of us are too keen on the idea. I am working from home now taking private lessons and giving myself more time to write, something I had always promised myself and something greatly enhanced by all the years of helping my pupils to choose their verse and prose; an education girls, for you and me! I can now use a computer for the first time, and my spelling has improved!

Thank you all, and take care of yourselves. It goes without saying that I shall never forget any of you, and my heart is now mended and full of happy memories.

I' m truly sorry that I must say, FAREWELL; but remember Girls.........WELL DONE

and GOOD LUCK for the future! With all best wishes

Catherine Hill 1978-1998

A Summer Fete Performance

Fete accompli

Although Bazaars and Garden Fetes only occurred once a year, they were an important part of School life. There was also the preparation ahead of the events and the organisation on the day. We thought that we would write down a few memories of those hectic days.

The first major fund raising event of the School year was the Christmas Bazaar. Every class had their traditional stalls but after half term, brains would be wracked as to how to make it slightly different – not an easy task.

We decided to have a go at good quality second hand toys. Several weeks beforehand generous parents deluged us with contributions from pre-Christmas clear-outs. However, this meant Sunday afternoons spent sorting, pricing and labelling of puzzles, dolls, etc. For the other staff there was cake pricing, books to sort and chocolates to buy and prepare for the popular chocolate tree.

In our time the Bazaar was in the gym on a Saturday afternoon. The Friday before was manic as our spaces in the gym had to be prepared and set up as attractively as possible. We all hoped we would not end up in the dark corner. Some years later we moved to the Sports Hall which gave us more room. Endless journeys were made carrying produce and goods – all this being done whilst occupying our classes of excited children. After all the hard work, the hall always looked welcoming and there was a feeling that Christmas was just around the corner.

The Summer Fete filled our hearts with trepidation for as well as the stalls we also had to put on a production involving every child in the Lower School. (Just as well teachers can multitask). As the summer term began, so did rehearsals, alongside academic life, swimming, sports etc. How did we manage it?! Productions ranged from David and Goliath to Dinosaurs and were always planned for outside. However, after several soakings in summer showers and competition from Church Wedding bells (one had to see the funny side) we were 'allowed' to do further productions inside. As soon as the Play had finished the Lower School staff had to make a hasty dash to their stalls which had been set up previously. There were the familiar cakes and books but being summer the chocolate tree was exchanged for ice cream. We had chosen plants and shrubs.

People's generosity and hard work throughout the year meant that the stall grew in size and reputation. This led to Alan (Jane's husband) being asked what Nursery he came from.

Was this time for a career change? One particularly successful year we did the unthinkable and beat the bottle stall!!!

Although putting on these events could be stressful and time consuming parents were amazingly generous in giving both time and money. Without these so many things like the Sports Hall and the Barn Theatre could not have been realised.

Sue Rogers, Lower School Staff, 1982 – 2008 Jane Wright, Lower School Staff, 1987 - 2007

1993 Carol Concert

A sound and enriching foundation

Casting my mind back to my mind back to my teaching days at the Convent was a nostalgic journey. Several memories were especially vivid and strong. I have chosen some that were very enjoyable.

Firstly, I can remember, clearly the annual Christmas performance, where the staff and children worked so hard to achieve a high standard.

There was an atmosphere of tense excitement, as we prepared – painting scenery, arranging costumes and rehearsing the lines and music. (Some children were natural performers; other more reserved. What a joy to see a quieter child enter into character and surprise us all.)

Two plays stand out, particularly. The first was 'The Night the Animals Sang' with Obadiah the Wise Owl predicting the wonderful arrival of the Christ Child. Mary Claxton played this part, wearing a beautiful costume, lovingly sewn by her mother.

I also recall that the sheep had broad Yorkshire accents that were true to the Dales. The camels were bad-tempered, after their long journey and kept grumbling! (It was a beautifully written play and the children responded whole heartedly.)

Another production was Dick Whittington, again well written and enhanced with catchy songs. I can see Miss Gooderson painting the black and white timbered houses for Medieval London and the children singing the vendors' cries as they sold their wares at St. Bartholomew's Fair.

Katherine Abel played the part of Dick in energetic style. Edward Sell was an imposing eastern Sultan.

The Christmas performance continues to be a special event in the school's calendar. The theme around the Christmas story changes with modern tastes. My granddaughter's play in 2013 was called 'Tinsel and Teacloths' set around an OFSTED inspection.

Among the subjects I taught was History and I was very enthusiastic. One of the modules was Invaders and Settlers and I worked hard to recreate those distant times. On one occasion, we had an Anglo-Saxon feast with close equivalents for food and drink. We dressed up, painted large shields, deciphered Saxon riddles and made decorations and jewellery. I t was very popular, especially as Miss. Burton and I were the slaves and waited at tables. The children loved the role reversal.

I always hoped that the children in some degree might continue to be enthusiastic about my passion of history, drama and literature but I was so surprised when one pupil told me, later on, that I had taught her a lot about God and how to be with others. I felt very humble.

I do hope that many of the children will have gone out into the wider world and become generous contributors with their energies, hearts and spirits. They were fortunate to have had such a sound and enriching foundation in a unique school.

Carol Pointer, Junior School Teacher 1986 – 1994 Written in 2014

A new chalk face!

Starting a new school must be one of the most nerve-racking experiences a person can go through, and is something that is usually associated with children, but what is it like for a new teacher you may ask yourself, well the Convent's very own roving reporter Abigale Halls was put on the case!

Mrs. Rizza is a name many of you, the parents, may not be familiar with but as of September 1994, she became an English teacher at our school, for the seniors. I interviewed her to investigate her first day feelings and her opinions of the Convent School and the infamous Convent girls!

What were the first obvious differences you found between our school and your previous place and level of teaching?

Well the first major difference, for me, upon entering the building, on my first day, was the size of many of the pupils. This may sound profound but I also teach at a University and so am used to my pupils being at eye level with me, whereas here many of the children were only around my knee level. This came as quite a shock!

I have previously taught and still teach G.C.S.E.s to adults so, for me, there was not a great jump from one level of teaching to another. However, I was very new to teaching Year 7's so that took me quite a while to get into my stride, they were the biggest jump!

Do you enjoy the atmosphere in an all girl's school?

I enjoy the school's atmosphere very much and although I'm not politically correct when I say this I do feel that it is very good for girls, in the main, to be in a single-sex school, they function better with no distractions. Being in an all girl's school does not restrict them, as it did in the olden days, having contact with boys, or having a social life. I very much enjoy the atmosphere because the girls do not have to compete with boys, and are not being put off by them or intimidated, which normally happens in mixed classes.

Is it more stressful/tiring/enjoyable teaching children who are so much younger in comparison to your other/previous pupils?

TIRING - very much more tiring, younger children make many more demands on you than older pupils. As the children get older they become more mature and thus you can relate to them as adults, they can also cope on their own. Whereas smaller children look on a teacher as a substitute parent, a sort of Mum or Dad to some extent, that I find takes up a lot of energy and is very tiring, but at the same time it is also very rewarding.

The school is very close knit in comparison to a university. Do you find that daunting?

It is certainly something that I had to get used to, but I find it very friendly. It was like moving into a family! In a school such as this there is no way of being anonymous, unlike in a big institution, a University or even large Comprehensive school, where you can blend in to the background, here you have a very high profile. When you're not there, for example, it is very noticeable and that takes some adjusting to, but it has its rewards.

How were you welcomed by the pupils and your fellow teachers, and what were your feelings when you were introduced to the school in assembly?

The welcome was very warm from all the members of the school, even the younger pupils who I don't teach. The staff were extremely welcoming, they put me right on the things I didn't know and were very helpful. As for my introduction to the school in assembly I did feel a bit like a queen, for a moment I didn't know what to do.

Have you found it easy to accept the attitudes and teaching methods of the school?

Yes. One, because I'm adaptable and two because I'm old! I was educated in a very similar background, my school was an all girls Grammar school. I know some of the school's methods and regulations are not the same as in the comprehensive school system, but it suits me because it reminds me of my own education that I found very easy to adapt to.

Do you find a smaller school more relaxing to work in / more pleasurable on a one-to-one basis?

Yes, in that you can get to know the pupils better which, of course, is a great advantage. The better you know them the easier it is to teach them, as in any subject I would think.

Thankfully in this school there isn't the feeling of 'them and us' between the pupils and the teachers, whereas in some schools it's a constant battle and fight, where the teachers are struggling for control all the time. It is relaxing in that you don't feel you are struggling against the pupils and it is tiring in the way that you do feel much more closely involved in everyone's lives. You can't easily shut off as you come to care for each of the pupils.

Finally, can you sum up your first day feelings?

Extremely nervous! When I first came I was particularly worried about dealing with eleven and twelve year olds, it has been a long time since my own children were that age, and the only experience I have had is when I did a term at a middle school and I found there that I had to teach many subjects that I wasn't very knowledgeable in. Thankfully I haven't had that problem here.

I think one of my main problems was that I came over prepared with excessive lesson plans, which I never actually fulfilled. I now know that when it comes to the younger classes you cannot really plan, but instead take everything as it comes.

So, its not easy is it? Mrs Rizza seems to enjoy the school and the pupils, but starting as a new teacher isn't as simple as you may think, so 'Convent-ites', be nice to them when they start because now you know how they feel!

Abigale Halls – Year 10 1995

My five years in a convent

My first impression of the school as I was shown around by Sister Francis in 1993 was one of peace, tranquillity and hard work. It was something of a rare experience for me to see pupils standing quietly, holding doors open to ease one's passage through a school. My previous thirty three years in the teaching profession had taken me to various parts of the world. These included a spell in the highlands of Northern Kenya amid the traumas of inter tribal riots, two spells in special schools for delinquents, a prolonged period with the British Forces Education Service in Germany and many years in mainstream English High Schools. The prospect of spending the twilight years of my teaching career in the 'relaxed' atmosphere of the Convent was something to which I looked forward with enthusiasm. I was, however, quite unprepared for the pace of life in the school. Where does the energy, which exists within the school, come from? I can but assume that it comes in the first instance, from the Sisters and the way that the school is run. Despite what we might sometimes feel, there is, a thirst for knowledge and a feeling of expectancy from the girls, a facet of school life that, apart from my time in East Africa, I had not been exposed to. It has been both a pleasure and a privilege to be a member of such a dedicated staff whether in teaching or support roles. They, operating within the Catholic ethos of the school, make it an establishment of which all can feel justifiably proud. The successes achieved by the school in both academic and non academic areas have, I am sure, much to do with the Sisters' uncanny ability to spot the smallest of talents that staff may possess and the way these talents are channelled into action. So it was that I found myself responsible for Lower School Football and Cricket, Careers Guidance and Special Educational Needs, in addition to my teaching subjects of Maths and Religious Studies. It came as something of a shock to me to find myself surrounded by 25 Lower School boys and girls, playing football and each one wanting to kick the ball at the same time. As a qualified Football Association Coach this was something that I had never seen in the manual.

One of the highlights of my time at the school came in 1993 when I was asked by Sister Francis to take part in the Carol Concert at Mr Foti's Hermitage Hall and, later, in the school. Regrettably, I was not asked to repeat the performance in later years and my career as a public performer was short lived. Some parents actually liked my ' Country & Western' style of singing carols.

Now as I prepare to put my chalk and board rubber away for the last time, my final thanks yous. I would like to thank the Sisters for giving me the opportunity to share their school, the Staff for their comradeship and support, the girls, both past and present for their hard work and friendship and finally, my wife Mary, who, for the thirty seven years of our married life, has been the one on whom I have relied. She, despite continuous ill health, has been largely responsible for what I have achieved and has supported me in my failures. Perhaps, now, I can begin to repay her. To you all, go my very best wishes and may Almighty God be with you always.

Terry Morrell 1993 - 1998

An honest account –
After one of our headcounts we were a child missing!

I first encountered the Convent in the very late fifties when I was sent by my school (Swaffham Secondary Modern School) to invigilate the 11plus exam. It was so quiet and peaceful in the school and I was served lunch in what I now know as the inner sanctum, by a striking nun with a white veil. She told me that she was about to take her final vows and I wondered why a pretty girl should choose the life of a nun. I was later to encounter this nun as a fully-fledged member of the Daughters of Divine Charity. That nun was Sister Thomas More! Sixteen years elapsed before we met again as I took up a teaching post at the Convent! I applied for a job as reception teacher and was appointed by Sister Margaret after answering two questions- could I teach children to read and when could I start? My very close friend Joanna Gribbon, later Deputy Head, persuaded me to apply and I'm grateful she did.

My first classroom was a wooden hut, cold in winter very hot in summer, with peacocks calling on the wall outside. Mrs Wade was a Welfare Assistant when I arrived and she remained a helpful and loyal servant to the school and especially to me and the children for many years, sadly she died after a long illness. We were extremely lucky to have such a hardworking and dedicated band of welfare assistants without whom the Lower School would not have run so smoothly, we owe them many thanks. We were very fortunate to move into a superb new Lower School building after much hard fund raising by the PTA. As a member of the committee we had lots of fun fund raising and many of those members remain good friends today. One of our money raising efforts was a sponsored walk when the Lower School went to Merton by bus and then walked the woodland path to the church. We certainly awakened the village but everybody was fascinated to see them enjoying themselves.

Mrs Jill Williamson
'Never a moment wasted'

We went on several outings the most memorable being trips to the Norfolk Show where the children were allowed to stroke the animals without numerous hand washes! On one visit after one of our head counts we were a child missing-help! I went to look for him but to no avail and then some member of the public told me he was marching with the brass band and there he was marching in the middle of the band blowing an imaginary trumpet. Needless to say I held on to his hand very firmly for the rest of the day.

Sister Francis was our new vibrant head and added a new dimension to school life by organising a Building Committee, which later became a PTA. It was great fun being part of these groups and much was achieved for the school. Alec my husband was given the nickname Axe-man and I am sure that the Sisters thought that he was a woodcutter. I am not sure where he got the name but he was often wielding a knife at hog roasts.

Sister Agnes was our very hard working and dedicated Head of Department working tirelessly for the good of the school. I have a memory of Sister Madelaine walking a family of twelve day old ducklings all the way to the pond at the bottom of the road to keep them safe only to find all but one had been eaten the next day. All the nuns, in the house or in the kitchens were very helpful in the overall running of the school.

My husband and I were very grateful to all the senior staff who taught our daughter, Emma, and enabled her to achieve good exam grades. We were very proud when she was appointed Head Girl and are pleased she had such a well-grounded education as many parents must be. One of my lasting memories of the school will be of whole school assemblies when 3 year olds upwards would sit through a mass and behave impeccably. That does not happen in many schools today and many employers have said that Swaffham Convent children do have something special to offer. Long may the school succeed My special thoughts go to my former pupils no longer with us, Freya, Alexandra and Daisy

Jill Williamson 1975 - 2007

Jill was a fantastic teacher, secondary trained but marvellous with Infants who understood her slightly unorthodox methods: 'put that rectangle into that rectangular hole' was well understood by her five year olds who loved her. The parents were always a little wary as Mrs Williamson would not stand for any nonsense, children were capable little souls and needed to practice disciplined independence - over protecting them was not an option. I remember well the day she challenged a senior member of staff, who thought that teaching young children was so easy, to change places with her. The gauntlet remains down to this day! Jill was a marvel and the rest of the Lower School staff admired her forthright ways which engendered positive, polite, questioning children with excellent reading skills. Sr Francis, one of her admirers!

Jill always remembered the Infant funnies and would recount them in the staff room and then submit them for the school magazines. Here is a small selection:

Mrs Willamson, we do change our feet a lot of times in this classroom.

Q. What has happened to your sweater, it seems too big?
A. I think I've shrunk

Q. What did you do at school today?
A. Not much, we've been too busy to do anything.

Q. What is a Vestry?
A. A place where the vicar keeps his chocolates.
A.   A place where the vicar keeps his vests.

Memories of Sacred Heart School

My first memory of the Sacred Heart School was arriving there, in the dark, for an interview the next day. I felt terribly ill and when Sister Kasjana opened the door, I said without ceremony, "I need to go to bed at once". After that initially unpleasant beginning, things looked up and I have very happy memories of my time at the School.

When I started, I had Year 6 as my class and thoroughly enjoyed having them in the room off the Science corridor. There were four 'naughty' boys and the rest were girls. We had some fun although getting them ready for the SATS test in English stands out for me, as a painful time. I decided after that, that I would recommend to the staff, that we stop doing the SATS because they were dull and not particularly helpful.

I went on a number of school journeys over the years, especially to France with Years 5 and 6.

These French trips remain my favourite of all the school trips I have been on. I found that watching the pupils trying snails or trotting round the market, practising their French on the long suffering stall holders, or at the end of the day, scampering around the beach, was a joy. Possibly, putting them to bed at night was not such good fun! Overall though, we had a wonderful time from which I felt the children benefitted hugely.

Fond memories

I enjoyed teaching GCSE Classical Civilization and remember taking my group to London to see a Greek play. We went to the British Museum to look at the Greek collection before diverting to Covent Garden market, where I spent a rather anxious hour, hoping that the girls were all behaving themselves! After eating and watching the play, I recall we were driven back to Norfolk arriving at some ghastly hour around midnight.

When I first arrived I helped the Librarian catalogue the Library, which had previously been Mrs Davey's Art Room. I could not possibly compete with all that the Sisters have contributed to the fabric of the school but I rather hope that I had let my mark on the school in the proliferation of built in cupboards in the Senior School and the painting of classrooms and corridors!

I remember, quite frequently, that tragic day in July 2006 when Daisy Stonach died. Without doubt, it remains the worst experience of my teaching career. It is, I think, the event that marked me more than any other and is in my thoughts remarkably often.

I recall both staff and pupils with great affection and look back happily on my seven years at school. I keep in touch with one or of the past pupils and feel that they really are a credit to the school as well as to their families.
Diana Wynter Deputy Head, Sept 2002 - June 2006, Headteacher June 2006 -July 2009 (January 2014)

Miss Wynter was a lady of some standing, her manner and dress inspired respect, good manners and perhaps awe amongst those who did not yet know her kindly manner. She was articulate and very well Informed and could turn her hand to any form of teaching, mastering the subject matter or the age of child. She brought a certain style to our country school, an air of the city, a knowledge of the wide world. The school is richer for her presence and I, personally benefited from her sound advice and talent for recording all things factual. She steered the school into a new dimension with the addition of boys to Year 11. (Sr. Francis)

Dual personality

My association with the Sacred Heart School has been a dual role – that of parent for 13 years and then as a member of staff for over 20 years and still counting!

It all began in 1979 when my daughter Claire then aged 3 started school. It was a daunting experience for both of us but soon friendships were forged both between the children and also between the mothers. Many pleasant 'get togethers' were enjoyed by the Mums newly relieved of their offspring and friendships begun. Three years later my son

Mark donned the uniform and quickly settled in. I have very fond memories of various activities which we as parents were invited to watch or take part in. It was often necessary to produce a costume of some sort and I remember having to provide outfits for such diverse characters as Ramases, a dog, and a Russian dancer just to mention a few.

There seemed to be several social activities which the parents enjoyed. There was one particular social event held around the swimming pool when one of the fathers who was gesticulating to demonstrate some point very nearly knocked Sr. Madeleine into the water as she attempted to pass by. He had to grab hold of her but fortunately she saw the funny side of it.

The years flew by in a flurry of sporting events, concerts, bazaars, garden fetes, parents' evenings and exams. Sr. Agnes managed to teach Claire to knit – something which I had tried but failed to do. Mrs. Williamson gave all the children in Mark's class some pumpkin seeds and he grew such an enormous one that it was a job to carry it in to school but the praise he got made it worthwhile. Sr. Thomas More returned to the school and taught Mark both in what was then junior 2 and again in junior 4. He thrived on his maths classes with her and it was on her recommendation that he applied for and got a scholarship to St. Joseph's College in Ipswich going on to study electronics and electrical engineering at Imperial College. Claire stayed at the Sacred Heart for the full 13 years before moving on to Fakenham Sixth Form and then to London to get her Diploma in general nursing at St. Bartholemew's hospital. They were busy happy years and in 1992 we said our goodbyes or so I thought!

In the following year there became a vacancy for laboratory and reprographics technician and so my role changed from that of parent to member of staff. It was strange to suddenly find oneself a colleague of teachers who had taught one's children and to see people in a completely different light. I hadn't really given much thought before how hard the staff worked and how dedicated they are.

There have been a number of science teachers whom I have worked with during the last 20 years. Mrs. Black and I were together for 14 years, Mr. Blackwell taught chemistry for about 5 years, Mrs Davidson for 2. Mrs Hall the young Australian biology teacher did 3 years until she went back to Australia. Now we are fortunate to have Mrs Burton who brings a lot of fun and unpredictability to the labs, Mrs Verne who brings a lot of love and Mr Murphy who brings technology and wonder! The labs are still standing however!

When I made the changeover from parent to staff member I was made very welcome and I think having been a parent of past pupils made me understand the feelings and expectations of the parents. The Sacred Heart School is unique and many a past member of staff has been told they should write a book about it – you certainly couldn't make it up but it does get under your skin!

Catherine Carter; past parent, science technician and current reprographics wizard (2014)

I could write a book but would anyone believe me?

After teacher training, followed by a year out in France, I returned to England in 1976 to discover that teaching jobs were in short supply and ended up with a temporary job as a filing clerk at the DHSS. My father was told by a colleague that a job would soon be available at the Convent as his wife, Mrs Rogers, was leaving to have a baby.

I knew nothing about Convents or nuns and it was under parental pressure that I wrote offering my services! I was duly invited for an interview by Sr. Margaret. On arrival I was offered tea, asked a few questions and shown around the school. I left wondering whether I would be invited back for an interview.

Working with me was another newly-trained teacher, Roz Downey (or Mangan as she then was) and as there were several posts to be filled I suggested that she also applied. She too was shown around but left having been told that the job was hers.

It was several weeks later and nearing the beginning of term and I had still heard nothing from the school and had assumed, rather with relief, that my services were not wanted. However, again under parental pressure, I rang to ask. I was greeted by Sr. Margaret whose response was, "But of course! We are expecting you to start next week!"

It was with great trepidation that I started life at the Convent, firmly determined that it would be temporary for a year until I found something away from Norfolk. I started in Infants 3 (Year 2), Roz in Infants 2 and another newly qualified teacher, Denise Mole, started in Junior 3 or 4. It really was a baptism of fire! With classes of 32 and waiting lists, no learning support or structured schemes and an expectation to "get on with it," many a lunch time was spent at Wagg's café in tears and despair! Florence Gardiner, a learning support in the Pre Reception class helped to keep us going. The staff were kind but appeared so efficient that we felt unable to confess our inadequacies. In the next classrooms were Mrs Whiteland, who had taught me as an infant at Marham Primary School, and then Sr Agnes who, whilst kindly and offering support, was intimidating to someone with no experience of nuns and convent life. There was intense pressure from parents who were not always happy with the structures we put in place and their word was always deemed final by Sr. Margaret!

Every third week I was filled with dread! The three classrooms had partitioned doors which were folded back and first thing every morning Infants 3, Junior 1 and Junior 2 had Assembly together and every third week it was my turn to take it. I have every sympathy with the younger children who are unfamiliar with the Lord's Prayer as I had never come across the Hail Mary. I would start it, with fingers crossed, and hope that the pupils would automatically continue as I was unable to puzzle out the actual words. Today the Internet would come to the rescue!

One Saturday I returned home late in the afternoon to find my mother anxiously waiting following a puzzling phone call from Sr. Agnes early in the morning. She had desperately wanted me to go to the school jumble sale to retrieve clothes. On arrival at school on Monday morning I discovered that the bags of dressing – up clothes for the forthcoming Sports Day had disappeared! Sr. Agnes had sent them to the jumble sale and, "Do you know, Miss Gooderson, Sr. Catherine actually laughed when I told her!" It was several years later before I discovered that Sr. Agnes had had to pay one parent a considerable amount of money for a pair of her designer shoes which she had been silly enough to send for her child to use! It was only then that I realised how much Sr. Agnes had protected us.

I was about to start teaching one afternoon when the door was flung open and a furious Sr. Agnes (normally so calm and collected) burst in dragging one of her boys by the collar. I am not sure who was more frightened, he or I, as she loudly proclaimed that, "He has the devil in him!" and he would have to spend the afternoon with me. I was so unnerved that I did not feel I could ask him what he had done and it was some days later that I found out that, with an audience of boys, he was trying to see how far over the dustbins he could urinate!

Having no staff room, morning break time was spent in my classroom and we always knew what the children would have for lunch (no staff would have braved the meals then) by the pieces of vegetables floating on top of the jug of coffee. Lunch break time could be spent in Mrs Williamson's hut, surrounded by buckets if it was raining. The staff toilet was in the children's cloakroom and on one occasion I looked up from the toilet to discover one of the boys looking down on me.

Not being a Catholic one of our foreign Sisters was given the task of teaching my class R.E. so twice a week, in the lesson after lunch, I sat outside my door in the corridor, next to the toilets, to do preparation or mark books. Unfortunately I could hear what was going on inside the classroom and time was wasted afterwards trying to settle the children down. Hell and damnation figured frequently, in more ways than one! Eventually, when I realised that the children were actually running across the desks, I knew that I would have to have a word with Sr. Agnes. Another Sister took over but the next year I must have passed the test as I was told that I was to teach it myself.

I was very bemused when the first Christmas arrived and pupils kept coming and asking me what I wanted for Christmas. I replied in my usual vein of "Oh a trip to America or a new car," but the children became more and more anxious and eventually I managed to piece together from the children that their previous teacher had allocated certain things to certain children e.g. one would bring her a pheasant, another a Christmas tree etc. An easy way to do Christmas shopping but morally…? Well!!

Things gradually became easier as we got to know our colleagues and they became great friends. Although I do remember Roz and I sitting in the market place rewrapping cakes bought from the bakers to take to the Bring and Buy sale being held at Jill Williamson's. Homemade cakes it had to be and neither of us were confident in that area!

Looking back over the years I realise how much things have changed under Sr. Francis' headship. There was little contact with the Senior school and staff were addressed by surnames. We felt like poor relations! On one occasion when a senior teacher was implying that anyone could do Reception teaching Jill Williamson offered to exchange places for a day. The challenge was not taken up. I wonder why??

In those early days I had to take my class swimming, in spite of being a non-swimmer myself at that time. Usually I managed to find a parent to accompany me. For one summer I was offered the services of a new Sister, Sr. Paul. I have to confess speculation amongst the staff as to what Sisters wear in the swimming pool (this was over 30 years ago and no-one had ever seen them in the pool!) I duly took the children to the pool and awaited Sr. Paul's arrival. I am sure my mouth dropped open as she (a rather large lady) appeared in a two-piece costume with a bright pink swimming hat. I don't think the staff believed me when I told them! I later learnt to swim, with encouragement from Sylvia Foxwell, the music teacher.

I have numerous early memories – mostly happy - of time at the Sacred Heart (as it has become.).

Sr. Agnes riding off on her bicycle to bring back a child who had run home (crossing the road at the front of the school which was then the main A.47)

Jenny Davey, a senior teacher, appearing at lunchtime with a Reception child whom she had

1991 Comic Relief Day
Miss Gooderson or was it Baderson with her water pistol

picked up in her car down Station Street. He was walking home as he thought it was home time.

The time a father (whom we had not met) arrived to pick up his child and the child insisted he did not know him– we had to ring the mother who confirmed that it was his father!

Having to rush a child to the cottage hospital as he had pushed an abacus bead up his nose was worrying..

Sr. Maria Goretti, with her piano accordion serenaded Penny Peirce on her birthday.

Sr. Paul charging across the playground astride a broomstick, shouting, "Tally Hoo!" and followed by a line of screaming children.

Staff acting out one of our reading scheme books, The Village with Three Corners, with Jill Williamson as a cross Mrs Blue – Hat; Staff in gales of laughter and the children watching rather bemused by it all.

The arrival of Sr. Thomas –More, to replace Sr. Agnes as Head of Lower School was awaited with trepidation as Sr. Agnes had frequently warned us that she was a "dynamo" and things would change. It did – things became less formal as Sr. Thomas-More actually joined us in our new staffroom and addressed us by our Christian names.

An anxious Sr. Madeleine rushing over to my classroom, late one evening – the cleaner had finished and locked me in. On arrival at home she had realised and rung through to the Convent. Fortunately I was unaware as we had no phones in our building or mobile phones then.

From my classroom watching senior pupils, at break time, climbing in and out of a coffin. It was a prop for a production of Oliver and had been brought in by the daughter of a local undertaker.

The beautiful cherry trees that grew near the sycamore tree – it was a sad day when we returned from our holidays to find them gone.

My temporary year extended and I gradually became familiar with all the idiosyncrasies of the Sacred Heart. Under Sr. Francis' headship new buildings grew up, structured schemes and support systems were introduced and life became easier.

Outings took on a greater importance and regular visits to local attractions became embedded in the curriculum. I vividly recall my first visit to the Tudor Re-creation at Kentwell Hall. Dressed as Tudors and accompanied by Sr Francis in the old style habit it was unfortunate that the year chosen was one when Catholic worship was not in favour and the children and I spent the day hotly defending Sister's presence. She of course rose to the occasion and even volunteered her services in succeeding years.

My first residential trip was with a group of year 5 and 6 pupils to The Kingswood Centre, on the coast, accompanied by Viv Phillips and Sr Francis. Here I had my first experience of Quad biking and Archery. The sleeping arrangements were far from perfect with the staff rooms well away from the children's dorm. Unfortunately on the first night there was a violent thunderstorm and the children were terrified. Sr Francis and I spent much of the night patrolling, Sr Francis having to console a group of Year 3 boys from another school. Their teachers, also situated away from the children's room, obviously slept through it – as did Mrs Phillips!! It was here at Kingswood that structure was given to a mammoth undertaking – our first and grandest Bookfair.

Following an inset for the staff on "Display" the Sports Hall was converted into bays, each decorated with a different literary theme. The timetable was suspended for three days and the whole school attended various workshops there. These included sessions with authors, journalists, illustrators, creative writing students from the U.E.A., booksellers, etc. To complicate matters we also invited several local schools to send groups. The logistics seemed impossible but all went ahead smoothly and it was a great success. The children benefitted enormously and we even gained a pupil from one of the schools – she had enjoyed it so much that she was determined to move!

The introduction of the National Curriculum brought more changes (although perhaps not so many as for some schools) and numerous training sessions in Lincolnshire for Lower School staff. On each session we would be given a Green folder full of lengthy notes and tick-sheets. They became the bane of our lives but we were lucky to be able to attend as Norfolk County Council were not helpful towards Independent Schools. The folders were certainly helpful when we had our first "proper" Inspection.

It was as a result of that inspection that the Senior Management Team was set up and Jenny Davey and I joined Sr Thomas-More, Sr Francis and Vincent Kelly. My brief at the beginning was to foster closer links and continuity between Lower and Upper school. Child Protection was also to become my responsibility and little did I realise at the time what an undertaking that would be!

Over the 37 years I have been with the school there have been numerous changes but one thing has remained the same and that is the strong sense of family, community and care which our Head girl so eloquently summed up last year and which I believe makes the

school such a special place.
Miss Sally Gooderson, Head of Lower School, 2014

School memories

My first memories of The Convent of the Sacred Heart are when I started in Infants 3, Miss Gooderson's class, after the February half term in 1977. At the start of the morning of my first day, we went into the next door classroom to join with Juniors 1 and 2 for assembly. I was slightly surprised to find that we sang the hymns with the help of a hymn book, not something I had encountered in my previous school. On that day it was "Ride on ride on in Majesty." If I ever hear this hymn now, I am immediately reminded of that first day!

Music and performances seem to be my greatest memory of the nine years I then spent as a pupil. Each summer at the Garden Fete, the Lower School gave a performance. In Infants 3, in honour of the Queen's Silver Jubilee, we all had to be sailors dressed in navy trousers and wearing our boaters behind our necks. We danced "The Hornpipe" on the lawn by the lower school classrooms. Both the lawn and cherry tree that grew there are long gone...the Lower School playground has grown larger and taken over this area. I remember at the same fete, the Pre-Infants (of which my younger sister was a member), sat in pairs on two benches and sang "The wheels on the bus go round and round." The second verse of the song was "We're going on the bus to see the Queen," all very topical and imaginative!

Another time in Junior 1 or 2, I was a flame in a bonfire and wore a red tabard. Other pupils in the class were also flames whilst others were smoke and wore grey. We danced round a boy perched high up on a gym stool who was the guy on top of the bonfire- less health and safety to worry about then maybe?

I think it was that year that the younger pupils acted out "David and Goliath." The children playing the Israelite soldiers all carried silver foil swords and blue and white shields they had made. The huge card and paint Goliath giant really did seem to be nine feet tall as he was in the song the children sang!

In Juniors 3 and 4 we seemed to do a lot of country dancing... "Heel and toe, heel and toe, one two three and away we go!" I'm not sure how, but some of us also managed a gym display at these events along with pupils in the senior school. I think the teachers must have spent hours with us all rehearsing!

Also in Junior 3, we did a Christmas play called "The Rebels' Inn." I felt really lucky, since I had to sit at the front of the stage playing a woman at the inn and eat small pieces of broken digestive biscuits throughout the performance!

I think the entire highlight of my time at school was the "Oliver" performance in 1984. What seemed to start as a fairly small show involving one or two classes, soon became an extravaganza involving numerous pupils and teachers as well. All sorts of props and costumes were acquired, the most memorable being a real coffin lined with silk for the scene in the undertaker's shop! We seemed to practise the songs under Mr Carter's direction and indeed the whole show, for what seemed like months and looking back there was so many talented pupils who took part!

Other memories of my time at school include pupils fetching the teachers' coffee in a big jug each day from the kitchens and bringing it to Infants 3 classroom (there was no Lower School staff room then). I remember eating chips with grated cheese and beetroot as a school meal in the dining room and later packed "cold" lunch in the classroom. As a special treat in summer, cold lunch people were allowed to take their food to eat on the field. The field was considerably bigger then or so it seemed to me. There were chickens in a run belonging to the house next door which we could see through the fence and a large tree to play around in the area where the Sports Hall now stands.

In the Lower School, Infants 3 and Junior 1 and 2 classrooms were all divided by screens which could be opened and pushed back. We had to be careful not to lean against them. One day when I was in Sister Agnes' class -Junior 2, there was a loud banging and shaking that seemed to come from the direction of the screen. Sister Agnes tutted and we carried on with our work. She told us the next day that actually it hadn't been somebody moving the screen, but a small earth tremor!

There were several mobile buildings housing Junior 4, the cookery room and later the science labs. I remember when the new Lower School was being built, people were asked to buy a brick at a summer fete and then sign it, presumably to be put into the new building. Later when it was finished we were able to have a tour – it seemed very modern and smart – I never dreamt at the time I would be lucky enough one day to teach in that very building!

I have many other good memories of trips to London and Paris, sponsored walks in all weathers and the cold, cold swimming pool! I can never forget the day when my family arrived to swim during the summer holidays to find a half full / empty pool... we went to the boarding house and told Sister Madeleine who after seeing it for herself said: "Somebody has pulled the plug out!"

Now I look back over the years, I think I could write much more about my times good, bad, sad and humorous at school. However perhaps most outstanding is that I really was very fortunate to be a pupil here and in many ways, also very privileged.

I am sure I can say without doubt, that my sister, Louise and I received not only a sound academic education, but an excellent social one and have much to be grateful for to Sister Margaret, who made the initial approach to my parents about the two of us joining the school. However, as the years have gone by, the Convent has become so much more than just a school to my entire family. My parents were involved running stalls at fetes and bazaars while we were there as pupils and have maintained their links with the Sisters as a result. Louise and I both formed life-long friendships with fellow pupils and in 1997, shortly after I had qualified as a teacher, Sister Francis approached me with the offer of a job teaching in the Lower School, so in many ways I feel I have come full circle! Most importantly to me, my own children, Charlotte and Isaac are now at the school as pupils themselves. I have no doubt that today they are benefiting from the caring and supportive environment that is such a prominent feature of the school. I am inordinately proud to have been associated with the Sacred Heart School as pupil, parent and teacher and hope this may continue for many years, long after the Centenary celebrations are concluded!

Catherine Riedlinger (nee Smith) Pupil, teacher and mother of pupils – 1977 – present

Memories of school 1974 – 1987

Being at the Sacred Heart School for 14 years, I have a few memories…

The earliest one, I think, would have to be drinking really cold milk with straws that always got stuck before we finished the bottle. Another one from my early years, when we went to the cookery room to make pancakes and because of our enthusiasm one got stuck to the ceiling!

In junior school, we had a teacher with whom we enjoyed singing songs, such as 'Here comes tiny wee Flea' and 'The mouse under the stairs', we also had Sister Agnes who taught us handwriting.

In senior school it was time to knuckle down and get on with lots of new subjects. Sister Francis taught us RE, Sister Catherine, Maths and Mrs. Davey, Art and Needlework. The first garment we made was our own apron for cookery.

In addition to all the subjects we learnt, we staged a production of 'Oliver' which was really good fun. In our class we had on loan, a coffin for the production, which we all tried out!

Entering into the community spirit, we attended the Swaffham Carnival as pupils of St. Trinians, involving a bank robbery (a film popular with all of us at the time). We used the really old school uniform, this was extremely effective. Other floats included grown men dressed as babies and dancing cavemen!

In senior school, P.E. was always interesting. We played hockey and attempted cross country, in the snow (all without joggers!) It was certainly character building! As a class, we played netball matches against other schools…and won!

Towards the end of term, we would play pirates in the gym with all the equipment out or climbing the ropes.

The summer term always seemed to be hot and we knew that in our final year that meant the examinations were looming. It also meant that the gym, where we took our Levels and CSE's was stifling, but we also knew that the long holiday was drawing closer.

After about 34 years I came back to school as a Teaching Assistant to support children in the classroom. When I arrived at the school there were some familiar faces from the past! Sister Francis was still in charge and Mrs. Mansfield who taught Geography was still there, as was Miss Gooderson which shows that the school has very dedicated staff. They all made me very welcome, and I feel like part of a huge caring family.

A few things have changed, such as the size of the classes and there are new buildings and play equipment, school dinners seem really good now, but they don't make the donuts, which used to be a Friday treat and all the school would be queued around the dinner hall, sometimes twice!

Since being back at school, I have made contact with a lot of past pupils from my year; some of their children attend the school now, which is really encouraging to see. The uniform hasn't changed much except the pupils don't have to wear open toed sandals anymore with navy tights or long socks, and the senior students don't have the pleasure of wearing boaters which grew soggy and sticky in the rain!

I really enjoy being in school, I've been on a few school trips, such as skiing and the

Geography field trip to Holt Hall. I have helped with Shakespeare and music evenings which can be very hectic at times, but it is always very rewarding to see children of all ages performing confidently.

Vanessa Adcock nee Chapman

Confessions of a bursar

It all began in 1979. My elder daughter had commenced at the School and Sister Francis convened a meeting to raise funds for a new infant classroom block. Being a responsible father I delegated attendance to my wife and stayed at home to watch football on the box! Sister Francis was not impressed by the lack of fathers attending and duly adjourned the meeting to be reconvened with fathers present.

I should have known better but went along as requested. As fathers entered the room they were pressganged on to what was to become the 'Building Fund Committee'. The Committee raised £20,000 in two years and the Infant Block was built and opened by Sister Angela in 1981.

Bishop Eddie of King's Lynn

Time to sit back and rest on our laurels – not so said Sister Francis as she had decided that as the Committee had been so successful it was time to form a PTA. I was elected Treasurer – a position I held until my retirement in 1997. According to my records the total sum actually raised by the PTA during that period was £104,527.35. That was a considerable amount of money and was of course used to develop the School premises and facilities.

One of the major achievements was raising funds towards the construction of the new Middle School block which was officially opened on the occasion of the 75th anniversary in 1989. This block was designed by our in-house Architect Roy Payne and constructed by my company, Walter Lawrence.

Another major success was the construction of the new Sports Hall which we were able to contribute towards. This was constructed by Andrew Scales of SCWS. The Sports Hall was officially opened by yours truly in 1997.

All the Committees put in a lot of hard work to raise those funds but also had a lot of fun in doing so. The sight of Sister Francis riding a three wheel tricycle around Swaffham Drill Hall at the end of our Charity Auction will live in my memory for ever.

The PTA was also instrumental in organising trips to Paris and Rome for staff, parents and pupils – and these again were memorable. On our first trip to Rome we had been booked into a hotel which turned out to be in the 'red light quarter' – enough said!

On the second trip to Rome Sister Francis had decided that I should be suitably rewarded for my long service and consequently whilst in a restaurant, much to the amusement of the other diners, I was 'ordained as Bishop Eddie of Kings Lynn'. This title originated from my attempts to obtain a reduced price for entry to the Vatican and when asked for details of my Bishop and Diocese as I had no idea (not being a Catholic) that is how I completed the questionnaire. The title has remained with me ever since and frequently confuses Sister Thomas More as when she receives a telephone call from the Bishop she does not know if it is the real Bishop or me.

The final trip was to Paris in 1997 and I particularly recall the journey home in the coach. My children had completed their education at the School, I was no longer on the PTA and I was retiring from business at the end of the year. I was sitting alone, considering my forthcoming lifestyle and various duties well done (in my opinion) when Sister Francis came and sat beside me to say "We are not letting you go you know". Sister then asked me to become Bursar of the School and to oversee the financial affairs of the Daughters of Divine Charity in England.

Mrs Irene Ranner enjoying an afternoon away from her computer.

My response was that I would think about it and after several weeks mulling it over I told Sister that I would take on the challenge. Sister's response "I know – the Sisters have been praying". And so I became the Bursar on 1st January 1998 and have seen many changes throughout the years but the ethos and spirit of the School remain the same.

The Sisters tell me they do not retire as theirs is a job for life – something tells me that this could also apply to the Bursar!

Eddie Howard, Bursar, Parent, Building Committee and PTA Member, Governor 1979 - present
16th April 2014.

Still working on the computer.............

I blame it all my daughter, Delwynne, and her godmother Ena Needham......

Way back in 1976 Delwynne was born and Ena was asked to be one of her godmothers. Little did I know then that her recommendation that Delwynne should become a pupil at the Convent would lead through to the present day with my continued association with the Sacred Heart School.

Delwynne duly started in Pre Infants and I found myself involved in various activities as one does as a parent! The normal ones like concerts, fetes and bazaars but then there was the second hand uniform shop which I helped to establish all those years ago and which is still going strong.

Delwynne progressed through the school, blossoming under the care of the committed staff who were determined to ensure that she developed all of her talents, despite her contrariness at times! There was her love of Music & Orchestra with Sr Thomas More; Maths with Mrs Sally Henderson & Mrs Marilyn Coughlin; even her English blossomed under Mrs Valerie Mann's eagle eye. Sister Agnes Lee ensured that she attempted needlework and craft. She progressed through to Form Five (Year 11) went on to Downham Sixth Form to study 'A' levels and then to University. Despite our advice she followed her father into Civil Engineering and now has a very creditable CV of sites and works completed also of contracts still being worked on! All due in no small part to the education and encouragement given by the staff in her formative years.....

Meantime I had found myself a permanent position within the school. In 1987 a vacancy for School Secretary arose; would I be interested? It involved getting to grips with a 'computer'. Not for me a typewriter but this new fangled keyboard with a memory!!!! Up for the challenge I was ensconced in the new, as it was then, Middle School building. My husband then got involved; writing a database where everyone's details were recorded; very basic and nothing like that now available, but it was a start.

I was eventually 'retired' from the front-line work of the School Office in December 2004 but not from the school. I continue to maintain a presence; this time ensconced in Sr Thomas More's Office in the Boarding House. Still working on the computer and fulfilling other tasks as required.

Who would have thought that all those years ago I would still be here working with and for the Daughters of Divine Charity. Thank you for all you have done for me & my family, also for what you continue to do for the education here in Swaffham.

Irene Ranner School secretary and PA to Sr Thomas More

Chaplaining at Sacred Heart School

Chaplaining at Sacred Heart School is a 'double-deal' with being Parish Priest of Our Lady of Pity - there is no getting away with it. Just as Ole' Blue Eyes used to sing - it's like "Love and Marriage, Love and Marriage, go together like a Horse and Carriage - you can't have one without the other". But like Love and Marriage it's both a great relationship, but equally you never know what is going to happen next! Especially with Sr Francis as the Head.

It all started early on in my time in Swaffham when Ryanair and Easyjet were just overtaking Buzz & Go & Debonair, and rivalling each other for the cheapest fares. With their usual hospitality I had been invited by the Sisters for Sunday lunch, and in making polite conversation, I said I had come across a web-site called 'Skyscanner.com' that found the cheapest air-fares, and that I had discovered that it was possible to fly to Rome for £4.99. The words were hardly out of my mouth before Sr Francis with her forefinger pointing at me said: "We're going! I'll ask the girls tomorrow how many want to come! They'll have to get the answer from their parents that night! I'll ring you first thing on Tuesday morning to tell you how many seats to book".

I was still having my morning cup of coffee on the Tuesday when the phone rang, and Sr

Francis blurted out "There are ten girls, and twelve members of Staff"! Having got all their names down, I returned to Skyscanner.com and found the outward fare had decreased to £2.99! So off we went for four or five days. the females staying in the Headquarters of The Daughters of Divine Charity at Grottaferrata, and the males with Franciscans nearby.

Fr Michael

We saw everything that could be seen in four or five days in Rome, including attending the Papal audience on the Wednesday. One girl, who had disgraced herself by an act of disobedient foolishness a few days before leaving, was in a wheelchair, and along with all others who were not able to walk, was wheeled right up on to the raised area near the Holy Father, and to everyone's amazement her naughtiness was rewarded by being presented to St John Paul 11, and receiving his blessing!

It was in Rome that I discovered the downside of travelling with a crowd of teenage girls: clothing shops ..... and loo stops! I spent many an idle hour awaiting those who had wandered astray. But I also discovered the usefulness of mobile phones for finding the whereabouts and rounding-up lost ewe-lambs!

So that was the start of it. Thereafter, while air fares truly remained startlingly low, we went to Krakow - to the Salt Mines, to Zakopane the mountain resort (in pouring rain), to Katowice (St John Paul's birthplace) and to Auschwitz. There's no need to expand on the influence of that on the children. And in another year it was off to Prague - to Independence Square, to the Opera House, St Vitus' Cathedral. Here we stayed with Sr Anna in her school: the most memorable thing being that all the female Staff members one night finding themselves locked in the building and unable to escape and join the party for supper! The only way of finding how to exit was to ring Swaffham, and ask someone to ring Sr Anna, who by then was safely home in her Convent and oblivious of the problem! And to Theresienstad - the 'model town' for the incarcerated Jews, with its own orchestra and schools - but also with its inevitable end, of holocaust. This was just as moving as Auschwitz had been.

There were other less diverting duties demanded of the Chaplain: the weekly Class Masses for example, those with the Junior School often wonderfully memorable with the innocent simplicity of 'the tinies', with their eager hands up to answer - often wildly off the point - any questions put to them, and Whole School Masses at the end of term, or on Feast Days like the Feast of the Sacred Heart, with some joyous choir singing and music-making under the inspiring direction of Mrs Harvey, and with the talents of so many of the pupils. Then also there were the bi-annual opportunities for the Catholics to make their Confession, most memorably when those awaiting would pray in silence before the Exposed Blessed Sacrament, often with conspicuous devotion and concentration. And when the Feast of Corpus Christi occurred during School time, the Procession in the

School grounds; or on other Holy Days of Obligation with the whole school filling up the pews in Our Lady of Pity Church, and raising the roof with their added volume enlarging the voices of the usual congregation.

Preparing Year 10 Catholics for Confirmation was another joyful task, which Sr Francis and I tried to make adventurous and eye-opening for Catholics living in a part of the country where Catholics are few and far-between, and where they seldom see people of their own age at Mass. We based our preparation on learning about the Sacraments, trying to find the opportunity for the group to experience each Sacrament in action. So the candidates would come to Our Lady of Pity for one of the two annual Masses of Anointing of the Sick, where they would act as hosts at the simple lunch afterwards; and they would visit another Church in the neighbourhood to see some of their contemporaries being Confirmed. They would attend a wedding, perhaps singing a Motet or other music as a group; and watch a Baptism from the gallery. We were lucky, too, in one year to be able to take the group to our Cathedral in Norwich for an Ordination. In addition to this we would go away for a long weekend to Ampleforth Benedictine Abbey in Yorkshire for the young to see and experience Monastic living and prayer, and visit other places of interest – historic or religious - on the journey there and back; or to Clare Priory in Suffolk for a different monastic experience, and time for instruction and prayer.

Hamish MacQueen, the Diocesan Youth Director comes to the School from time to time to organise Youth Events in the School's considerable facilities, which the older girls were able to share in. This was particularly the case in years when there was an International World Youth Day; and on two occasions - in 2005 and 2008 - some of the girls joined the Diocesan Group, going on the earlier occasion to Cologne, and on the latter to Townsville in Queensland and Sydney. Both of these occasions were truly formative and memorable occasions.

So all in all, there was much "on the go" in the life of the Parish Priest/Chaplain, shared between 'town' (the Parishioners) and 'gown' (the pupils at Sacred Heart School). But all in all joyous and joyful - and often with a good mixture of the secular with the sacred. And for me, certainly, they were ten most memorable years.

Fr Michael Johnstone, School Chaplain, 2002 – 2012

Fr. Trevor Richardson

Fr. John Cureton

Staff between 1989—2014

Administration Staff

Gloria Boulton Assistant Secretary Jan 2012—present	Catherine Carter Lab/Repro Assistant Sept 1993—present	Valerie Chaffer Office Assistant 2000—Sept 2000	Susan Cipolla Office Assistant/ LS 2001—June 2001	Erica Dineen Lab/Repro Assistant Sept 1992—July 1993
Karon Dugdale LS 99 Assistant/ Secretary 2001—Sept 2012	Deborah Fountain School Secretary May 2011—present	Edwin John Howard Bursar/ Governor Sept 1998—present	Helen Kelley (Harvey) Assistant Secretary Nov 2012—July 2013	Irene Ranner School Secretary 87 Admin Jan 2005—P
Philip Riedlinger IT Support Jan 2000—April 2001	John Sorrell IT Support 1999—2003	Jane Stockdale Secretary Jan 2005—July 2010	John Williamson IT Support 2002—July 2006	Peter Young IT Manager Sept 2001—present

Diane Twining, Reprographics, PTA chair, 1991-1992

Boarding House Assistants, Learning Supports, Playtime Supervisors

Vanessa Adcock Learning Support Sept 2012—present	Penelope Barton Boarding House Jan 2004—July 2004	Margaret Bond Playground Sup 1980—April 1998	Teresa Cannon Learning support 1988—July 2004	Jennifer Chalkley Learning Support 2002—July 2005
Jacqueline Cockman Kitchen / EY Mar 12 Dec 2013—present	Lorraine Dennis Playtime Sup/ Dom Jan 2000—Oct 2009	Maureen Doran Listener	Sylvia Filmer Nursery Assistant Sept 2000—Mar 2009	Julia Fitzpatrick Playtime Sup / Dom 1995—2005
Florence Gardiner Learning Support 1974—1996	Janet Heaver Librarian/ LS Sept 2002—July 2013	Cheryl Jenkins Boarding Nurse 2002	Margaret Keating Playtime Supervisor Mar 2013—present	Susan Knock Playtime Sup/ Dom Sept 1993—Oct 2009
Liridona Laska Early Years Assistant Sept 2008—present	Nicola Leeder Learning Support May 2014—present	Beth Phimister Boarding Assistant July 2002—Nov 2008	Michelle Redford Learning Sup (Vol) Jan 2014—present	Margaret Smith Boarding 1999—2002 Vol Feb 2009—present

Boarding House Assistants, Learning Supports, Playtime Supervisors

Jacqueline Tansley
Support Assistant
1988—1999

Ute Tingay
Playtime Supervisor
June 2009—present

Amy Underdown
Learning Sup
1996—April 2004

Barbara Wade RIP
Learning Support
1974—1998

Patricia Woodwards
EY/ Boarding Mistress
Sept 1995—July 2013

Sarah Wookey
Learning Support
Sept 1997—present

Jacqueline Amini, Boarding Mistress, Jan 2004— July 2004
Sandie Salthouse, Learning Support, Sept 2005 – Dec 2005
Terri Tighe, LS Volunteer, Nov 2012 – Mar 2013
Rosalind Ware, Boarding Nurse, Dec 2009

Sheena Zelos
Learning Support
1991—2000

Catering, Domestic, Maintenance

Richard Allison Domestic Feb 2009—present	Caroline Bowman Kitchen 1997—Dec 2000	Emma Craske Kitchen Assistant Jan 2014—present	Bruno Coelho Maintenance June 2013—present	Lily Cleaver Kitchen Assistant/ Cook 1998
Mally Doreste Catering 1997—June 2008	Brian Dunlop Catering 1998—June 2007	Wendy Dunton Domestic 1978—March 2008	Dorothy Fuller Domestic 1996—2002	Sally George Kitchen Assistant Oct 1999—present
Angela Gilding Domestic 1997—2002	Susan Greer Assistant Cook 1998—April 2003	Jean Harrod Domestic Jan 1986—Feb 2009	Melanie Hurren Domestic 2003—2003	Doris Knight Assistant Cook 1996—2000
Jack Knock Painter Jan 2001—July 2011	William Knock Gardener 1997—2004	Ann Powell Domestic 2001—July 2002	Angela Shough Domestic 2003—Dec 2007	Kirsty Smith Kitchen Assistant 04 - Manager Mar 2013—P

Catering, Domestic, Maintenance

Michael Titmarsh Maintenance 1979—present	Hazel Todd Domestic 1996—2002	Jemma Wright Kitchen Assistant Jan 12—present	Weronika Zawadzka Cook/ Domestic Sept 2007—present	Piotr Zawadzki Maintenance Jan 2008—-present

Helen Baldwin, Kitchen, Sept 2005 – May 2007
Ellen Blake, Kitchen Assistant, Nov 2011 – Dec 2011
Emma Buckley, Domestic, Jan 2009 – Oct 2013
Caitlin Chapman, Domestic, Feb 2009 – July 2009
Maria Coelho, Domestic, Nov 2006 – May 2012
Kelvin Copeman, Domestic, Feb 2009 – Mar 2013
Lindsey Gilding, 2002 – July 2007
Sally Ann Gilding, Domestic, 2002 – 2002
Sandra Gonclavas, Domestic, 2003 – July 2003
Brian Johnson, Maintenance, Sept 2003—Dec 2008
Patricia Johnson, Domestic, Mar 2003—Dec 2008
Edward Keating, Mini Bus Driver, Sept 2012—present
Stella Lee, Domestic, 2008—2009

Carol Lund, Kitchen Assistant, 2002—2002
Karen Matthews, Kitchen Assistant, Jan 04—Mar 2010
Katherine McDermott, Domestic, June 2012—Jan 2013
Donna Nally, Catering, April 2008—Mar 2013
Tamsen Nally, Kitchen Assistant, Jan 2009—Mar 2009
Kayleigh Shough, Kitchen Assistant, 2003—2004
Marluci Silva, Domestic, Nov 2007—Mar 2012
Julie Stangroome, Kitchen Assistant, 2001 –2001
Joyce Jean Steed, Kitchen Assistant, 1998—2002
Estinislau Stramonski, Domestic, Feb 2009—July 2009
Sandra Winter , Kitchen Assistant , 2003—2004
Paula Wood, Kitchen Assistant ,2000—July 2002

Peripatetic Staff

Alexandra Bhundia Speech & Drama May 2009—present	Helen Brandwood Piano Sept 2007—present	Bernadette Buxton Maths/ English 1992—Dec 1999	Jean Elizabeth Dean Latin Club 1997—June 2009	Mark Dawson Cricket/ Football
Michelle Burrel, Dance, 1996—July 2002	Francis Buxton, English & Maths, 1992—July 1999	Bonnie Bygrave, Sept 2009—present	Kenneth Canfor, Self Defence Instructor, 1994—2000	James Grant, Gymnastic Coach, 2003

Peripatetic Staff

Paul Donley RIP Peripatetic Music May 1995—Jan 2008	Eddie Godden Drama, Security July 2001—Nov 2011	Juliet Golder Speech & Language Sept 2001—present	Andrew Graham Guitar May 2011—present	Catherine Hill Speech & Drama Sept 1978 – July1998
Jeremy Hodges PE Coach Sept 2008—-present	Monica Horsley Buck Typewriting 1990—July 2002	Adrian Kitchen Violin Teacher 1993—1995	Lissa Kinsey, Singing, 2002—2003	Frances Levy Piano, violin Nov 2009—present
Helen McDermott Latin American Dance Sept 2007—present	Wendy Nixon Ballet Teacher 2002—2010	Valerie Pickering Speech & Drama Sept 1995—present	Karen Stanghan Piano, flute Sept 2005—present	Richard Stibbon Guitar Teacher 1995—April 2011
Ashley Swift Tennis Coach Sept 2014—present	Debbie Upton Gymnastics 1994—Dec 2000	Joan Upton Visiting Nurse		

Laura Hayes, Drama Club, Mar 2012—July 2013
Catherine Hill, Speech & Drama, Sept 1978– July 1998
Andres—Salazar, Peripatetic Singing, Dec 03—04, 06– July 12
Anna Hudson, Woodwind Teacher, 2002—July 2005
Kate Jones, Maths Teacher, Sept 2008—June 2009
John Kirby, Tennis Coach, Sept 2002—March 2013
Fay Lincoln, Singing & Instrumental, 2005—2005
Rosemary Millikin, Visiting Nurse, Sept 2007—present
Richard Moore, Roller Skating./ Hockey, June 2010
Jason Orage, Gymnastics, Jan 2000—Sept 2000
Matthew Parkinson , Oct 2010—Jan 2011
Olga Robinson, Dance, 1991—1993
Eddie Seales, Orchestra, 1991—1993
Mandy Slater, Music, Sept 2005—April 2009

Sisters Past and Present

Teachers

Anne Baker Science/ Deputy Head Sept 1974—July 1998	Leslie Balfour Lower School Teacher Sept 1998—July 1999	Tessa Black Science Teacher Sept 1982—July 2007	Malcolm Blackwell Science Teacher Sept 1993—July 2001	Shirley Brandon Year 5 Class Teacher Jan 1977—July 1998
James Brown Mathematics Jan 2014—present	Vanessa Burton Science Teacher Sept 2008—July 2014	Anna Carter Lower School Teacher Sept 2008—July 2014	Donald Carter Junior Teacher Sept 80 P. Music Sept 91– July 07	John Clements Maths Teacher 03 Peripatetic Dec 13—P
Marilyn Coughlin Maths Teacher 1987—1997	Maggie Dalton PE Teacher 1985—Dec 2004	Jennifer Davey ,RIP Art/ Textiles Mar 75—Mar 11	Bernadette Davison Science Teacher Sept 2001—July 2006	Clair Foster PE Teacher Sept 2005—July 2010
Mary Gargett– Stringer English Teacher Sept 2003—present	Sally Gooderson Head Lower School 06 Sept 1976—present	Valerie Green HE Teacher Sept 2008—July 2010	Julie Grover Music Teacher Sept 1992—Dec 1999	Carla Hall Science Teacher Sept 2006—July 2008

Teachers

Jane Harvey Music Teacher Jan 2000—July 2014	Marguerite Heale LA 99 Art/ Pottery/ HE July 2006—present	Irene Henden (Hillen) Junior/ SENCO/ RE '14 April 1983—present	Sally Henderson Maths Teacher Sept 1987—July 1993	Jane Howarth French Teacher Sept 1987—July 2014

Julie Jennings Lower School/ SENCO Sept 2002—July 2013	David Johnson English Teacher Jan 2002—July 2004	David Jordan ICT Teacher Sept 2012—present	Oona Kelly Class Teacher / RE Sept 1998—July 2002	Vincent Kelly Maths Dir of Studies Sept 1998—July 2002

Hilary Kenny Geography, Dep Head 06 Sept 1992—present	Katherine Laban Science & Maths Nov 2011—present	Pat Leonard Maths Teacher Sept 1998—July 2003	Valerie Mann English/ Deputy Head Sept 1976—July 2003	Marie Mansfield Geography, History, RE

Terry Morrell Maths/ Football/ SENCO Sept 1993– July 1998	Lewis Murphy Maths, Science Teacher Jan 2010—present	Wendy Padley English/ Drama Teacher Jan 2005—July 2014	Penny Peirce Little Pedlars Teacher Sept 1986—July 2014	Vivienne Phillips ICT Sept 1987—present

Teachers

Catherine Racey HE Teacher Sept 1989—July 2007	Catherine Riedlinger Lower School Teacher Sept 1997—present	Carol Rizza English Teacher Sept 1994—Dec 2001	Sue Rogers Lower School Teacher April 1982—July 2008	Rachel Scrafield L Sup Maths/ Science April 2005—July 2012
Susan Stanley HE Teacher Sept 2007—July 2008	Frances Verne Science, Maths, PSHE Sept 2007—present	Robin Stratford Maths Teacher Jan 2003—Dec 2009	Jill Williamson Lower School Teacher Feb 1975—July 2007	Natalie Wilson History Teacher Sept 2010—present
Rachel Wilson PE Teacher Sept 2010—present	Jane Wright Lower School Teacher Sept 1997—July 2007	Diana Wynter Deputy/ Head Teacher 06 Sept 2002—July 2009	Zoe Young PE Teacher/ Supply 11 Sept 1987—Sept 2011	-Adrian Cooke, PSHEE Teacher, Sept 01—April 13 -Andrew Howarth, Supply PE Teacher, Sept 12—Nov 12 -Carole Pointer, Junior Teacher, 1986 – 1994 -Gary Saunders, ICT Teacher, Sept 11—July 12 -Susannah Wade– Martin, History Teacher, 1880—1992

Chapter 18 THE SISTERS

Province of the Sacred Heart at St Teresa's Convent, Hunstanton
Back Row: Sisters Madelaine, Gorretti, Margaret, Verdrana, Catherine
3rd Row: Sisters Emilia, Bernarda, Monica, Jacinta, Kasjana, Winifide, Hildeberta
2nd Row: Sisters Francis, Clare, Agnes, Lydia
Front Row: Sisters Mary Joseph, Thomas More, Dobrimira

SIXTY SIX YEARS ASSOCIATED WITH THE SACRED HEART CONVENT

As we reach the 100th Anniversary of the Daughters of Divine Charity in England I realise that I have known almost all the Sisters who have ever lived and worked here.
My first meeting with a Sister was with Sr Irmgardis who was the Superior and Headmistress of St. Mary's Convent, Long Eaton. The school had been established in 1939 and I started there in 1942. The Community included Sr Hildeberta, Sr Josephine, SrMary Joseph, Sr Philomena, Sr Chrysanthia, Sr Dobromira, Sr Irmengard and Sr Bernadette. The last two Sisters returned to Vienna after the Second World War.

After six happy years I left St. Marys and went to Swaffham to the Convent of the Sacred Heart as a student teacher. Sr Irmgardis had been transferred and was Headteacher and Superior there. I worked with Sr. Clare in school and helped with the boarders. Sr. Agnes was Novice Mistress to Sr. Barbara, Sr. Frieda, and Sr Patricia and later to Sr Margaret and

Sr Stanislaus. Other Sisters in the Community were Sr Madelaine, Sr Laeta, Sr Michelina, Sr Anne and Sr Justina who later returned to Vienna.

The only Sister buried in the Swaffham cemetery at that time was Sr. Margaret Mary McSweeney who was the first English girl to enter the Convent. Sadly she died in 1928 at the age of twenty six and it must have been a great sorrow for the community. Her sister Pattie who was a teacher, visited Swaffham every year during the school holidays and I met her on several occasions.

I was fortunate to know Sr Ositha who had come to England in 1914 with the first Sisters and I was present at the celebration of her Golden Jubilee in August 1951. When I went to say goodbye to her during the Christmas holidays I said 'See you at Easter'. She replied, 'No, next time we meet in Heaven' and in fact I did not see her again as she died in January 1952 while I was at College.

For the next four years, two years studying to be a teacher and two years teaching in the Catholic School in Ilkeston, I only saw the Sisters during the holidays but I visited them whenever I could at Long Eaton, Swaffham and St Teresa's Convent in Leicester.

I knew God was calling me to follow Him in Religious Life so during a visit to Swaffham in the Easter holidays 1954 when Sr.Angela was Headmistress and Superior, she offered me a post as a Junior Teacher for September, I knew this was the next step I had to take.

Sr. Catherine was clothed in January 1955 and I joined her in the Novitiate in August of the same year. In 1963 we made our Final Vows together with seven other Sisters in the Motherhouse in Vienna. In 1969 I was transferred to St. Joseph's Convent Chesterfield and spent eight happy years as Superior and Headmistress before moving on as Headmistress to St. Mary's Catholic State School just next door to the Convent. I thought I would end my teaching career there but it was not to be, as in 1987 I came back to Swaffham and here I am. On the occasion of my Golden Jubilee one little pupil wrote 'Congratulations Sister, Keep Going.' Well I do try but age has a habit of catching up with one.

In each community I have lived and worked I have had the love and support of all the Sisters. I have so many happy memories of all of them and it makes me proud to be a Daughter of Divine Charity and it is such a great joy to see our two young postulants, Lucia and Ewelina who are ready to join our Congregation and will become Sisters in August this year. I hope and pray that they will be as happy as I have been.

England has always relied heavily on the help given by Sisters from other countries belonging to our Congregation. We are grateful to all those Sisters, too numerous to mention by name, who have lived, worked and prayed in our communities

SISTERS WHO DIED IN ENGLAND BETWEEN 1957 AND 1989 WERE:
Sr Michalina 1973, Sr Anne 1974, Sr Adelberta 1975, SrPhilomena 1978
Sr Gertrude 1982, SrAnthony 1986, SrLaeta 1986, Mother Irma Berko (1st Provincial
Superior) 1986

SISTERS WHO DIED IN THE PAST 25 YEARS WERE:
Sr Irmgardis 1990, Sr.Angela 1990, Sr Dobromira 1992, Sr.Mary Joseph 1996,
Sr Clare (aged 101) 1996, Sr. Madelaine 1996, Sr. Winifride 2001,Sr Hildeberta (aged 100)
2004, Sr Agnes 2009, Sr Margaret (4th Provincial Superior) 2011,
Sr. Monica 2012.

Mother Huberta Buchanan who was in Swaffham with Sr. Margaret Mary later became
Mother General in 1948 and died in Vienna in 1969.
Mother Fidelis Weninger who had been Mother General and later, our 2nd Provincial
Superior, also died in Vienna 2011.
Sr. Thomas More Prentice, Provincial Superior. (Written 2014)

Sisters

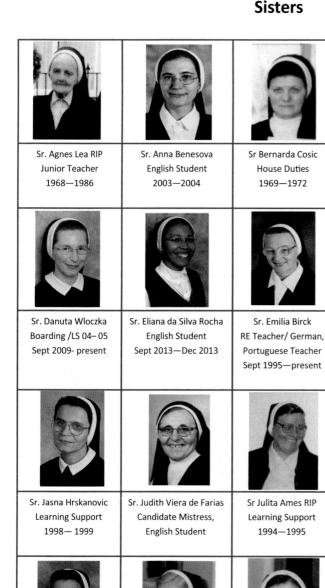 Sr. Agnes Lea RIP Junior Teacher 1968—1986	Sr. Anna Benesova English Student 2003—2004	Sr Bernarda Cosic House Duties 1969—1972	Sr. Catherine Maguire Superior, Maths Teacher Jan 1954—July 1968 Jan 1979—July 1996	Sr. Danica Sanader Learning Support 1992 - 1994
Sr. Danuta Wloczka Boarding /LS 04– 05 Sept 2009- present	Sr. Eliana da Silva Rocha English Student Sept 2013—Dec 2013	Sr. Emilia Birck RE Teacher/ German, Portuguese Teacher Sept 1995—present	Sr. Francis Ridler Junior /Art/ RE/ Maths 69 Headteacher Jan 79—May 06 Sept 2009—present	Sr. Jacinta Cirko Boarding House Keep- er Sept 1992—Sept 1996
Sr. Jasna Hrskanovic Learning Support 1998— 1999	Sr. Judith Viera de Farias Candidate Mistress, English Student	Sr Julita Ames RIP Learning Support 1994—1995	Sr. Kasia Zdanowska Postulant Mistress June 2007—July 2009	Sr. Kasjana Ziembin- ska LS, Boarding Duties Jan 1996—present
Sr. Linda Pergega RE/ Music Teacher, LS Sept 2006—present	Sr. Lydia Dupont RI{ Learning Support 1990—1992	Sr. Luzia Valadao Learning Support 1990—1991	Sr. Madeleine Ciquel RIP Nurse 1979—1996	Sr. Maria Gorretti Learning Support 1998

Sr. Mary Joseph RIP Cook 1964—1992	Sr. Mira Markic Nurse, Learning Sup 2005—2006	Sr. Monica Grebenar RIP Boarding House	Sr. Thomas More Prentice Class Teacher/ Deputy Provincial Aministrator Sept 1987—present	Sr. Vedrana Ljubic Learning Support 1991—1997
				Sr. Martina Cervienkova, Sept—Dec 2008 Sr. Weronika Mikova, Learning Support, Jan 2008—July 2009 Sr. Jeronima Juros, English Student, 1990—1991 Sr. Alberta Ibersperger, Community Member Dec 2009—June 2010 Sr. Ana M Autonovic, ICT Support, Sept 2006—July 2007
Sr. Victoria Dedic House /Garden duties Three periods of time	Sr. Zora Stojanovic Learning Support 1997—1998	Ewelina Switaj Postulant Sept 2012—present	Lucia Pivarnikova Postulant Oct 2011—present	

Compiled by Ewelina Switaj

Chapter 19 THE PTA

A most and generous and enthusiastic PTA supporting major projects like the Sports Hall, and Arts Centre Barn
1989 -1990
Chairman: Roy Payne, architect for Middle School.
Opening of the Middle School by Bishop Alan Clark
Easter PTA Trip to Rome, Sorrento and the Amalfi coast - fun packed adventure with 45 parents and pupils - sometimes trying to get onto local transport all together! 1st Splash Evening great success and 1st Grand Ball at Grady's, Swaffham.
1990 - 1991
Chairman: Len Bircham, wonderful at Jumble Sales and getting things done
2nd Annual Ball, Auction raised £600. £4500 raised at the Bazaar to go towards the Reference Library. Fashion Show presented by Dove's Boutique.
1991-1992
Chairman: Len Bircham,
£37000 presented to school at Garden Fete
The Christmas Bazaar raised £2775. The Annual Sponsored Walk was held through Thetford Forest. The Summer Fete raised £2000
1992 - 1993
Chairman: Len Bircham
Purchased 6 boxes to extend the gym stage, 7 new keyboards and a portable PA system.
3rd Annual Ball organised by Tony Abel – even bigger success; Quiz Evening; two jumble Sales; Rick Wick's rafting Extravaganza at the Splash Evening in the Swimming Pool – very dangerous, Dads were so competitive, BBQ held; Treasure Hunt; Auction at Drill Hall organised by Eddie and Helen Howard with auctioneer Chris Nash, completed a library annexe by opening up a cloakroom in the Senior School entrance.
1993 - 1994
Chairman: Andrew Scales, a passion for a large project – the Sports Hall
Car Treasure Hunt organised by the Abels, an Aromatherapy evening, a Quiz evening with a Year 11 team and another Ball.
Ladies Group organised by Helen Howard monthly on Fridays, mums took on 2nd Hand Uniform
1994 -1995
Chairman: Andrew Scales
Literary Dinner; Archive Film Evening & usual fund raising events;
Decision to build Sports Hall and undertaking gaining external funding
1995 - 1996
Chairman: Andrew Scales
1st Auction of Promises with auctioneer Chris Nash.
Sponsored walk organised by Jackie Moss raised £3500. £17000 raised during the year.

1993. Rick Wick's Rafting Extravaganza

1996 - 1997

Chairman: Gerry Burns – wrote regular newsletters to parents. £19000 raised with various events like the Sponsored walk, Ladies Tennis Day, Auction of Promises, Jumble Sales, Beetle Drive, and 100 Club. Opening of Sports Hall by outgoing treasurer. Eddie Howard, special family luncheon for past and present pupils, parents staff, Sisters and friends.

1997 - 1998

Chairman: Gerry Burns

£15000 raised towards Sports Hall heating through the usual activities including a Summer Ball, Auction of Promises, Jumble Sales, Horse Race Night, Irish Night, Barn Dance, Sports for Parents organised by Val Chaffer and Carol Price, Ladies Tennis Day and Meal organised by Carmen Sell.

1998 – 1999

Chairman: Gerry Burns who wrote: 'This school has always been blessed with an enthusiastic PTA'. The PTA offered constructive advice on a range of matters, drawing on members' experiences and talents to help the school's wonderful record of success continue. 'Sports for Parents' partially funded the red gym mats. 2nd Hand uniform run entirely by parents.

1999 - 2000

Chairperson: Tony Gayton – International Cuisine and Latin American Dance in conjunction with the Lionesses, Quiz Evening, Irish Night, Car Boot / Jumble Sale. 'Sports for Parents' organise weekly sessions of aerobics & Badminton. Purchase of PTA shed for storage. Youth Club at RC Church led by Tony.

2000 - 2001   Chairperson: Julie Grapes – renowned for explaining to parents the importance of increasing the facilities.

60's - 80's Night, Grand Jumble Sale and Grand Valentine Disco Dance, St Patrick's Night.

Money raised for Maths Garden, science pond, markings on the playground. Events included: Halloween Disco, Forest Ball, Irish Night, Splash Evening,

2001 - 2002

Chairman: Preston Andrews - very active in applying for grants. £30 500 raised for the Barn, (£10500 in grants) through the usual events as well as a Car Boot Sale, Quiz Evening, Jubilee Sponsored Walk followed by a 'street' tea party down the drive.

2002 - 2003

Chairman: Preston Andrews

Family Valentine Disco, organised talk from Police on drug abuse – good turnout of parents. A two week Summer School organised by Dee Ruppert.

Helped to organise a School Reunion – over 100 past pupils present. Survey sent to parents regarding a CCTV system to safeguard our children, continue to raise money for the Barn / Theatre

Tony Gayton PTA Chairperson 1999-2000 and Sr Kasjana

2003 – 2004

Chairman: Cherry Leeder, parent who seemed to be able to locate all kinds of resources including a very large furry camel for the Live Crib in the town.

It was agreed to go ahead with a CCTV Security System to be installed at the School.

Events included a Horse Racing Evening with pork supper, Film and slide show with Chris Knights, farmer and conservationist, a Beetle Drive and Splash Evening. The Bazaar raised £3654 and the Garden Fete £2300.

2004 – 2005

Chairperson: Sarah Knights, past pupil with new ideas; Firework Party at Beachamwell; Cabaret by Jimmy Germain as Cliff Richards at Lydney House; Beetle Drive and Bingo as family events; VE Celebrations instead of the Summer Fete. A Peruvian Art Diner Exhibition organised by Carman Sell to celebrate Jose Gomez's work. Money raised for the installation of CCTV, Lighting for the theatre, 2 projectors, and £3000 for the IT Department for upgrading computers plus £100 for each Lower School class and a Yamaha piano

2005 - 2006

Chairperson: Sarah Knights, a loyal and hardworking past pupil. Some very enjoyable and profitable events including a Bonfire Party by kind permission of Mr and Mrs A Wales, a Reindeer Drive, Bingo, Sponsored Walk through Thetford Forest, BBQ and Summer School organised by Mrs Dee Ruppert. Christmas Bazaar raised £3541 and the Fete £2020.

The IT Department has benefitted greatly, plus the current fundraising drive for the Swimming Pool Project.

2006 - 2007

Chairperson: Jae Payne used her contacts in show biz to help the school. The refurbishment of the Pool Changing Facilities commenced and plans to cover the pool with a telescopic cover considered; because of leaks in the pool the overall cost would be £50 000+, funds of £30000.The Ball at Lynford Hall raised £2200, and the PTA organised a Prom at the Leziate Club for Y11 and guests. Auction of Promises raised £4600 with excellent items such as a helicopter ride, liveried chauffer for the night, a day's shoot, £4600 raised. The Bazaar raised £3990 and Fete £1989.

2007 – 2008

Due to other commitments Acting Chairpersons were proposed this year: Night to Remember Evening raised £300, PTA involvement in change of uniform to Birds of Norwich. The first mention of a Reindeer Drive. The PTA Newsletter was re - introduced. Approximately £40000 was collected towards the swimming pool refurbishment programme. Dee Ruppert organised another successful Summer School.

2008 - 2009

Chairperson: Sally Hayes, past pupil with enthusiasm and drive;

Bank account looking poorly following a massive amount of it going towards the swimming pool. Fundraising bar raised to improve our finances. Summer school. Mr Hodges was introduced to the lower school to help with the provision of boys sports. Website for SHS parents only was set up. Parent Class Reps were introduced. Mrs Knock given a PTA gift for her 30 years service. Sponsored bike ride completed by Mark Sorrell, £2304 raised. Quiz and Chip night £121, Bags to school and

Everyclick.com were registered as new fundraisers as well as the children designing a Christmas card to be purchased in multiples, £120 raised by the latter. Table top sale held on school field. Bird boxes with infra red lights donated by Mr C Knights. Ball at Knights Hill £1393 Beetle Drive and PTA café. Fun Run. Bingo. A massive effort for the Christmas Bazaar with Santa, his elves and huskies making an appearance. Lots of outside stall holders. £3323. A successful fundraising year bank balance £10.941. A cheese and Wine evening, organised by the PTA was held at the meeting to say farewell to Miss Wynter. Sr Francis returning as SHS Head Teacher.

2009 - 2010

Chairperson: Sally Hayes:
Beetle Drive, Disco, Pamper Evening, Astronomy Fundraising Evening with cheese and wine, Easter Egg Hunt, New notice board. £5000 donated towards a new mini bus, Janis Bell sponsored Safe Start for school usage. Jungle Climber and other pieces of play equipment purchased and installed (£7000 from PTA and £8000 from County, £2600 from pupils). Strollers at Picnic in the Park event. Senior Sports day refreshment sales. Splash evening. Summer Fete and Christmas Bazaar input as always.

2010- 2011

Chairperson: Sarah Napper, a seemingly inexhaustible ability to get things done with an eye to keeping children safe
Strollers Night at Assembly Rooms £800, Pupils designed self-portrait tea towel; Children's disco £200, Bingo £90, Splash Evening, Ball at Leziate Park Club £1000, Pamper Evening £308, Bags2 school £460; Christmas Bazaar £2445 and Summer Fete £1900
Purchased own Bouncy Castle

Official opening of the Jungle Climber by Sally Hayes, former Chairperson of PTA and past pupil

2011 - 2012

Chairman: David Perowne, a man of ideas; Strollers Night at Assembly Rooms, £370, Reindeer Drive £141 Children's disco £100, Bingo £201, Splash Evening £218, Bags2School £250, Pamper Evening £199 Human Fruit Machine constructed. Two ICT suites in the Senior School were renewed and a bank of computers for the new ICT room in the Lower School was organised. Ball at Lynford Hall £1398, Pamper Evening £199 Christmas Bazaar £3074, Summer Fete £1992

2012 - 2013

Chairperson: Sarah Napper, find a busy person and things will happen. Smarter uniform researched mainly by Monica Richardson - tartan kilts chosen; Autumn Ball at Lynford Hall £2396, Strollers Evening in the Barn, fish & chip supper, Reindeer Drive £159, Lower School Disco £14, Bags2School £110; Splash Evening £207, Christmas Bazaar £2403, Sumer Fete £2403;

2013 - 2014

Chairperson: Sarah Napper
Focus has been on advertising the school and particularly renewing the website. Parents have continued to help at Open Days and their expertise amongst new parents has been invaluable.
Bags2School £390, Reindeer Drive £151, Senior Halloween Disco, Lower School Disco
Christmas Bazaar £2055
Compiled by Sr Francis and Sally Hayes Grateful thanks are extended to all PTA members and parents and staff who have supported, in every way, all the events.

Chapter 20 GOVERNANCE

1997 to advise the Head and Governing Body or Trustees who are the Provisional Council of Daughters of Divine Charity, on the educational and financial administration of the school. Membership included the Head, Sr Francis, Deputy Heads of the Senior and Junior schools; the finance officer, Eddie Howard; the parish priest, Fr Michael Michael Johnstone; the Provincial, Sr. Thomas More; and three independent lay members, Pauline Coe, Eddie Doran and Maurice Lynch. It was a period of national changes in education with a more prescriptive focus on the curriculum, regular detailed, outside inspection of all aspects of school life, a concern about health and safety in every area with the consequent beaurocracy and administration, and the implementation of policies to ensure the safety and welfare of all pupils and staff. All of this was very demanding on staff time and planning, alongside the maintenance of the warm, caring and Christian ethos of the school and its continued exceptional academic standards and results. It was also a time when the costs of a private education were heavy for many parents with a consequent fall in the school numbers. This was a cause for anxiety and required trying by every means, to counter it through open days, and many and various recruitment drives. In 2009 the school became co-educational, opened a nursery department and continued to offer flexible boarding arrangements.

Meanwhile, the numbers of vocations from the English province had declined and age was making its own inroads. When Sr. Francis departed to recuperate after a couple of operations and to oversee new educational ventures at Chesterfield, it was decided that a layperson be appointed Head. Miss Diana Wynter was appointed in 2003. She proved very capable, sympathetic and concerned to develop the school's ethos and achievements. Inevitably, an initial process of the separation of School and Convent began to emerge. It became clear that new sets of relationships and channels of communication between the School and its concerns and those of the Convent needed to be identified and processes to implement them be put in place. In particular, there was confusion of role regarding ownership, finance and administration and school governance. The executive had underestimated the need for detailed preparation in identifying the issues that might emerge from these areas and it was suggested that a more formal governing body with a broader range of experience and expertise should be appointed. In the event, Miss Wynter retired in 2009 and Sr. Francis returned as Head. As a result, these issues remain as business pending for the new governing body.

Maurice Lynch, Member of the Executive Committee and later a Governor, 2014

Second steps – Governing Body

The world of Education is like all other parts of our national life. It is subject to change and, if it is to prosper, then it must embrace change. Nowhere is this more necessary than in the management and governance of our schools. Once upon a golden time, it seemed everything could be left to the undoubted wisdom of the revered figure of the Headteacher. Now it is not so. Change is everywhere, from the construction of the school curriculum, the appointment of suitably skilled and qualified teachers and support staff, the demands of Health and Safety legislation, financial due diligence, and the rigours of the modern school inspection regime. The Head need support, encouragement and, from time to time, challenging, so that the strategic direction of the school is subject to scrutiny and analysis. It is foolish indeed, to believe the internal school leadership can achieve by themselves all that is required.

Thus, at the Sacred Heart, an Advisory Governing Body has evolved to assist the school to move forward, to build on its great traditions, and to continue to provide the very best education for its young people. The Board has a variety of skills it can offer, from knowledge of the law, the wider world of education, accountancy and finance, and a range of business expertise. As a Body, it meets termly, reviewing in detail, every aspect of the life of the school. It receives detailed reports from the Head and excellent contributions from Teachers, informing us of the work of individual departments. Exam results are poured over and the wonderful extracurricular life of the school reported upon. The Governors believe that this is a fruitful partnership that can only help the Sacred Heart School sustain the exceptional quality of the education it offers.
Robin Gregory, Chair of Governors 2014

Members

Tom Bedingfeld, Janis Bell, Robert Dale, Eddie Doran, Robin Gregory, Simon Fowler, Eddie Howard, Maurice Lynch, Marie Mansfield, Roy Payne, Rev Roger Sparks, Craig Wardle, Fr Gordon Williams, Michael Wright and Helen Howard, Secretary.
Former Members: Fr Michael Johnstone, Aiden McGovern and Delwynne Ranner

The Sisters are indebted to the help, generous time and good management of the school, firstly by the Executive Committee and secondly by the Advisory Governing Body. Their expertise, wise counselling and challenges have focused the Sisters and the Senior Management Team regarding the everyday running of the school as well as its future .

Plan of Sacred Heart Convent and School
Reformatted by Eddie Godden

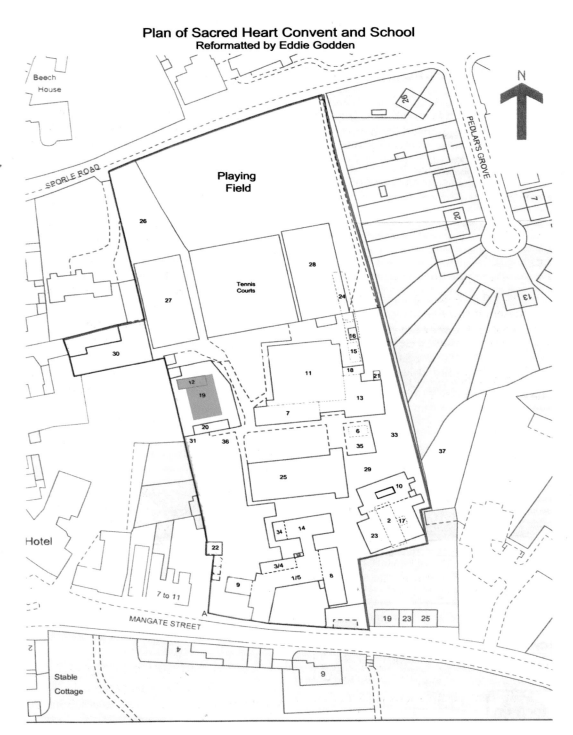

Chapter 21 PREMISES

The number given in brackets refers to the plan on the opposite page.

1914

A small house, Ivy House, was rented and then purchased in Station Street. The Sisters moved in on 11th July and the house was blessed on 24th July. There were two classrooms in the house and a stable building at the back of the garden was converted into a Chapel.

1920

The Sisters moved to their present convent on 17 Mangate Street. [1]

1923

The first building was erected, now demolished and sold for the same price as purchased. It was a white long hut with a black roof on the site of the present Infant School. [2]

1928

The first addition was made to the rear of the Convent building. The two storey addition contained a kitchen and dining room on the ground floor and a dormitory, two smaller rooms and bathrooms upstairs. [3 and 4]

1934

An additional storey was added to the main Convent building of four large bedrooms and other small rooms. [5]

1939

A classroom in the house was used by the boarders and the classroom transferred to a hut in the garden. [6]

1943

The field at the back of the Convent with an entrance from the Sporle Road was purchased, but could not be used as a playing field for three years as it had been used for pasture land.

1946

Playing field in use.

1948

Prefabricated building consisting of three classrooms was constructed on the former tennis court. Rooms were knocked into one room and used as the Art and Needlecraft room, and now the space is housing a whole school Library. [7]

1953

The large right wing of the Convent was erected and was used as a Senior Common Room and a Junior Common Room with a two large dormitories upstairs. [8]

Central heating was installed in some parts of the building

A laundry and bedroom wing were constructed on the west side of the Convent. [9]

The hut was converted into a laboratory. [6]

The two hard tennis courts were laid.

1958

Another prefabricated building housing three classrooms was added to the first building. [10]

1960

The Gymnasium, changing rooms and three further classrooms and cloakrooms were added to the Senior School. [11]

1961

The first above ground liner swimming pool was erected. [12]

1962

Further classrooms, a laboratory, staff room, office and cloakrooms were built. [13]

1964

A modern kitchen and dining hall were built. [14] The old kitchen became the Sisters' Refectory, and the former Dining

1972
The fifth form classroom was added as an extension to the senior school. [18]
1974
A new larger swimming pool was constructed. [19]
1975
The Swimming Pool Pavilion was erected as changing rooms and storage. [20]
Fire safety work began in the Boarding House.
1976
An extension to the school office was completed. [21]
1977
Drying area and Tudor barn built the former Dining Room was made into the Junior Common Room.
The central heating in the house was extended.
The domestic science outbuilding was erected. [15]
1969
A mobile unit was purchased and used as a Library and later as Y5 classroom. [16]
1970
The infant cloakroom was built. [17] A new playground was constructed on what used to be the chicken run, and an equipment store added to the gymnasium.
1972
The fifth form classroom was added as an extension to the senior school. [18]
1974

A

The Sports Hall

new larger swimming pool was constructed. [19]
1975
The swimming pool pavilion was erected as changing rooms and storage. [20]
Fire safety work began in the boarding house.

1976
An extension to the school office was completed. [21]
1977
Drying area and Tudor barn built Maintenance Department. [22]
1978
Carpets were laid in the Senior School classrooms.
1979
The roof began to slide off part of the north side of the boarding house and timbers and roof had to be restored.
1981
The new infant block was completed with four classrooms and toilets, replacing the first building. [22]
1983
A large mobile unit housing a large science room, preparation room and typing room was erected. [24]
1987
New climbing cube frame installed on the grass adjacent to the swimming pool.
1989
The 75th Anniversary Block, known as the Middle School, was built to replace the library and science mobiles. This consisted of two science rooms, a cookery room, two classrooms, a computer room and office and reception area, built on large lawn area. [25]
1990
Staff car park constructed. [26]
1991

Astro turf tennis court installed adjacent to the fenced courts. [27]
1997
Sports hall complex built. [28]
1998
First minibus purchased. Outdoor tarmac nursery play area set up on patch of green. [29]
2001
Building site Barn purchased for bargain price - £60 000. [30]
New wildlife pond constructed. [31]

Maths garden made next to

conservatory maths room.

Conservatory walkway added to Sisters' refectory.[32]
Mangate Street Station and train built on Lower School playground. [33]
2002
New school Library opened in Art and Textile Rooms and Art Room temporarily in the gym. [7]
2003
Art and Music departments moved into the Barn, £30 000 received from WREN for staging and retractable seating for the theatre. [30]
A new computer suite established in the english room and linked to the main computer room.
Garage demolished from the front of the premises and railings and gates installed to make space for visitors and minibus to park.
2004
Pottery room opened in the Barn. [30]
A second minibus purchased and CCTV installed with six cameras to secure the site.
2005
The Barn Theatre was completed with seats, stage, lighting and sound. The roof had to be raised to allow for productions. [30]

2006   Part of Middle School corridor partitioned off for Headteacher's Office.
2007
Extension to the dining room completed. [34]
Refurbishment of the swimming pool changing rooms. [20]
Senior School was rewired at a cost of £42 000
2008   Renewing all pipework, relining the pool, and replacing surrounding slabs with rubberised matting.- £27 000 (PTA Funds). [19]
2010   Assault trail set up for the Lower School. [35] Jungle Climber purchased for older pupils. [36]
2011
Extended Lower School Playground by moving the gate and fence to the furthest end of the Sports Hall. Strong security gates in position at entrance to property, old gate Dustbin area tidied up and unsafe   wall removed and replaced with   matching fence.
2013
Reception and office decluttered, Headteacher's Office re-sited to
2014
School allowed use of the Woodland area adjacent to the Lower School for a peppercorn rate, on land leased to Manor Farm Surgery but owned by Nexus Group. Rotary Club gave
£5 000 for the woodland project in memory of past pupil who died in the tsunami. [37]

THE EPILOGE

The professional repertoire for Primary teaching is transferable skills, if one is familiar with the subject matter, and Art and Textiles were my recreational activities. The next move was more traumatic in many ways. Our young Mathematics teacher died suddenly after only a few weeks illness and I was called to take up the reins at very short notice.

I was the right person for the job, as I had borne bad experiences of Mathematics in the Primary School, but had risen to the top of the class in the Senior School, partly out of fear but also because I hero-worshipped Sr Irmgardis, the Mathematics teacher and wished to emulate her. I discovered that I enjoyed Maths and thought it was fun. However, teaching Mathematics required hours of revision and practising papers as the Maths undertaken at College was very alien to GCE.

With the grace of God, I succeeded and one of my proudest moments was helping a girl to gain an A in Maths after a psychologist had stated that she would never understand Maths! Maths really is my favourite subject, but when the Religious Education Teacher left, it was assumed that all those skills were easily transferable. Perhaps this is the subject that I felt most uneasy with; there are no definitive answers in RE. God was definitely in the driving seat and we were given particular praise for the discipleship answers.

In November 1978, Sr Margaret, Headteacher was being transferred to Chesterfield and she asked me to undertake the Headship in January 1979. Secretly I thought that I could do a better job, but I was very young and inexperienced. Some parents saw an opportunity to change things and the battle of the ear rings commenced, and I knew that I had to win!

Nearly half a century later, I have seen great educational changes and so many building projects. I have always been blessed with generous and stalwart parent helpers who were eager to take on new developments including the Swimming Pool, two large teaching blocks, the Sports Hall and a Barn Arts Centre. I have worked with many colleagues who have given me support, advice and friendship and followed many an ambitious scheme. The eyes glazing over when I say, 'I have an idea' is a sure sign to tread carefully, but together we have achieved so much such as transforming the Sports Hall into a wonder World of Books, undertaking voyages to foreign parts on very tight budgets to be welcomed by our Sisters, performing under the Buttercross sporting fruit and vegetable hats, journeying to London on the first day of term to be the choir, or being part of our latest project placing a stone into the Sacred Heart of Jesus Mosaic.

I have been overwhelmed by the pupils' willingness to follow, be stretched, do embarrassing things and think laterally – their holiday challenges are examples of creativity, originality and enthusiasm. I experienced another of my proud moments when a senior girl wanted a favour, prefixing the request with: 'You told us in Assembly to ask if we hope to receive'. Of course, she gained a positive response!

So this book which has been written and compiled by so many past and present pupils and staff is all within my personal experience. Although absent for three years I still returned to my roots as a Trustee and to be with my fellow Sisters, who are the bedrock of this school. What would the school be without the Sisters to care lovingly for the place, to be a reminder of God's presence in the world and pray for all, to welcome in parents and pupils and be a support for the Community, Parish and Diocese?

Signed off with grateful thanks and trust in Divine Providence,
Sr M. Francis Ridler, FDC Headteacher 1979 – 2006 and 2009 - present